The
CRESCENT
And The
COMPASS

Other Books by Angel Millar

Freemasonry: A History
Freemasonry: Foundation of the Western Esoteric Tradition

The CRESCENT *And The* COMPASS

Islam, Freemasonry, Esotericism, and
Revolution in the Modern Age

By

Angel Millar

TORAZZI PRESS

MMXVII

This edition published by Torazzi Press, 2017.

Originally published by Numen Books, Australia, 2015.
This Torazzi Press edition is revised and expanded.

978-0-9993247-0-7 Paperback
978-0-9993247-1-4 Hardback

Millar, Angel, author.

The Crescent And The Compass: Islam, Freemasonry,
Esotericism, and Revolution in the Modern Age

Social Science – Freemasonry & Secret Societies
Religion – Islam – General
Religion – Mysticism

For Chris; for your support, conversation, and friendship over the years.

CONTENTS

ACKNOWLEDGEMENTS xi

INTRODUCTION...1
Islam and Alternative Spirituality

ONE: Gnosis in Shi'ism and Sufism.....................................5
- Sufism: Initiation and Gnosis...8
- Initiation..9
- Gnosis 13
- Fraternity...16

TWO: European Brotherhoods; Impressions of Islam 19
- Enter The Fraternity of The Freemasons 22
- The Craft Masonic Ritual and Islamic Esotericism.......27
- The Arab and Sufi Influence in Europe and America 31
- Persian Sufism, "Arab" and "Old Turkish" Freemasonry.............36

THREE: Muslim Revolutionaries, Masonic Lodges, and the Near East.. 45
- A Sufi and Resistance Fighter.......................................46
- Jamal ad-Din al-Afghani and His Disciples 50

FOUR: Shaykh Abdullah Quilliam and the Ancient Order of Zuzimites .. 57
- Conversations with Angels 61
- The Ancient Order of Zuzimites 63

FIVE: René Guénon, Esotericism, and Islamic Traditionalism 69
- Swedenborgianism and Anti-Freemasonry 71
- Disciples 74

SIX: Ayatollah Khomeini: From *'Irfan* to Islamic State 79
- *'Irfan* 80
- Secularism by Force 84
- Ayatollah Khomeini: Emergence and Exile 89
- Sending an Earthquake 93
- After the Iranian Revolution 96

SEVEN: Birth of a Conspiracy Theory 101
- Making and Disseminating *The Protocols of the Elders of Zion*. 104
- Militias in the Middle East 111

EIGHT: Islamists Against the "Masonic" West 115
- Ideology 117
- Terror in Turkey 119
- After The Arab Spring 122

NINE: Black Nationalism in the USA 125
- Prince Hall 127
- Black Nationalism 129
- From Moorish Science to The Nation of Islam 133

TEN: Anders Breivik, The Knights Templar, and Terrorism 141
- Freemasonry and Anti-Freemasonry 143
- New "Templar" Orders 145

ELEVEN: Islam, Esotericism, And The Heir to The British Throne. 149
- Defender of Faith 150
- A Guénonian Prince 153

CONCLUSION: Secularism, Spirituality, And Struggle In The Modern Era 157

AFTERWORD: A Time For Islamic Spirituality? 161

APPENDIX I: Islam, Europe, and The Influence of Julius Evola 167

APPENDIX II: The Freemasonry On Bin Laden's Bookshelf 173

ENDNOTES 175

INDEX 193

ABOUT THE AUTHOR 203

ACKNOWLEDGMENTS

I have been fortunate, throughout the years, to have received support and guidance from numerous thinkers, discussion groups, and institutions. However, I am especially indebted to Greg, Craig, Chris, and Donald, who read the manuscript and provided me with their insights, observations, and encouragement.

Piers Vaughan kindly helped with translating from the French for the revised edition and has proved a source of inspiration over the years.

My thanks also go to Jason, for introducing me to more esoteric areas of Islam, to Toyib, for his depth of knowledge on the Islamic tradition, and to Mohamad Yatim for allowing me to see his research on the subject of Islam and Freemasonry when I was revising and updating *The Crescent and The Compass* for this new edition. Thanks also to Sharif Anael-Bey for his feedback on my work and his insights into Moorish Science and the life and work of Noble Drew Ali.

All of the above have helped to develop my understanding and to make my work better.

INTRODUCTION

Islam and Alternative Spirituality

In its broadest scope, *The Crescent And The Compass* is concerned with spirituality and radical thought within Islam, as well as movements that claimed in some way to represent the religion or its teachings, during the modern era. However, at the heart of the work are the many, and, oftentimes, highly significant connections between Muslim revolutionaries, activists, groups, thinkers, and the fraternity – or, more accurately, perhaps, fraternal movement – of Freemasonry, globally over the last century and a half.

Before we look at Freemasonry in greater depth, we should note that we will generally be exploring the more secretive, esoteric, and spiritual forms of the fraternity that influenced the underground spiritual milieu of the 18th and 19th centuries. (Ranging from Hermeticism to Rosicrucianism, and from Theosophy to the "positive thinking" or New Thought movement, these provided a foundation for the New Age and Western alternative spirituality movements later on.) This book is, in other words, about a largely unknown chapter in the history of the meeting of East and West, and the spirituality, politics, and radical thinking of the two.

In many respects, we are living with this legacy today, and, perhaps also, of the consequence of the fact that this chapter in our relatively recent history remains unknown to many, if not the vast majority of, experts on religion and foreign policy in the West today.

Muslim revolutionaries initiated into Freemasonry include Sayyid Jamal ad-Din al-Afghani, founding father of modern political Islam, whose ideas remain relevant in the Middle East, having been diffused into organizations and the writings of theorists; Algerian military leader and Sufi Abd al-Qadir al-Jazairi, who led the resistance against the French invasion (1830-1847); and Shaykh Abdullah Quilliam, the founder of Britain's first mosque, and a political agitator for the rights of Muslims under the British Empire.

Again, the French esotericist René Guénon was involved with fringe Masonic and other spiritual groups before adopting Islam in later life. He is best known, however, as the founder of Traditionalism, a school of esoteric spirituality that claims all of the major living religions are manifestations, though imperfectly, of a primordial religion or revelation. Accordingly, the Traditionalist must enter one of these faiths, adhering to its teachings even as he rejects religious literalism and sectarianism. Important Muslim thinkers of the Traditionalist school include Titus Burckhardt, a prolific author on various aspects of Sufism and Islamic culture, and Martin Lings, who wrote a biography of the Prophet Muhammad. Prince Charles, who is currently heir to the British throne, and a man sometimes praised and sometimes criticized for his expressions of sympathy toward Islam, has also been influenced by Traditionalist thought.

Another figure of influence, regarding the meeting of Islam and Freemasonry, is Noble Drew Ali, the founder and prophet of Moorish Science. This faith absorbed elements of Freemasonry and proto-New Age spirituality, as well as some Islamic trappings, though, beyond its title, its holy book, the *Circle Seven Koran*, has little relation to the Qur'an of traditional Islam, Sunni or Shi'a. Nevertheless, still practiced, Moorish Science had some influence on the early Nation of Islam, and constitutes a significant if short episode in the history of Black nationalism in the USA.

So, how did Islam – or, at least, revolutionaries invoking the name of the religion – come into contact with Freemasonry, both in the East and the West? The fraternity that traces its origins to the medieval stonemasons' guild of Great Britain had acquired its basic structure by about 1725, only some years after the founding of the first Grand Lodge of Free and Accepted

Masons (more often referred to as "Freemasons") in London.

Having adopted the mythology and rudimentary initiation procedures of the stonemasons' guild, Freemasonry developed a complex Ritual consisting of three Degrees (or interdependent rituals) that incorporated Biblical symbolism, sacred geometry, and natural law theory. Within a few decades it had become all the rage in continental Europe, and was taken further afield by members of various military regiments. These applied for, and received, charters to establish Masonic Lodges among their ranks and on their travels.

Such "Lodges" were not physical buildings, but rather groups of men who met to perform the initiation rituals, to discuss their meaning, and to engage in more ordinary fraternal activities such as dining and drinking together. While membership of these traveling Lodges was initially restricted to members of European military regiments, eventually settled Masonic Lodges in the Middle East, Asia, and elsewhere, allowed non-Europeans to join. In some cases, those initiated were dignitaries and diplomats of countries that the various European powers wished to cultivate a relationship with. As such, Freemasonry became a tool of international diplomacy.

Jessica L. Harland-Jacobs argues in *Builders of Empire: Freemasons and British Imperialism, 1717-1927* that globalism – at least global connectivity – was created largely, if accidentally, through the spread of Freemasonry. It was the first movement of the modern age to extend across the globe, creating networks that connected men, and enabled them to travel across country and even across continents, more or less sure that they would be greeted and welcomed by "Brothers." More importantly, Freemasonry was able, eventually, to embrace men not just of different races and ethnicities, but of different religions, with the first Muslims and Hindus being initiated during the 19th century in India.

The more spiritual and intellectual Freemasons admired, romanticized, and took an active interest in non-Western religions, their symbols, rituals, and esoteric interpretations. Articles appeared in British and American Masonic publications of the late 19th and early 20th centuries, on aspects of the world's religions believed to reflect or shed light on aspects of the Masonic Ritual. Masonic encyclopedias, published for members of the fraternity who wanted to understand its history and symbolism, contained frequent references to non-Western faiths.

Freemasons were also among the major figures of the modern occult and spiritualist worlds. These included Aleister Crowley, the British occultist, author, poet, artist, and mountaineer, who founded his own religion of Thelema; co-founders of the Hermetic Order of the Golden Dawn, William Wynn Westcott and Samuel Liddell MacGregor Mathers; and founders of the Ordo Templi Orientis, Theodor Reuss and Carl Kellner.

We will soon see how a number of Freemasons and Western esotericists were inspired by Islam, and by Arabic, Persian, and Turkish culture, but, here, it will be worth noting that as far back as the 17th century, the mystical Fraternity of the Rosy Cross incorporated Arabic elements into its legend. Crowley himself composed a little-known work inspired largely by Iranian Sufism. And, during the 19th century, Freemasons created a number of Rites that drew directly or indirectly from either Arabic or Persian culture.

ONE

Gnosis in Shi'ism and Sufism

uhammad, the Prophet of Islam, was born into the Koreish tribe of Mecca circa 570 C.E. His father died before his birth. It was not an auspicious beginning, but Muhammad would one day unify the desert tribes of Arabia, who would regard him as the "seal of the prophets," the lineage of which had begun with Adam and passed through Jesus ('Isa).

At twenty-five, Muhammad began retiring to meditate in the Hira cave located in the Jabal al-Nour (Mountain of Light), at the edge of Mecca. There, in 610 C.E., according to Islamic tradition, he received a visitation from the Angel Gabriel, who recited passages from the Qur'an. A few years later, in 613 C.E., Muhammad began his mission, proclaiming that – though the Arabian tribes then worshiped a multitude of deities – there was only one true God. According to Islamic tradition, over the next two decades, until the death of the Prophet in 632 C.E., he would receive further revelations, each of them being a part of the Qur'an.

The first person to accept Muhammad's revelations was his cousin and son-in-law 'Ali ibn Abi Talib (often referred to simply as 'Ali). He would go on to serve the Prophet and Islam faithfully, fighting, according to accounts, in the battles of Badr, 'Uhud, Khaybar, Khandaq and 'Hunayn, helping the Muslims to secure victory.[1] On the death of Muhammad, as his household, 'Ali, and many of those close to the Prophet attended to the funeral arrangements, another group of the faithful gathered to elect a successor (*caliph*) to govern the community. Muhammad's father-in-law was chosen. With this, the community effectively split into the Sunnis (traditionalists) and the Shi'ite (supporters and followers (of 'Ali)) group, since the latter believed that Muhammad had publicly chosen 'Ali to be his successor, before a large crowd of followers, at Ghadir Khumm on the return journey from Mecca to Medina during the last pilgrimage (*hajj*) of his life.

After the death of the Prophet, 'Ali taught "the Divine sciences"[2] to disciples at his home. This continued for twenty-five years, until the death of the third caliph, at which point he was elected to the position, and became the fourth of the "rightly-guided" caliphs. For Shi'ites, however, 'Ali is the first "Imam." In Sunni Islam, the term generally refers to the leader of a congregation. In Shi'ism, however, although the Imam guides the external behavior of the faithful, unlike the caliph – whose function is purely to govern the worldly affairs of the Muslim community (*ummah*) – "he possesses the function of inward and esoteric leadership and guidance," Allamah Sayyid Muhammad Husayn Tabataba'i tells us. "He is the guide of the caravan of humanity which is moving inwardly and esoterically toward God."[3] Thus it is necessary for there to be either a prophet or Imam on earth at all times.

Mainstream "Twelver" Shi'ites believe there to have been a lineage (*Imamate*) of twelve Imams in total. The last of these, the Mahdi – Imam al-'Asr (b. 256/868) – went into occultation in 329/941, and will only reveal himself at the end of time. Then the Mahdi will battle against the world's oppressors, ushering in a period of peace and justice.

As a leader, 'Ali is known to have advocated for the fair treatment of Muslims and non-Muslims alike, instructing, for example, Malik al-Ashtar, his governor in Egypt, not to consider his subjects "easy prey" since "either they are your brothers in religion or your equals in creation."[4] Besides his instructions on worldly affairs, 'Ali is, with the exception of Muhammad, the central figure of Islamic gnosticism (the tradition of Divine knowledge). This is partly a historical matter. 'Ali, of all the companion's of the Prophet of Islam, "is known particularly for his eloquent expositions of gnostic truths and the stages of the spiritual life," says Allamah Tabataba'i.[5] Both a master of Islamic jurisprudence and law and an initiate of Islamic gnosticism under

Mirza 'Ali Qadi, Allamah Tabataba'i tells us that

[...] we must not consider gnosis as a religion among others, but as the heart of all religions. Gnosis is one of the paths of worship, a path based on knowledge combined with love, rather than fear. It is the path for realizing the inner truth of religion rather than remaining satisfied only with its external form and rational thought.[6]

Although, today, esotericism is often regarded as existing outside of, and as even opposing, religious orthodoxy, in the traditional view, the esoteric (inner) teaching was not regarded as existing independently, complete in itself, but as being discoverable, and emerging, only *through* the outer, or the exoteric (e.g., through the interpretation of religious scripture). Thus says Amir-Moezzi, Shi'as believe that "all reality is composed of a *zahir* (an apparent, exoteric aspect) and a *batin* (a hidden, esoteric aspect)."[7]

Shi'a Islam has developed a complex theory of transmission of initiatory knowledge ((*'ilm*), i.e., the esoteric interpretation of the Qur'an) to the elite believers (*khassa*). The exoteric side has been given to humanity through law-giving, prophecy, and the Qur'an itself. According to Shi'a esotericism, the Prophet Mohammed, says Amir-Moezzi, "is both the prototype and the end" of the exoteric aspect of Islam, for though he knows the esoteric also, he teaches this only to the Imams. Thus, in the Shi'ite "Imamate" or "Twelver" doctrine, the twelve Imams, and Imam 'Ali in particular, proceed from the exoteric (outer), and represent the esoteric (inner) aspect.[8]

As with the Imamate Shi'ites, from which they split in 765, with the death of Imam al-Sadiq, the early Ismailis believed that the literal meaning (*zahir*) of the Qur'an and the laws it prescribed had to be distinguished from "true spiritual reality (*haqiqa*) hidden in the [esoteric] *batin*." The Ismailis believed, says Farhad Daftary in *Intellectual Traditions in Islam*, "that the *zahir*, or the religious laws enunciated by the messenger-prophets, underwent periodic changes while the *batin*, containing the spiritual truths, remained immutable and eternal."[9]

Sufism: Initiation and Gnosis

During the 10th century, with the conquest of Iraq in 945 C.E. by the Buyid dynasty, Shi'a Islam came to dominate the Muslim world. The prosperity of the sect continued until the Seljuks – a Sunni warrior tribe from Central Asia – emerged on the horizons. The tribe ascended to political power, from mercenary guards to town protectors, and later to protectors of the Abbasid caliphs. Then in 1055, Tugrul Bey – the Seljuks' leader – forced the caliph to appoint him Sultan. Bey would legislate regarding secular concerns, military and administration, (with the Seljuk dynasty establishing Hanafi jurisprudence (*fiqh*) as the state's own[10]), while the caliph remained in the background, legislating on spiritual and personal affairs, and serving to legitimate the Seljuk sultanate.

For the Shi'ites, the emergence of the Seljuks meant a rapid decline in status and loss of power. In return for the Caliph's recognition, the tribe enforced Sunni Islam as orthodoxy, and began to root out Shi'a influence, forcing Shi'ite Muslims out of positions of authority.[11] While Muslim mystics and ascetics had existed prior to this period, organized Sufism emerged around this time, probably largely to fill the void left by the removal of the more esoteric Shi'a branch of Islam.[12] "Sufis […] came to adopt a gnostic approach, tapping Shi'i as well as other gnostic sources," says J. Spencer Trimingham in *The Sufi Orders in Islam*, "especially after the open profession of Shi'ism was banned."[13]

The rationale of both (Sunni) Sufism and Imamate Shi'ism was to engender a sense of spirituality in relation to the Qur'an and prophetic tradition, with disciples discovering the inner truth or the Real (*haqiqa*) through the mediating of the revealed law (*shar'*) and the belief in the Oneness of Divinity (*tawhid*). But, despite considerable differences, Shi'ism and Sufism share not only a general orientation but also some important details, such as the reverence of 'Ali, to whom, in different ways, both traditions trace their lineage (and thence to Muhammad).

The earliest Muslim mystics embraced an array of approaches to the Divine, from asceticism to theological contemplation and elaboration. For Sufis as for other Islamic (and non-Islamic) esotericists, there existed an outer (exoteric) and an inner (esoteric) understanding of Deity, as evidenced to them by Surah 57:3 of the Qur'an, which describes Allah as "the First and the Last, and the Outward and the Inward." Often used to refer to Islamic mysticism in general, "Sufism" derives from the Arabic *Tasawwuf*, meaning *to become a Sufi*. Its etymological root, however, is believed to be the Arabic word *suf*, meaning "wool,"[14] which the Sufis used for the fabric of their clothing. Rough, practical, and contrasting the opulent dress of the sultans, their form of attire was adopted from the pre-Islamic mystics of the Near East – both Christian and Hindu[15] origins have been suggested.

According to 'Abdullah Ansari of Herat (d. 1089 C.E.), while there had been "great Sufis" before him – i.e, those who had renounced earthly pleasures, and who were on the path of Love (*mahabbat*) for God – the first figure to bear the title *Sufi* was Abu Hashim al-Sufi (d. 767). Ansari made this observation in his translation of the work of Abu 'Abd al-Rahman al-Sulami, who had lived in eastern Iran and had died in 1021. Al-Sulami had written the first major collection of the lives of the early Sufi saints, as well as a number of other works in Arabic. Like his biographer, al-Sulami recognized that the term had not been used at the time of Muhammad, but that it had emerged much later. Some of those described as Sufis by al-Sulami and other early biographers had not been known as such during their lifetimes.[16] Moreover, together, they represented a relatively broad array of expressions of Islamic mysticism.[17]

Initiation

Those aspiring to the knowledge and experience of Islamic mysticism often sought the guidance of a Master (*shaykh*). Circles formed around these more learned figures on the path of Sufim, and during the 12th century these groups took on the more definite shape of the Sufi Order (*tariqah* – meaning, literally, "path") that still exists today. Such Orders claim to represent a chain of initiated masters that go back through 'Ali to the Prophet Muhammad himself. As can be found in esoteric and secret societies around the world, entrance into a Sufi Order occurs through a formal initiation ceremony.

Shaykh Amin ad-Din Balyani (d. 1344-5)[18] of Shiraz is reported, by his hagiographer, to have compared the Sufi initiation to the laying of the foundations of a fortress, upon which the initiate would have to build through the efforts of mind and body. Balyani's hagiographer relates that during initiations into his Sufi community in southern Iran, the shaykh would sit before the initiate, and would recite prayers greeting the Sufi masters of the past and present. He would then ask for the blessings of God on His Prophet and on those that had elected to obey His commands. After this, the initiate would swear an oath that he would obey God, and would relinquish behavior disobedient to Him. Then Balyani would cut three hairs from the forelock of the disciple (*murid*), and, with each, would ask "permission of God, the Prophet, Shaykh Abu Ishaq, and Shaykh 'Abdullah." Next, he would clasp in his hand an amount of the initiate's hair, on the right side of his head, and would recite, "a long prayer in Arabic that recalled God as Light and as the one who bestows Light and guidance on human beings."[19]

During the initiation into a Dervish Order, the seeker's hand would be clasped by the shaykh so that the former would be able to receive the *baraka* (blessing power).[20] He would swear an oath of allegiance. And he would be invested with the robe (*khirqa*) and cap (*taj*) of a Sufi. This, like other elements of Sufi dress, is infused with esoteric symbolism. Varying in color and shape, the Sufi cap is sometimes composed of seven, nine, or twelve pieces or pleats, the latter of which was associated with the twelve Imams.

In the Bektashi Sufi Order, likewise, a girdle is worn, to which a seven-sided or seven-cornered stone called the *palank* is attached. This number is associated with the seven heavens, seven planets or seven earths created by

Allah (Qur'an, Surah 65:12), and the seven seas. The girdle and stone serve as mnemonic devices. Binding it on a disciple, the shaykh would say, "I now bind up thy waist in the path of God." When binding it upon himself, the shaykh would remind himself that he was tying up seven vices (greed, anger, avarice, ignorance, passion, hunger, and Satanism) and unbinding seven virtues (generosity, meekness, piety, fear of God, love of God, contentment, and Divineness).[21]

Historically, a few Sufis have claimed to have been initiated into such a chain, and into Islamic gnosticism, by the spirit of a deceased Sufi master. Such initiations took place in dreams or visions. On occasion both types have been alleged to have occurred, with the initiation by a spirit of the deceased master solidifying the reputation of the initiate as especially blessed in spiritual matters. There is also a legend that a green bird would descend onto the head of the successor (*khalifa*) to a dying shaykh, appointed by the latter but which, until this auspice, had been regarded as unworthy by the brethren.

For Sufism, the venerated shaykh is key to the transformation of the disciple. Sufism has been compared, by its masters, to alchemy, and the shaykh of the Order, on occasion, to the red sulfur, believed to have the power to transform base metals into gold. Jalal ad-Din Rumi, probably the best-known Sufi master, was credited with the power to transform base materials into precious gems. He also frequently used alchemy as an analogy of the transformation of the initiate from the ordinary, base man, through the power of God and the discipline of Sufism that purify him. Comparing himself to copper becoming gold through God, Rumi said that the initiate had to live, with the Divine, in the "furnace."[22]

To aid the initiate on the path to becoming spiritual gold, the disciple would be introduced to certain oral teachings as well as meditations and other practices through which he could experience a sense of being dissolved in the Divine. For the Sufi, the Prophet's Night Journey (*al-Isra*) or Ascent (*al-Mi'raj*) provides the archetypal example of the mystical journey toward God.

According to Islamic tradition, one night in 621 C.E., Muhammad was sleeping in the sanctuary next to the Ka'bah. There, a figure approached the Prophet, cut open his body, and removed his heart. It was then washed in a golden tray of Belief (by which it became filled with Belief) and then returned to its place in the body. Next, a creature called the Buraq – which was white and bigger than a donkey but smaller than a mule – was brought to Muhammad. Then, with the Angel Gabriel beside him, the Prophet was, according to tradition, taken on the Buraq to the nearest heaven, where he was welcomed by Adam. From there, he was taken up through the remainder of the seven heavens, where he greeted, and was greeted by, Yahya (John), 'Isa, Idris, Harun, Moses and Abraham.[23] At the summit, Muhammad saw the "lote tree of uttermost limit," the boundary marker signifying the limit of Being.[24]

Using prayer and contemplation, Sufis seek to ascend the seven heavens, in a spiritual voyage that, ritualistically and internally, emulates Muhammad's Night Journey. And it is from descriptions of the *Isra* or *Mi'raj* that they have drawn, to articulate their gnosis.[25] Experiencing such otherworldly states did not mean that the Sufi abandoned or went against the forms of the religion binding on ordinary members of the faith, however. Even today, most Sufis observe the exoteric, religious strictures of Islam – such as fasting during the month of Ramadan, and some Sufis – such as the Naqshbandis in Turkey – are *shari'a*-observant.[26] Religious law, Rumi said, is like a candle that reveals the way. One must follow the *shari'a* (meaning literally "road") before diverging to enter the *tariqah* (the narrower path). Following it, one will reach the mystical truth. For Rumi, the religious law can be compared to alchemy, and the path to the operation of applying the Philosopher's Stone (believed to transform base metal).[27]

The path, according to some of the later Orders of Sufism, meant that the personality of the disciple could become totally absorbed into the personality of the shaykh. For those who had reached a sufficiently high level of spirituality, such Sufis could, it was believed, traverse the stages embodied in and symbolized through the prophets, from Adam to Jesus. While many were believed to remain in one of these stages, the perfect shaykh would transcend them, so that he would, according to Sufi tradition, become united with the *haqiqa muhammadiyya* (the (esoteric) truth of Muhammad).[28]

The relationship between Sufi master and disciple was solidified not just through the formal initiation ritual but also through the practice of spiritual transmission (*tawajjuh*). Master and disciple would concentrate upon each other, with the meditation creating a spiritual bond between them, and the shaykh entering "the door of the disciple's heart." The Naqshbandi and some other Sufi Orders regarded *tawajjuh* as an essential prerequisite to *dhikr*[29] (the formal practice of reciting the Names of God). By the 11th century, the latter was largely established within Sufism.

Through *dhikr* the Sufi seeks to remember, and to become immersed in, the Divine. Egyptian Sufi, Ibn 'Ata' Allah of Alexandria (d. 709/1309) is credited with writing the first treatise on the practice. He had been an opponent of Sufism earlier in his life, but later emerged as a master of the Shadhiliyya Order, though preaching a restrained form of Sufism, "which melded Sunni orthodoxy with Sufi spirituality." He spoke to ordinary members of the Islamic faith about conventional Sunni matters, while also addressing and often introducing listeners to *dhikr*, pilgrimages to the shrines of saints, and other aspects of Sufism in its manifestation of popular religion.[30]

Gnosis

In his *Key to Salvation and the Lamp for Spirits*, Ibn 'Ata' Allah presents *dhikr* as involving the entirety of the initiate's being, from the use of the tongue at the outermost level, through the engagement of the heart, intellect, soul, spirit, and what Carl W. Ernst calls "the innermost conscience." This ritual of remembering God must be undertaken with complete sincerity, and must take place only when the disciple has been careful to observe religious dietary laws, and has dressed himself in the proper attire. Then he should sit with his legs crossed, eyes closed, and palms resting on his legs. To ensure that it is pleasing to the angels and jinn, the place of his *dhikr* should be pleasantly perfumed. Next, the disciple should visualize his master as sitting between his eyes. This is done even if the master is present and can be seen by the disciple, since the shaykh is regarded as a living link in the chain that leads back to the Prophet of Islam.

Dhikr purifies the disciple from his disposition of forgetting God due to worldly distractions, by reciting Names of the Divine. Specific Names should be chanted by those at particular stages along the path. The Name *al-Mawla* (the Master), Ibn 'Ata' Allah tells us, is usually recited by those who are new to Sufism, since this is the object of their concern at this stage. Evoking intimacy and bringing illumination closer, *al-Muhsin* (the Beneficent) can be recited by ordinary people who wish to achieve trust in God. *Al-Sadiq* (the Sincere) will confer knowledge upon the gnostic, and will create in the Sufi a sincere heart.

Allah, the first of the ninety-nine Names of God, is the most frequently recited. Next to this, in frequency of usage, is the formula "there is no God but God [Allah]." This is best known as the first part of the *shahada* (or "double *shahada*"), the Islamic profession of faith, the latter part of which proclaims that "Muhammad is the messenger of God [Allah]." Both statements appear in the Qur'an, though separately; and inscriptions, coins, and papyri, suggests that the first part (the "single *shahada*") only may have been in use during the early years of Islam.[31]

Sufi masters later extended – in a mystical direction perplexing or offensive to many ordinary Muslims – the statement "there is no God but God" to "there is nothing but God."[32] The latter statement is a reflection of the Sufi's striving for a state of total absorption (*fana*) in God. Only God exists in Reality, they believe. The things of the created world merely reflect the Creator that brought them into existence. Hence, Ibn 'Arabi claims that "he who says, 'I have seen nothing but God' speaks the truth."[33]

Regarded as the founder of theosophical Sufism,[34] Abu'l-fayd b. Ibrahim Dhu'l-Nun (796-861), was born in upper-Egypt to a Nubian father. He studied medicine, alchemy, and magic, and became a spiritual teacher, who spoke openly about mysticism. Like other Sufi masters after him, Dhu'l-Nun regarded the self as the main barrier to spiritual development. He advocated solitude as a remedy against the affliction of the self, saying, "he who is alone sees nothing but God, and if he sees nothing but God, nothing moves him but the Will of God."[35]

The esoteric extension of the Islamic profession, "there is no God but God", toward gnosis (knowledge of God through direct experience) is typical of Sufi interpretation. Formally, Sufis believe that the verses of the Qur'an possess between seven and seventy levels of meaning. Occasionally, they suggest that there can be an even greater number of interpretations, leading the disciple to an ever-higher level of spiritual understanding. Modern Sufi shaykh M. R. Bawa Muhaiyaddeen (d. 1986) claimed that "Within one word in the Qur'an, there are thousands of meanings." Muhaiyaddeen advised devotees to "look within" each meaning of each word to uncover new, rarefied nuances, ultimately to discover the Real.[36]

"For the Sufis," says Idries Shah, the Qur'an possesses "levels of transmission, each one of which has a meaning in accordance with the capacity for understanding of the reader." Shah elucidates this Islamic esotericism, and what he believes to be its potential to avoid conflict between the religions, through Surah 112 of the Qur'an:

> Say, O messenger, to the people:
> "He, Allah, is Unity! Allah the Eternal.
> Fathering nobody, and not himself engendered –
> And absolutely nothing is like him"

This surah denies the Christian claim that there is God the Father, Son, and Holy Spirit, and, equally, that God would become flesh, even in the figure of Jesus. "The devout Moslem," says Shah, can use it against the Christian, whom he considers to be a heretic of the monotheist tradition." The Christian, in turn, is liable to react, "considering it an insult to his central beliefs." In this case, there is a "clash," facilitated through a "psychological climate" that lays the groundwork for conflict.

But, Shah tells us, this is not the only interpretation, and, moreover, that it was not the one accepted by the Sufis. They, Shah asserts, understood this surah as affirming the "final objectivity" and "uniqueness" of Allah, which could not resemble anything "familiar to man." Only through such a comprehension of this surah, Shah believed, could Muslims and Christians – and presumably those of other religions – bridge the gap between them. Otherwise, it will be understood in such a way that it will be "bereft of Sufic connotation," and, ultimately, more militant in its interpretation.[37] For the Sufi, then, comprehension of the Qur'an and other Islamic texts is dependent on the level of spiritual understanding that he has reached and that he embodies.

Fraternity

As we have mentioned, from its roots in the lives of various ascetics, who renounced the world for the chance of union with the Divine, Sufism began to solidify into different schools, each focused on a particular master and his teachings. The earlier Sufi associations were generally informal, with devotees joined together by a common spirit, aim, and sense of the numinous. This began to change with Sunni victories over the Buyids in Baghdad in 1055 C.E. and the Fatimids in Egypt in 1171 – both Shi'ite dynasties. By the time of the latter victory, Sufi associations had already enjoyed "some linkage with and transmission from artisan *futuwwa* [chivalrous, ethical] orders," says J. Spencer Trimingham. They adopted the Shi'ite oath of allegiance (*bay'a*), and began swearing faithfulness to their shaykh.[38]

From the trade guilds, the Sufi Orders also derived a certain structure, emulating the crafts' division of members into a grand master, master craftsman (*mu'allim*), companions (*sani'*), and apprentices (*mubtadi'*), and establishing tiers of Sufi masters, initiates and novices.[39]

This was neither the first nor the last time that trade guilds, religion and esotericism would be fused together. From weaving to warfare, and from farming to mining, ancient mythology suggests that the professions and tools of early man held a sacred significance for him. The blacksmith, as Mircea Eliade has demonstrated, played a role as religious officiate and initiator in primitive tribes throughout the globe.[40] There were also rites for planting, mining, and other professions in antiquity.

Later on, during the medieval, and even into the early modern, period, trade guilds in Britain and continental Europe possessed their own mythology, initiation rituals, and code of ethics. In France, the rituals of the *Compagnonnage* trade guild were strongly influenced by Roman Catholicism. The guild survived into the 19th century, by which point its rituals had to some extent been influenced by – and probably influenced in return – the fraternity of Freemasonry, which, as we saw earlier, had roots in the medieval builders' guild of the British Isles.

Freemasonry also became associated with Rosicrucianism, the founding mythology of which may have been partly inspired by the *Unzertrennlichen* or *Indissolubilisten* (Order of the Inseparables). Founded in 1577, the membership of the Order included owners of mines and smelting works, and seems to have been primarily concerned with alchemy and metallurgy. This society became linked to the *Fruchtbringende Gesellschaft* (Fruit-bringing Society), which was founded in 1617 by Prince Ludwig von Anhalt, and included among its early members Johann Valentin Andreae (1586-1654), the author *The Chemical Wedding of Christian Rosenkreutz*, one of the manifestos of the Rosicrucian fraternity.[41]

TWO

European Brotherhoods; Impressions of Islam

During the early years of the 17th century, in a series of pamphlets, a self-styled Fraternity of the Rosy Cross was beginning to inveigh against clerical authority. The influence of priest, theologian, and church reformer Martin Luther can be discerned in the fraternity – which claimed to be made up of authentic Christians – not least of all in its name (Luther's seal was a cross inside a heart, enclosed in a rose) and its invective against the "Pope's tyranny."[42]

The *Fama Fraternitatis* was the first Rosicrucian pamphlet. It was published in 1614 but had circulated in manuscript form since, probably, 1610.[43] According to the *Fama*, the founder of the fraternity had been a German by the name of Christian Rosenkreutz. He had entered a cloister at the age of five, and, later, as a young man, had traveled to Fez, Damascus, Egypt, and throughout Arabia, learning various arts and sciences.

Because of "his skill in physic he [Rosenkreutz] obtained much favor with the Turks," and "became by chance acquainted with the wise men of Damascus in Arabia." Rosenkreutz is also supposed to have learned Arabic, and to have translated a book called *M.* "into good Latin". Yet, while Rosenkreutz eagerly absorbed the various sciences, as a convinced Christian he could not accept the other religions he encountered. In the *Fama*, Rosenkreutz is said to have complained that the "Magia" of Fez "was not altogether pure, and also that their Cabala was defiled with their Religion."[44]

Originally a Jewish mystical system, the Cabala was adopted by a number of Christian thinkers, such as the Italian Renaissance philosopher Giovanni Pico della Mirandola (1463-1494) and the German humanist

Johann Reuchlin (1455-1522). It was adopted, and reinterpreted, partly in an attempt to convert Jews to Christianity and, often, to lend support to Christian theology.

By the time the first Rosicrucian manifestos appeared there was a long history of conflict between Muslim and Christian powers. Muslim armies had taken much of Christendom, including the Holy Land, well before the end of the first millennium. By 902 C.E. they had made inroads into Europe, having captured Spain and Sicily. During the 11th century, the *Reconquista* (re-Conquest) was well underway, with Christian forces recapturing lost territory. By the end of the century, they had advanced into Palestine and Syria. However, the tide turned once again, and in 1453, the Ottomans took Constantinople, Christendom's second city after Rome, and made it into their power base.

Still the Ottomans pushed westward, capturing the Balkans and most of Greece. During the 16th century, Muslim armies advanced as far as the gates of Vienna, while naval raids reached the British Isles. Fear of conquest was felt even in the farthest corners of Europe. In Iceland, the Lutheran Book of Common Prayer besought God to save the faithful from "the cunning of the Pope and the terror of the Turk."[45] Yet, although the Battle of Lepanto struck a serious blow to the Ottoman Empire in 1571, it fought on until defeated at Vienna in 1683.

Rosenkreutz was a fictional character, but punctuating the peculiar stories and flowery language of the three Rosicrucian pamphlets was a serious political message. Like its mythical founder, the fraternity was Christian, Protestant, and it was "chiefly in Germany" that the pamphleteers believed the faith was "most clear and pure[ly] professed." The Fraternity of the Rosy Cross was quite specific in this regard. According to the *Fama*, the fraternity used only "two Sacraments, as they are instituted with all forms and ceremonies of the first reformed Church." In imitation of Luther's translation of the Bible into German, the second manifesto, the *Confessio Fraternitatis*, published in 1615, proclaimed that the *Fama* had to be published in "everyone's mother tongue" so that no country could be "defrauded of the knowledge thereof," as God, the reader is informed, did not wish to deprive anyone of the happiness that the fraternity's knowledge offered.

This happiness would be grasped to differing degrees, according to the receptivity of different cultures, it was suggested. The *Confessio* nevertheless praised the inhabitants of "Damcar in Arabia, who have a far different politick order from the other Arabians," as the city was governed by "wise and understanding men" that enacted laws only with the king's permission. Such a government, the manifesto proclaimed, "shall be instituted in Europe." Abraham Ortelius's map of the world, *Theatrum Orbis Terrarum*, published in Antwerp in 1570 shows the location of Damcar. This city – the home of the Queen of Sheba – is in *Arabia Felix* ("Happy Arabia" – a nickname for Yemen), the homeland of the Sabeans. (The manifesto reproduces the typographical error of Ortelius's map. Damcar is, in fact, Damar.[46])

The type of authority the Fraternity of the Rosy Cross envisioned was not a theocracy. The authors of the *Confession* insists that the fraternity could not be suspected of having any "purpose against the worldly [i.e., secular] government" and offered "good will to the chief head of the Roman Empire" – the emperor for the territories of central Europe. Although the manifestos went almost uncommented upon by Catholics, they provoked immediate and enthusiastic responses from many of Europe's Protestant intellectuals. However, perhaps the best-known figure to have been influenced by the manifestos was Francis Bacon (1561–1626), the Queen's Counsel, a leading figure in natural philosophy, lawyer, and member of Parliament in England.

In *A New Atlantis* – a story reminiscent of the adventures Christian Rosenkreutz – Bacon describes how a party of sailors come across the mysterious island of Bensalem, populated by Christians except for a small minority of Jews "among them, whom they leave to their own religion." Advanced in the arts and sciences, as well as spiritual matters, the Jews of the island believed "that Moses by a secret Cabala ordained the Laws of Bensalem which they now use." The peculiar fusion of Christian symbolism and Eastern, even a proto-Orientalist, glamour, embodied in the manifestos, also turns up in *A New Atlantis*, with the inhabitants wearing turbans, practicing Cabala, and with the sailors being taken onto the island by a man whose "turban was white, with a small red cross on the top."

In Sweden also, the mystic and antiquarian Johannes Bureus produced a series of his own Rosicrucian-inspired manifestos that were also influenced by the Cabala, as well as Christian and Old Testament mythology, and that incorporated the ancient northern European runic alphabet (letters of which had sometimes been used as symbols, historically). In 1610, Bureus read Guillaume Postel's translation of the Jewish Cabalistic text *Sefer Jezira* (published 1552). Bureus was inspired by a prophecy recounted by Postel: After a thousand years, Christians would come to learn the Qur'an and Arabic, at which point the rule of Islam would collapse and Christ would rule. Lending a hand to fate, Bureus redesigned the runes as a flowing script resembling Arabic. [47]

Minus its Arabic elements and occasional hostility to Islam, the Rosicrucian mythology would have a broader and, ultimately, a profounder effect on Western culture during the 18th century through Freemasonry. Members of this brotherhood would found their own society in the states of Germany, and elsewhere in Europe, called the Golden Rosicrucians. This was a semi-Masonic, semi-occult and alchemical society, that claimed to teach the secret of the Elixir of Life to its highest initiates, and to raise spirits through the use of a machine. Splitting into competing jurisdictions, Masonic Rites and Orders also absorbed Rosicrucian and alchemical symbolism and doctrine, creating such rituals as the Rose Croix, a popular, partly-Catholicized Degree that has existed in a variety of forms.

Enter The Fraternity of The Freemasons

Although rooted in the medieval stonemasons' trade guild, Freemasonry came into existence as a fraternity in its own right during the first quarter of the 18th century. According to the traditionally accepted version of events, four London Lodges met to form a Grand Lodge in 1717. Christian at first, a century and a half later Freemasonry had accepted men of religions as diverse as Hinduism and Islam. However, the seeds of such ecumenism were planted early on, though unintentionally.

According to the rules or "charges" laid down by Rev. James Anderson in *The Constitutions of the Free-Masons*, 1723, members of the fraternity had "to obey the moral Law". If they understood the "Art" of Freemasonry they would neither be "a Stupid Atheist, nor an irreligious Libertine," but were obliged only "to that Religion in which all men agree, leaving their particular Opinions to themselves; that is, to be *good Men and true*, or Men of Honour and Honesty, by whatever Denominations or Persuasions they may be distinguished." There can be little doubt that "that Religion in which all men agree" – or the "Catholick Religion" as Anderson also put it – referred specifically to Christianity, and that the intention was to prevent dissension between men of different Christian "denominations," not different religions, as is often claimed today.

Anderson himself, in the *Constitutions'* history section, refers to the birth of Jesus – "God's MESSIAH, the great Architect of the Church" – under the reign of Augustus Ceasar.[48] Much of the rest of the history is derived from the Old Testament, though the author speaks of architectural wonders being found across the world, and throughout the ages, and holds a favorable impression of many cultures. Nevertheless, Anderson takes a dim view of some, lamenting, notably, "the general Devastation of the *Goths* and *Mahometans* [i.e., Muslim armies]".[49]

The Germanic pagan tribes of the Goths and Vandals, he says, had overrun Rome, destroying some of its edifices and defacing others, while "the *Asiatic* and *African* Nations fell under the same Calamity by the Conquests of the MAHOMETANS [emphasis as original], whose grand Design is only to convert the World by Fire and Sword…"[50] Even leaving aside Anderson's biases as a Presbyterian minister and chaplain – which were undoubtedly considerable

– such a view is not entirely surprising given the long history of conflict between Christian and Muslim armies.

Nevertheless, Anderson did not, and could not, speak the fraternity, which had not established anything close to uniformity in regard to, or control of, its Ritual. Not only were Masonic "higher Degrees" and Rites about to appear and multiply at an extraordinary rate, especially in France and Germany, but even in England, there remained significant differences in the foundational Craft Masonic Degrees.

Notably, too, Masonic catechisms were also being recorded, and sometimes published in newspapers, both before and after 1723. And, most strikingly, in a Masonic catechism printed in 1726, called *The Grand Mystery Laid Open*, we find references to Cabala and Jesus ("INRI" – an acronym for *Iesvs Nazarenvs Rex Ivdaeorvm* ("Jesus of Nazareth, King of the Jews"), ordered to be inscribed over the head of Jesus on the cross). Hence:

How many Signs has a true Free Mason, Nine, which are distinguish'd into Spiritual and Temporal. How many Temporal Signs are there? Three [...] Have the six Spiritual Signs any names? Yes, but [they] are not divulged to any new admitted Member, because they are Cabalisttical. [...] Who is the Grand Master of all Lodges in the World? INRI. What is the meaning of that Name? Each distinct letter stands for a Whole word and is very mysterious.

While references to Cabala and, of course, to Jesus, appear in other early Masonic catechisms and writings (and in some early anti-Masonic polemics), far more unusually and strikingly, *The Grand Mystery Laid Open* also references Islam. Hence:

Who is your Founder? God and the Square. What is God called? Laylah Illallah.

The final phrase above is, of course, the first part of the *shahada* or Islamic profession of faith (*lā ilāha illā llāh* ("there is "no God but God

[Allah]). And it is mentioned three times in the short text. Hence, we read, also:

Who was the first Mason? Laylah Illallah. Who invented the secret Word? Checchehabeddin Jatmouny. What is it? It is a Cabalistical Word composed of a Letter out of each of the Names of Laylah Illallah as mentioned in the Holy Bible.

Although Henrik Bogdan has suggested that the catechism is "probably a spoof,"[51] such an early reference to Islam – and citation of the *shahada* – within the Masonic textual tradition cannot be dismissed lightly. Indeed, Mohamad A. Yatim has suggested[52] that "Checchehabeddin" may be a reference to Persian Sufi Shaykh Chehabeddin (Shahab al-Din Abu 'l-Futuh Yahya ibn Habash ibn Amirak al-Suhrawardi (1154-91 C.E.)). A Persian influence is supported by the appearance, in the Masonic text, of the word "Asphahani" (referring to someone or something from the city of Isfahan – where al-Suhrawardi himself had spent time on his travels). Though there appears to be no good reason for this, and we do not find this assertion made elsewhere, "Asphahani," the reader is told, is the name given to the Masonic emblem of the hammer or trowel.

It is interesting to note that al-Suhrawardi placed the symbolism of light at the heart of his worldview. Often referred to by the title of Shaykh al-Ishraq ("Master of Illumination"), he conceived and spoke of God as the "Light of Lights."[53] If "Checchehabeddin" does refer to al-Suhrawardi, then, this may be why he would find his way into a Masonic catechism. Like the Persian shaykh, Freemasonry has always strongly emphasized the symbolism of "Light," speaking of the Bible as the "great light in Masonry," and the Freemason as seeking "light in Masonry," etc.

Whether or not we regard the catechism as a "spoof," as Bogdan suggests, it is clear that we have, in this early Masonic text, something of importance, especially in its embrace of Cabala, esoteric Christianity, and

Islam. Indeed, the inclusion, three times, of the first part of the *shahada* suggests both significant knowledge of, and sympathy for, the latter religion.

We must admit, of course, that judging by the contents of the early Masonic and anti-Masonic texts, Islam was a far more marginal interest than even Cabala, and perhaps had, at most, a small circle of interested Freemasons, perhaps in some way associated with, or an influence on *The Grand Mystery Laid Open*. Later, however, a greater number of Freemasons and Western esotericists would find inspiration in Islam, especially Sufism.

Moreover, some scholars have drawn parallels between Islamic esotericism – especially Sufism – and Freemasonry. "The Sufis are an ancient spiritual freemasonry," says Idries Shah (1924-1996), an Indian-born writer who introduced a modern, universalist, spiritual Sufism to the West.[54] "[W]hat interests the Sufi," claims Shah, "is the fact that, out of the material which claims to be partially or wholly Masonic, a very great deal is at once seen to concur with matters of everyday Sufi initiatory practice."[55] Likewise, in *The Heart of Islam: Enduring Values for Humanity*, Seyyed Hossein Nasr compares the "Islamic guilds" to "the medieval European guild of masons," although he notes that Freemasonry began when members officially divorced their gatherings from the trade and became a purely "speculative," philosophical and esoteric society. However, says Nasr, "the Islamic guilds themselves never underwent such a transformation. They remained closely wed to Sufism and the spiritual practices of the Islamic religion."[56]

Some of the more philosophically- and spiritually-minded Freemasons have also found themselves attracted to Sufism. Part of the reason for the appeal lay in the belief that Sufism is "The Eastern parent of Free-Masonry," as Sir Richard Francis Burton claimed.[57] Burton's translations of Eastern religious and mystical texts appealed to both serious occult students and spiritual adventurers, including fringe Freemason Aleister Crowley, as we shall soon see.

The Craft Masonic Ritual and Islamic Esotericism

Similarities between Freemasonry and Islamic esotericism, especially Sufism and Shi'a Islam, certainly exist. However, we should understand Shah's and Burton's claim in the context of Masonic scholarship itself. Far from being the only claim for the origin of Freemasonry, an extraordinary number of theories have been advanced since the 18th century, and that of a Sufi origin is only one of the latest.

Other alleged origins range from the Crusaders (especially of the Order of the Knights Templar) to the Pharaonic Egyptians; from the ancient Druids, the pre-Christian Norse and Germanic peoples to initiates of the Dionysiac Mysteries; the Biblical story of Christ and the Resurrection, through the Cabala, European alchemists, the German Rosicrucians, Sir Isaac Newton, and Britain's scientific Royal Society. It is interesting to note, though, that in 1891, in volume IV of *Ars Quatuor Coronatorum* – the journal of the world's premier Masonic research Lodge – Rev. Haskett Smith claimed, in a paper titled "The Druses of Syria and Their Relation to Freemasonry," that the Masonic fraternity derived, ultimately, from this Middle Eastern sect.

The Druze faith emerged from Ismaili culture – itself a mystical offshoot of Shi'ism – but it incorporated beliefs from classical Greece, Christianity, and Judaism. Smith claimed that "so far as regards initiations and degrees, the Druse system is closely allied to Freemasonry." Unfortunately, as with so many other such theories, Smith's rests on descriptions of both the Druze and Freemasonry that are either applicable to virtually every religious or esoteric phenomenon (e.g., "the practical moral code of both may be represented by the same formula, 'Brotherly Love, Relief, and Truth' "), assertions that are not backed up by evidence, or relative similarities in the physical appearances of certain symbols.

Smith had come into contact with Druzes, but was not, however, able to witness their rituals for himself, despite repeated attempts. Believing that he had found the origin of Freemasonry, the Masonic scholar even took to giving the fraternity's passwords to individual Druze, in the hope of being recognized as a Brother, though he was unable to solicit any response."[58]

Nevertheless, Robert Ambelain, a scholar of Martinism and related Western esoteric movements, suggests that certain Masonic Rites may have derived partly from what he calls "Druze Masonry" in Lebanon. While, like many other writers on Freemasonry, he does not offer any concrete evidence for his assertions on its alleged origin, he nevertheless gives us a window into the thought of the Rite of Memphis (which is generally not recognized by regular Masonic jurisdictions in English speaking countries), saying that because they believed it to have derived from the Lebanese faith members of the Rite of Memphis named their Lodges and chapters "The Reunited Druzes," "Knights of Lebanon," and so on. Ambelain also claims that one of the high grades of the Rite, "Sublime Day," was named after a secret grade of initiation among the Druze.[59]

Although their methodologies and claims may be questionable, Smith and Ambelain are typical of the more intellectual and spiritual Freemasons, who, even today, remain very interested in non-Western, as well as pre-Christian European, religions and cultures. Hence, we might note that in the same volume as Smith's, another article titled "Masonic Landmarks Among the Hindus" by Rev. P. J. Oliver was also published. Remarkable for its time, by the turn of the century the *Ars Quatuor Coronatorum* had published articles on Hermeticism, Rosicrucianism, Hindu "Brahminical Initiation," the ancient symbol of the swastika (typically associated with Hinduism, Buddhism, and pre-Christian European religion and culture), and "West African Secret Tribal Societies."

Again, when the North Carolina branch (or "College") of the Societas Rosicruciana (a Rosicrucian society, membership of which is only available to Freemasons) was founded in 1933, its Chief Adept presented a lecture to members, and read off a list, "of short and lengthy subjects upon which we would like to have papers written." Notably, among the thirty-three suggested were "The Druses of Mount Lebanon" and "The Yezzidees," a Gnostic faith found largely in Iraq.[60]

Despite the serious interest in the world's religions and esoteric traditions and their mysteries, the above mentioned theories of Masonic origins share one thing in common: their proponents have rarely, if ever, made a proper study of the early Masonic documents, exposés, fragments of rituals, etc., or of the development of the Masonic Ritual and its symbolism. Instead, advocates nearly always rely on superficial similarities in symbolism and elements of mythology. Hence, the three pillars represented in the Masonic Lodge have been regarded as deriving from sources as divergent as the Jewish Cabalistic Tree of Life (the most commonly-known type of which has three trunks or pillars) and the pre-Christian Norse temple, devoted to the deities Odin, Thor, and Frey.

Shah falls into this category of theorist. He is really more of a philosopher, making use of the system he finds. As far as an exercise in creative esoteric philosophizing may go, this may be acceptable, but it is not historiography. His chapter in *The Sufis* devoted to demonstrating the alleged Sufi origin of Freemasonry exposes, instead, only a lack of knowledge of Masonic history. Instead of exploring Freemasonry in context, Shah reinterprets Masonic and Islamic symbolism through the "method of codes within codes," an obviously dubious manner of research, which he suggests is common to both.

Hence, employing numerology in regard to Roman and Arabic letters, Shah circumnavigates history, creating fanciful links where there are none. For Shah, for example, the Masonic emblem of the letter G – which is displayed on the eastern wall of the Masonic Lodge, and which represents the "Great Architect," "Grand Geometrician" (or "God"), and "Geometry" – is, he says, really "the Arabic letter Q." Much of his argument employs such acrobatics of logic.

Nevertheless, part of the enigma of Freemasonry is that its symbols and rituals can, with very varying degrees of success and legitimacy, be compared to those of various religions and esoteric schools. Since we have already looked at Sufi initiation and Islamic esotericism more broadly, and since we will soon explore Freemasonry in greater depth, and the influence of Islam on some late offshoots of the fraternity, it will be worth looking briefly at the Masonic initiation, and noting similarities to Islamic esotericism.

When the fraternity of "Free and Accepted Masons" emerged as a society independent of the stonemasons' trade, it had in its possession the basic building blocks of Masonic symbolism and ritual. There existed, for example, a basic initiation ritual (consisting in some parts of Britain of two Degrees, one for the initiation of Apprentices and one for Fellows). The nascent fraternity also possessed a mythology, recorded in various manuscripts or "old charges." (The oldest known of these is the Regius MS (circa 1390 AD).) During the first few decades of the 18th century Freemasons developed the initiation rituals, creating the "Masonic Ritual" or "Craft Freemasonry" of three Degrees, the first being for the initiation of an Entered Apprentice, the second for initiation into the Degree of Fellowcraft, and the third to raise Brothers to the Degree of Master Mason.

The basic structure of the Ritual owes much to the initiations of the stonemasons of Britain. However, the content of the Ritual is derived partly from there, partly from the actual work of stonemasonry, partly from Old Testament symbolism and legend, and partly from natural law philosophy, as we noted earlier. These were amalgamated, to a degree organically and over time, into a Ritual of complex and nuanced meaning, though the interpretation was essentially Christian, with an open Bible placed on the Lodge altar. The Lodge room was also said to be situated East-West partly in emulation of church buildings and partly because the Gospel had been brought from the East to the West.[61] (Such symbolism was later dropped in English-speaking Masonic jurisdictions, with the holy book of the initiate's religion being placed on the altar.)

The initiate into Craft Freemasonry is dressed in a way that exposes some or all of his extremities. He will also be blindfolded. In this condition, he will be led into the Lodge room, where he will meet with various symbolic dangers, swear an "Obligation," and will be taught various signs and esoteric symbols, thus "receiving light in Freemasonry." There are parallels with certain forms of Islamic esotericism as well as with the esoteric and mystical schools of other religions.

Although women were very occasionally initiated into Craft Freemasonry during the first half of the 18ᵗʰ century (usually because they had somehow overheard the proceedings, and formal initiation would mean swearing an Obligation, which included the promise not to reveal the secrets of the fraternity), membership of the society was normally limited to men who believed in God. To all intents and purposes, this meant Christians as well as a smaller number of Deists.

The initiations of the esoteric Shi'a Alawite sect of Syria are also reserved for adult males and its ritual, like that of Freemasonry, is partly drawn from notions of natural law (the belief that nature embodies Divine Law). Likewise, the structure of late Sufism was, as we have noted, influenced by the trade guilds and, like Freemasonry, used ritual forms of dress, and occasionally used building as a metaphor for their path. The formal transmission of secrets and esoteric interpretations of symbols through initiation rituals may also be common to Freemasonry, the Alawites, and Sufism, but it is also a phenomenon found worldwide, including in antiquity. Nevertheless, with Freemasons drawing on an array of religious culture, history, and symbolism, creating new Masonic Rites and rituals from the 18ᵗʰ century, it was almost inevitable that some of these would draw on esoteric interpretations of Islam.

The Arab and Sufi Influence in Europe and America

During the 19ᵗʰ century, Arab and Persian culture was beginning to appeal to some Freemasons, especially of a more esoteric inclination. It is certain that, in some parts of the Near East, Masonic Lodges and Sufi sects – especially the Bektashi – occasionally came into contact. But, in the West, the fringe Masonic and Western esoteric societies that emerged during this time, claiming some connection to Sufism, or Arab or Persian culture, were simply inspired by then-contemporary ideas about the exotic East.

Membership of the Ancient Arabic Order of the Nobles of the Mystic Shrine – often referred to as "the Shrine," "Mystic Shrine," or "the Shriners" – was only open to Freemasons who had taken the "Knights Templar" Degree (later, Freemasons could take either the Knights Templar Degree or the Consistory Degrees of the Ancient and Accepted Scottish Rite prior to application for membership in the Shrine), additional to the three Degrees of Freemasonry proper. This restriction suggests, perhaps, that it was originally envisioned as an elite Masonic body, but if this was the intention it very soon took on an entirely different character.

Undoubtedly due in part to its high street parades, charity, and reputation for good-humored entertainment, the Shrine's membership expanded rapidly. Yet, although its requirement – that prospective members had to have taken the higher Degrees of Freemasonry before admission – may have attracted some, who may have thought that some esoteric secret were to be found in its Ritual, it proved a barrier to entry for other Freemasons. Two decades after the founding of the Mystic Shrine, another, very similar society, would be founded, but with no requirement to take any Degree higher than that of Master Mason.

On September 10, 1889, members of Hamilton Lodge No. 120 in New York founded the Fairchild Deviltry Committee, with LeRoy Fairchild as its head. An initiation ritual was devised and then revised over time, with "some things that were considered objectionable" being removed. Conceived of as a purely local society for a small number of Freemasons, at first, on May 28, 1890, members of the F.D.C. met to establish a Supreme Council for what would afterward be known as the Mystic Order of the Veiled Prophets of the Enchanted Realm.

According to one history of the M.O.V.P.E.R. its Ritual, "is founded on a very ancient Persian manuscript, discovered in a secret vault in one of the sacred temples of Teheran, the City of Mystery, and the action involves many famous characters of ancient mythology."[62] In reality, the theme of the Ritual had been inspired by Thomas Moore's poem "Lalla Rookh" (1817) and its mention of a veiled prophet in Iran.

Its initiations were meant to be elaborate, theatrical affairs, "where fun and fantasy revel in joyous freedom," although not to the point where the members transgressed the far more sober expectations of conduct placed on the Freemason during the Craft Degrees. As with the Mystic Shrine, the M.O.V.P.E.R. – sometimes referred to as the Grotto – did not regard itself as Masonic per se, but, drawing their membership exclusively from Freemasonry, these societies were keen to show that they violated neither the laws nor the spirit of the fraternity.

In regard to regalia, the M.O.V.P.E.R. adopted the turban, though, later, this changed to a black fez, reminiscent of the red fez of the Mystic Shrine.

As with the Grotto, the spirit of the Shrine is fraternal, social, and charitable, rather than mystical. Its initiation ceremony – often referred to as "crossing the burning sands" – has participants wearing exaggerated Arabic clothing along with a red Turkish fez bejeweled with insignia, all of which gives the impression of pantomime performances of Ali Baba. Shrine rituals are more like carnivals.

A notice from 1921 advertising a "Shrine Ceremonial" depicts, in cartoon style, some rather unpleasant scenarios. One scene shows a number of naked men boiling in a pot, for example. In another, a naked man clings to a rope, trying not to fall onto a sword embedded upright in the ground, on which he would be impaled. In other scenes we see one man riding a camel blindfold, another impaled on a cactus, and two men hoodwinked, their arms bound, dancing on burning sand. None of this seems to reflect the often somber rituals of Freemasonry proper.

Nevertheless, the Ritual of the Mystic Shrine did contain more serious elements. According to one early 20th century monitor, or ritual book, the Mystic Shrine "was instituted by Mohammedan, Kalif-Alee," i.e., 'Ali, the son-in-law of Prophet Muhammad. Nevertheless, since both the Bible and the Qur'an were to be placed on an altar, and since the initiate was to swear "the obligation of the Nobility of the Mystic Shrine"[63] on the former, it is probable that this claim was intended to be understood as purely symbolic. Freemasons, after all, had long regarded the claim, made in the Craft Masonic Ritual, that Hiram Abiff, the architect of Solomon's Temple, was the first Grand Master of Freemasonry as symbolic or mythical.

Despite Christianity underlying the Shriner Ritual, one early history of the society claimed that it was a Westernized form of Sufism, saying, " 'Mystic Shrine' is merely an attempted translation of the Arabic word 'Bektash,' the name of a great secret fraternity which flourishes today in the Orient." The history goes on to say that the Bektashi sect was "noted for its liberal attitude towards foreigners," and that this had often placed the Sufi sect "in direct opposition to ecclesiastical and official Islam."

The Shrine's "nomenclature," we are told, "is a translation, more or less faithful, of the Arabic words." This includes the titles of Shrine officers. "Thus, the 'potentate' of the [Shrine] temple is simply the English equivalent of the 'sheik' of the Bektash," while "high priest and prophet" is derived from the Arabic, "imam." The alleged authenticity of the Shrine is also due to its origins, we are told. Accordingly, the actor William J. Florence "happened to be wintering on the Nile" in 1870, and "was initiated into the mysteries of the Bektash at Cairo."[64] He, along with Dr. Walter M. Fleming, founded the Shrine's "Mecca Temple" in New York the following year.

In other "histories," Florence is supposed to have been initiated into the Bektashi in Marseille, receiving its esoteric doctrine later in Algiers and Aleppo. However, evidence suggests that, along with some other Freemasons, the Ancient Arabic Order of the Nobles of the Mystic Shrine was founded in New York by Florence and Fleming in or around 1870.[65]

Despite some initial success in recruiting Freemasons, however, with the American economy soon taking a downturn, the new society began losing members and was forced to close a number of its fledgling temples. The Shrine might well have disappeared altogether had it not have been for

Albert Rawson. Having been presenting himself as an expert on Islam and the Middle East for a considerable time, around 1876 or 1877, Rawson was hired by Florence and Fleming and given the task of writing a new Ritual for the Shrine.[66] He was still appealing for work from the Shriners for a decade after its completion, and, consequently, Rawson was finally dismissed as someone more interested in finance than fraternity by the society he had helped give new life to.

A flamboyant figure who made questionable claims about the source of his knowledge, he was nonetheless praised by Mme. Blavatsky, founder of the Theosophical Society,[67] for his superior knowledge of the Middle East. Blavatsky believed him to have been initiated into the Druze religion, and to have a knowledge of the region unrivaled among Westerners.

Rawson himself claimed to have been initiated by a Bedouin shaykh and to have visited Mecca disguised as a Muslim, though it seems that he was in jail in New Jersey at the time that his *hajj* was supposed to have taken place. Nevertheless, Rawson was significantly involved with the Western spiritual underground milieu, including fringe Masonry and fraternalism.

In New York, during the 1870s, Rawson founded the fraternity of The Sheikhs of the Desert, Guardians of the Kaaba, Guardians of the Mystic Shrine. Like the Ancient Arabic Order of the Nobles of the Mystic Shrine, the narrative of the Ritual for this society was based on the *hajj* – a first hand account of which had been published by Richard Burton, who had gone there in disguise before Rawson began claiming to have visited Islam's holiest site in the same manner.

Notably, too, Rawson also claimed to have founded an esoteric society in London, based on instructions from an Arab in Paris, who, he believed, was connected to the Ismailis. This account is strikingly similar to the story of the founding of the Order of Ishmael, as recounted by John Yarker. A collector of fringe Masonic Rites, Yarker even approached Rawson, to apply for membership of his Sheikhs of the Desert, which he was granted.[68]

Persian Sufism, "Arab" and "Old Turkish" Freemasonry

In his multi-volume *Glossary of the Tribes and Castes of the Punjab and North-West Frontier Provinces* (1911), H. A. Rose asserts, "Members of the [Bektáshi Sufi] order are affiliated with French Masonic Lodges. Its headquarters are at Rumili Hissár [in Turkey]."[69] He would not be the last to claim that some kind of union of Freemasonry and Sufism existed in relation to Turkey.

The self-styled Baron Rudolf von Sebottendorff (born Adam Alfred Rudolf Glauer) had been born into modest circumstances, in 1875, in a market town near Dresden. But he had grown up with a sense of adventure. In 1900 he found his way to Cairo, where he met and began working for a wealthy Turkish landowner, Hussein Pasha. In the same year, he saw whirling dervishes of the Mevlevi sect of Sufis. It ignited his interest in the mystical. Pasha, who was a Sufi himself, encouraged Sebottendorff, as did an elderly member of the Greco-Jewish Termudi family, who he had met at Bursa, Turkey, where he had resided for a time. The elderly Termudi was a devoted student of the Cabala, alchemy, and Rosicrucianism, and a member of a Masonic Lodge. Sebottendorff was soon initiated.

Having already been studying the traditions of Turkey, learning the language, and exploring its religious culture with a local imam, Sebottendorff began to believe that Islamic mysticism was connected to the ancient Germanic tradition, and, most specifically, to the runes, which were enjoying a renaissance in occult circles in Germany and Austria. In 1916 he moved to Bavaria and again came into contact with purported representatives of the Mysteries. He had seen an advert for the *Germanenorden* (Germanic Order) in a local newspaper, at the bottom of which were three runes. Sebottendorff was intrigued and decided to make contact. It was not long before he met its leader, Hermann Pohl, in Berlin. Sharing an interest in the esoteric interpretation of the runic alphabet, there was an immediate rapport between the two men, and Sebottendorff was soon busying himself, promoting the

Order in Bavaria, as well as working as Pohl's secretary and publishing its periodical, *Runen*.[70]

Like many of those involved in runic-based mysticism and occultism, Sebottendorff was anti-modern, anti-materialistic, and opposed to the rising tide of communism. He had witnessed nationalist politics in Egypt, and, now in Germany, convinced of a glorious Aryan past – which he believed, peculiarly, encapsulated the Islamic mysticism of Turkey, as well as Germany's indigenous occult traditions – he became increasingly involved in its nationalist politics. Nevertheless, in 1924 Sebottendorff published *The Practice of the Ancient Turkish Freemasons – The Key to the Understanding of Alchemy*,[71] a slim volume, in which he claimed to set out the practice known as "the science of the key" of the Turkish Bektashi sect of Sufi Islam.

By then, however, another occultist had attempted to draw Freemasonry and Islam together in a highly unorthodox and highly esoteric manner. Aleister Crowley (1875-1947), an English occultist, as well as Freemason, mountaineer, adventurer, and poet, had joined the Hermetic Order of the Golden Dawn while still in his early twenties, in 1898. The Order had been founded by William Wynn Westcott and S. L. MacGregor Mathers – both active esotericists and, notably, prominent members of the *Societas Rosicruciana in Anglia*, a Rosicrucian society only open to regular Freemasons – along with William Robert Woodman, who died shortly after.

Later, in 1910, having left the Golden Dawn behind, and having established himself as a controversial authority on "Magick," Crowley joined the Ordo Templi Orientis.[72] This organization had been founded by Theodor Reuss and Carl Kellner, both Freemasons with a strong interest in the esotericism. Reuss had originally envisioned the Order as a Masonic body, to be known as *Academia Masonica*. However, despite overtures, the O.T.O. was never recognized by regular Masonic jurisdictions as having any legitimate connection to the Masonic fraternity.

In its Degrees, the O.T.O. had originally taught the legend of Hiram Abiff – the chief architect and builder of Solomon's temple, and, according

to Masonic tradition, the first Grand Master of Freemasonry. Since this was
– and still is – central to the Masonic Ritual, the Order effectively challenged
the legitimacy of regular Masonic jurisdictions, making it an illegitimate or
"clandestine" organization according to regular Freemasonry.

At least partly to prevent the O.T.O. clashing with established
Freemasonry, and to enable the more esoterically-inclined members of the
fraternity to join, in 1919 Crowley revised the Order's Degrees, and replaced
Hiram Abiff with the Persian Sufi Mansur al-Hallaj (858-922 C.E.).[73] Later,
in 1944, as Crowley prepared to pass on what was left of the O.T.O. to a
new generation he began to talk of finding a "Caliph" (the Islamic term for
"successor," used to denote the leader in the line of successors of the Prophet
Muhammad) and a "Caliphate" (the classical pan-Islamic jurisdiction).
Crowley was well aware of the meanings of these terms, but, as with the
story of al-Hallaj, he bent them to his own purposes.

Still, this does not mean that his admiration for aspects of Islamic
culture and mysticism was in some way insincere. Crowley writes in his
Confessions that, long before this, "Persian fascinated me more than any
other language had ever done and I revelled in the ideas of the Sufis. Their
esoteric symbolism delighted me beyond measure."[74]

In August 1905, Crowley led an expedition up Kangchenjunga, the
world's third highest mountain. This was the first ever attempt to scale the
mountain located in the eastern Himalayas, on the border of India and Nepal.
Four climbers died in the endeavor, and the party failed to reach the summit.
In September, following the calamity, Crowley traveled to Calcutta and
stayed briefly with the Maharajah of Moharbhanj. There, planning to return
to England via Persia, and having castigated himself for his ignorance of
Sufism, he "began to study the language with a munshi," Crowley says in the
Confessions, "to imitate the poets of Iran."[75]

Never insecure about his intellect or abilities, Crowley was soon writing
"The Ghazals of Ishtar," a collection of poems named after the ancient
Babylonian and Assyrian goddess, but in the style of the Sufi poets. This

project was to turn into *The Scented Garden of Abdullah The Satirist of Shiraz*, probably Crowley's least-known book, though described by the author himself as nothing less than "a complete treatise on mysticism, expressed in the symbolism of Persian piety."[76]

It was typographed in both Persian and Roman lettering and printed by the scholar-printer Philippe Renouard in Paris. Two hundred copies were printed on Van Gelder paper and packaged in parchment, with the Persian title – *Bagh-i-Muattar* – printed on the upper cover. A deluxe edition of ten copies was also printed on Japanese Vellum. The care and consideration of quality and details indicate how seriously Crowley regarded the work, which would not bear his name. Publishing it pseudonymously, Crowley created Abdullah el Haji, whom he imagined would have composed the work circa 1600. Since a translator would be needed for the ruse, Crowley invented the Reverend P. D. Carey, a somewhat unsavory member of the clergy, interested in boys and young men, and beset by the peculiar habit of evoking the ancient Greek pagan god Pan in curiously Crowlean manner.

Despite its oddities, for the English poet, irregular Freemason, and occultist, the work transcended even the Tao Te Ching and the Bhagavad Gita, texts that had influenced Crowley's understanding of spirituality. (Crowley even translated the Tao Te Ching into English.) The symbolism of *The Scented Garden*, though, was erotic – specifically homoerotic – as well as mystical. Its poems are dense and, by today's standards, dry and academic, however. Despite the occasional reference to "buttocks," it is difficult for the modern reader to discern anything erotic in them. "As I placed the rigid pen of my thought within the inkstand of my imagination," begins the first of the poems, "The Abyss." If one knows the nature of the poetry, the sexual metaphor is obvious, but it would hardly excite the modern voyeur. Nevertheless, while *The Scented Garden* was sold through the London Orientalist bookseller Probsthain and Co. in 1908, because of its symbolism, most copies were seized and destroyed by Britain's Customs authorities.[77]

While the reader may not learn much about genuine Sufi Islam from the work, in the introduction to *The Scented Garden* Crowley implies a kinship between Sufism and Freemasonry, and claims to have belonged to both societies:

Being myself admitted formally [...] to the joyous company of the Sufis, (I cannot here discuss the curiously patriarchal systems of mystic fraternity in vogue among Muslim[s], if only because I am a Freemason) I was enabled to use several fine MSS. for the translation, a privilege of which I availed myself without scruple or diffidence: without scruple, as knowing I was well entitled to them; and without diffidence, because of the invariable courtesy which adepts in these mysteries exhibit to their fellow workers in the divine Arcanum.[78]

Moreover, *The Scented Garden* may help us understand *Liber AL vel Legis*, or *The Book of The Law*, a text that Crowley claimed had been dictated to him, in Cairo, by a spirit called Aiwass on April 8, 9, and 10, 1904. Although Crowley claimed to be initially repulsed by its message, the text would later become the foundation of his religion, *Thelema*.

The idea of receiving a revelation from a spirit or deity was known in British occult circles, and the English magus had himself made an early, though aborted, attempt to contact his "Holy Guardian Angel." Yet, it is strikingly similar to the Islam's claim that Muhammad had received the Qur'an, from the Angel Gabriel over a period of roughly 22 years.

Crowley's *Book of The Law* would, however, be rejected by any believing Muslim, not least of all because the text declares that earlier religions and revelations have been abrogated. The implication is that Crowley has been ordained the prophet of the new aeon.

Yet, even so – and despite being populated with pre-Islamic, Egyptian deities, such as Isis and Osiris – the wording of Crowley's *Liber AL vel Legis* appears to have been significantly modeled on the Qur'an. Hence, for example, reminiscent of the Qur'anic command to "sacrifice a heifer... neither too old nor too young..." (surah II, 8, 67-68),[79] we read in *Liber AL vel Legis* (Ch. III, 12), "Sacrifice cattle, little and big."

Again, whether taken literally or interpreted metaphorically, in both the Qur'an and in Crowley's *Liber AL vel Legis* we find commands to make war against certain enemies and to be strong or have strength in that task. Hence, *Liber AL vel Legis* reads, "Also ye shall be strong in war,"[80] and again, "I will give you a war-engine. With it ye shall smite the peoples; and none shall stand before you,"[81] while the Qur'an says, similarly,

> Against them make ready
> Your strength to the utmost
> Of your power, including
> Steeds of war, to strike terror.[82]

At times, we find explicitly Islamic terms appearing in the text. Crowley, as the recipient, of the message of *The Book of The Law*, is instructed to "Establish at thy Kaaba a clerk-house," the Kaaba being the black, cubic structure at the center of the mosque in Mecca, constituting Islam's holiest site. The text – or Aiwass – also instructs Crowley to establish a temple, which, "shall be your Kiblah for ever." "Kiblah" is normally understood as referring to the direction of Mecca, which Muslims are required to face when praying. Later Crowley would identify the "Kiblah" of his *Book of The Law* with his home – Boleskine House – in Scotland. It would be there that his disciples would face.[83]

Similarities between the Qur'an and *Liber AL vel Legis* are not, then, coincidental. In fact, in accord with Islamic tradition, Crowley had memorized some parts of the Islamic holy book while in Cairo, and, as such, it is unsurprising, that even where *Liber AL vel Legis* does not draw on Islamic terminology, it seems, at times, like half-remembered passages from the Qur'an.

Although Crowley had once claimed to have known no one in Cairo besides "a General Dickson, who had accepted Islam," as well as a few carpet merchants, pimps, and other persons of low stature[84] in that society, in his *Confessions*, he states that,

> As to my study of Islam, I got a sheikh to teach me Arabic and the practices of ablution, prayer and so on, so that at some future time I might pass for a Moslem among themselves. I had it in my mind to repeat Burton's journey to Mecca sooner or later. I learnt a number of chapters of the Koran by heart…
>
> My sheikh was profoundly versed in the mysticism and magic of Islam, and discovering that I was an initiate, had no hesitation in providing me with books and manuscripts on the Arabic Cabbala. These formed the basis of my comparative studies. I was able to fit them in with similar doctrines and other religions…
>
> From this man I learnt also many of the secrets of the [Islamic co-fraternity of the] Sidi Aissawa.[85]

Lastly, then, we might note that although Crowley would come to believe that Aiwass (spelled as "Aiwaz") was "the true most ancient name of the God of the Yezidis,"[86] the name of his Holy Guardian Angel is strikingly similar to that of the Islamic society (Aissawa) – from which Crowley claims to have learned certain secrets. Indeed, "Aiwass" seems to be more or less an anagram of "Aissawa."

Although he may have gone further in his pursuit to understand the religion, Crowley was not the only British esotericist interested in Islamic mysticism, of course. One serious, if short-lived attempt to create a Sufi-type secret society in Great Britain and Europe was the so-called Order of Ishmael. It claimed that the "Chiefs of the Order reside habitually in the East, and two of the three chiefs must always be east of Jerusalem." This was certainly untrue, but the custom of fabricating secret chiefs was already a long-established custom in the overlapping fringe Masonic and occult scenes. Sometimes the chiefs were alleged to be actual people – as was the case here – while at other times they were said to be spiritual entities that existed on a higher plane than our own, and who appeared occasionally to guide humanity.

It is possible that there is a tangential connection between this fringe Masonic society and the Ancient Arabic Order of the Nobles of the Mystic Shrine, via the figure of Albert Rawson. However, according to John, the Order of Ishmael was founded by Kenneth MacKenzie, a Masonic scholar who had been highly active in secretive, fringe Masonic and Rosicrucian-type societies.

In an article on "Arab Masonry," published in 1908 in *Ars Quatuor Coronatorum*, Yarker claims that "In 1872 the late Bro. Mackenzie organized the 'Order of Ishmael,' of 36 [Degrees of initiation], the basis of which, he informed me, he had [obtained] from an Arab in Paris, and in 1884 I was myself in relation with Prince Moustafa ben Ismael, ex-Prime Minister of Tunis, then in Paris." According to Yarker, MacKenzie believed that the "Biblical legends were the transmissions of the 'Order of Ishmael'," "the oldest secret society in the world," after which he had modeled his own organization.[87]

The 36 Degrees were divided into four sections – Initiatory, Historical, Explanatory, and Philosophical – with nine Degrees to each section. The names of the first section are rather Masonic-sounding, e.g., Minor Fellow, Major Fellow, Companion, and Master, while the Degrees of the second read like scenes of a play: Ishmael, Isaac, The Burial, Marriage, The Meeting, The Desert, etc. Together, the first 18 Degrees were concerned with "The history of Ishmael and his mother, and that of Jacob and Esau."

The Degrees of the Explanatory section focus on positions of authority, with some emphasis on the militant as a metaphor of initiation. They are "Novelty," "The Attack," "Aid," "Chief," "Prince," "Teacher," "Illustrious," "Commander," and "Patriarch." The final section, however, was more concerned with religious and esoteric themes: e.g., "Faith," "Hope," "Charity," "Providence," and "Fate." It is undoubtedly significant that the name of the final Degree was "Submission," the literal meaning of *Islam* (submission to the Will of Allah). However, if MacKenzie did believe that the Order was in some sense Islamic, it was of an extremely unorthodox type.

It was not necessary to be a Freemason to join the Order, and, though Catholics were prohibited, Protestants and Orthodox Christians, Muslims, Hindus, Jews, and Zoroastrians were all permitted to join. Considering that the membership remained confined to a small clique of esoteric Freemasons and occultists, it is certain that it was not as cosmopolitan in reality as it was in theory. Nevertheless, the rules of the Order allowed for candidates to swear their "obligation" over the object that was sacred to their faith. "If a Mohammedan [Muslim], he is obligated on the Qur'an;" MacKenzie tells us in his *Royal Masonic Cyclopaedia*, "if a Brahman, on the Vedas; if a Jew, on the Old Testament; Parsees [Zoroastrians], by Fire; Hindus by the Cow; if a member of the Orthodox Greek Church, or a Protestant of any denomination, on the four Gospels."[88]

THREE

Muslim Revolutionaries, Masonic Lodges, and the Near East

Freemasonry began to spread across the globe relatively early on in the life of the fraternity. In 1730, a Masonic Lodge was founded in Calcutta. And already, in 1728, Lord Kingston, Grand Master of England, had granted a Deputation to George Pomfret, enabling the founding of Masonic Lodges in Bengal, although this does not appear to have come to fruition. The relatively rapid globalization of the fraternity was due to the granting of charters to army regiments, especially by the Irish Grand Lodge. This enabled soldiers to hold Lodge meetings and rituals as they traveled abroad. Foreigners were not expected to join.

At this point, still, British, Irish, and continental European Freemasons were overwhelmingly Christian, or otherwise Deist. The first Jews were probably admitted in London during the late 1720s or very early 1730s, with the first recorded initiation being that of Edward Rose in 1732.[89] The fraternity would eventually liberalize further, proving attractive to non-Europeans in Persia, India, Egypt, and elsewhere. However, while European Freemasons were often interested in the antiquities of the East, the non-Europeans who joined the fraternity were often inspired by its apparent modernity, especially its ability to transcend ethnic, religious, and other such divisions.

Regardless of what went on in the world, Freemasons addressed each other as "Brother" inside the Lodge. Members of the fraternity met "on the level." Social and other distinctions were unimportant, at least in theory. This appealed to many non-Europeans who were employed in colonial government administration or had other, minor official functions. But the prospect of membership proved attractive for other reasons. A number of non-European diplomats joined – often at least partly to cement relations between their country and one of the colonial powers – as did the occasional member of a royal family. Persian dignitaries were initiated into Freemasonry from early on in the 19th century, in Europe. Askeri-Khan, an ambassador of the Shah, became a Freemason in Paris in November 1808. He is known to have had discussions with his French brethren about the possibility of establishing a Lodge at Isfahan, although there is no evidence that the conversation was ever acted on. In 1810, Mirza Abul Hassan Khan, Minister to the Court of Persia, was made a Freemason in the city of London.[90] Again, Habibullah Khan, the emir of Afghanistan, was initiated into Freemasonry on a visit to Punjab, India, in 1906.[91]

Intellectuals and radicals comprised another group keen for admittance to the Masonic Lodge. The networks and relative privacy of Freemasonry presented such outliers with an opportunity to express, to a private audience, views that were taboo, and even to agitate for political reform. Elie Kedourie suggests that "Freemasonry and freethinking seem to have been closely linked at that time [the middle of the 19th century] in the Near East. To be a freemason was to show one's dislike of orthodox, traditional religion, the power it gave to ecclesiastics, and the hatreds and divisions it promoted and perpetuated in society."[92]

A Sufi and Resistance Fighter

There is more than a grain of truth to Kedourie's assertion, but it does not give the whole picture. Freethinkers, who were at least nominal Muslims, certainly joined Masonic Lodges, but so, occasionally, did those who found some resonance between the ethics of Islam and those of Freemasonry. One of those was Abd al-Qadir al-Jazairi (1808-1883), Sufi, resistance fighter, and Emir of Mascara in northwest Algeria.

Abd al-Qadir was born into a family of prominence in the Qadiriyya Order of Sufism, which had been founded by Shaykh 'Abd al-Qadir al-Jaylani in 1165. He was also a descendant (*sharif*) of the family of the Prophet of Islam.

While still a young man, in 1826-27, Abd al-Qadir and his father, shaykh Muhy al-Din – then head of the Qadiriyya Order in the region – traveled to Mecca for the *hajj*, visiting Cairo, Damascus, and Baghdad along the way. Wherever they stopped, Abd al-Qadir met and discussed with the scholars of different Sufi traditions, gaining a deeper understanding of the esoteric and philosophical traditions within Islam.

However, only a few years later, in 1830, the French invaded Algeria, which had been under Ottoman rule for three centuries. Initially Muhy al-Din led the resistance against the French, but, realizing that he was too old to be effective, he soon abdicated this responsibility, as well as his leadership of the Qadiriyya Order, to Abd al-Qadir. Of necessity, the son turned from contemplative to a military leader, uniting Arabs and Berbers behind him in his jihad against the French.

Tens of thousands of Algerians were killed, either on the battlefield or because of the scorched earth policy of the French, who destroyed orchards and crops, causing widespread famine. Consequently, Abd al-Qadir was forced to sue for peace in 1847. Taken to France, and placed under minimum-security house arrest, he devoted himself to the study of the works of Sufi master Ibn al-Arabi, though, from this new vantage point, he also observed the material progress that France was making due to of its embrace of scientific rationalism.[93]

In 1851, Napoleon III ordered Abd al-Qadir's release. The Sufi master traveled to Istanbul – where he met with the sultan – and then to western Anatolia. Four years later, he returned to Paris to seek permission to live in an Arab country. The French allowed Abd al-Qadir to settle in Damascus, Syria. His humane treatment of French prisoners had earlier earned him a reputation as a man of honor. Now his reputation as a man of learning was beginning to spread. Before his departure to Damascus in 1855, Paris's Asiatic Society registered Abd al-Qadir as a Fellow and requested him to send a sample of his work. He composed an essay titled "Reminding the Rational Man and Alerting the Neglectful Man," and submitted it to the society. In it, Abd al-Qadir contemplated the relationship of revelation to reason, and of Muslims and Christians, to one another. As for revelation and reason, he regarded them as complementary. God had given man the capacity to understand the material world and to know the spiritual, partly through the use of reason.

At the invitation of a number of 'ulama, on his arrival in Damascus Abd al-Qadir began giving lessons on the Qur'an and Sunnah at the Umayyad mosque.[94] He had traveled to the country with an entourage of fellow Algerians, who settled with him. With his fame and reputation preceding him, and with a large pension from Napoleon III at his disposal, Abd al-Qadir soon enlarged his circle, patronizing some 'ulama, and establishing an intellectual salon for the discussion of Sufi texts at his home. In the summer of 1860, anti-Christian riots broke out in Damascus. Abd al-Qadir intervened, appealing to the Ottoman governor, local Muslim notables, and local Druze communities, in an attempt to prevent more violence.

In addition, the Sufi master also sheltered a number of Christians, including several monks and nuns, and, with his armed entourage, held a local mob at bay. Abd al-Qadir had seen in Algeria how the slightest pretext could be enough for the French to send in the troops, to occupy Muslim land. Besides giving Christians refuge in his house, he also protected the French and British consulates, warning the mob that their persistence would mean the French would invade and would turn the mosques into churches.

Still, even if some Muslims began to suspect that France's former enemy was now working for its interests, the protection of the Christians won Abd al-Qadir new respect and attention in the West. European rulers sent him medals, awards, and gifts in response to his actions. And Henry IV, a Masonic Lodge under the jurisdiction of the French Grand Orient, was another interested party. The Lodge wrote to Abd al-Qadir, praising him, and asking him to affiliate. The Freemasons informed the Sufi leader that their society was based on a belief in the existence of God, the immortality of the soul, and the brotherhood of man. He had previously regarded Freemasons as atheists who intended to "disturb the order of society." Now Abd al-Qadir had an entirely different impression.

He corresponded with the Lodge for the next four years, affiliating himself with the French-based group of Freemasons until the possibility of initiation. This came in 1864. Returning from the *hajj*, Abd al-Qadir visited Alexandria, Egypt, where he was initiated into the Lodge of the Pyramids, which acted as a proxy for Henry IV. Afterwards, he wrote to the Parisian Lodge, referring to its members – in line with Masonic etiquette – as "Brothers," and telling them that he understood that the basis of Freemasonry was to do what is constructive for God's creatures, to act with humanity and fraternal love, and to drive away whatever is harmful.

It would not be long, however, before the relationship was broken off. The following year, in 1865, Abd al-Qadir traveled to Paris, meeting the brethren of Henry IV Lodge. They had always hoped that having a man of his stature in their ranks would help spread Freemasonry in the Middle East. Now, bluntly, they asked for his help. Abd al-Qadir refused, saying that the people would not be receptive. The Grand Orient was becoming progressively secular and had even removed the invocation to "The Great Architect of the Universe" (a Masonic term for God) at the beginning of their meetings. The Algerian Sufi wondered what value there could be in an initiatic society that was expelling God from its rituals, symbols, and gatherings. Moreover, he was now convinced that the Freemasons "no longer were interested in exchanges with Islam and its spirituality which could enrich them," says Ahmed Bouyerdene, "but rather that they were seeking Muslim representatives capable of extending their influence and propagating Masonic ideals in the East."[95]

Nevertheless, some anti-colonialist Muslims and free thinkers in the region would soon join Masonic Lodges in the hope of propagating their ideas. And Egypt, where Abd al-Qadir had been initiated, would be the main center of this activity.

Jamal ad-Din al-Afghani and His Disciples

According to legend, the fraternity was introduced to Cairo in 1798 by soldiers traveling with Napoleon Buonaparte's army. Since Freemasonry was popular in France, it is certain that a number of these soldiers would have been members of the fraternity, and it is possible that they held Masonic meetings and rituals during their spare time. However, evidence puts the first Masonic Lodges in Egypt in 1802, when Lodge La Bienfaisance was established under a charter of the Grand Orient of France.

During the latter half of the 19th century, Freemasonry would attract some of Egypt's most notable figures. Prince 'Abdu'l-Halim Pasha, was elected Grand Master of the Grand Orient in Egypt in 1867. He was the son of the founder of modern Egypt, Muhammed Ali Pasha, and a rival to the Khedive Ismail, who had him exiled to Istanbul the following year. Nevertheless, during the 1870s, Halim Pasha used the Masonic Order to agitate for the deposition of the khedive.[96]

Yet, of the non-European intellectuals and radicals to join Freemasonry in Egypt, Sayyid Jamal ad-Din al-Afghani (1838-1897) is both one of the best-known and perhaps the most significant. Born in Shi'ite-majority Persia, al-Afghani, as his name suggests, presented himself as an Afghan, and, by implication, an adherent of Sunni Islam, the largest branch of the religion. He is often regarded as a freethinker, however. And there are plenty of signs that this was the case, or, at least, that this was one side of al-Afghani. One of his lovers had been a Dutch woman, and he associated with Babis, Christians, Jews, and secularists, throughout his life. Al-Afghani also admired and immersed himself in Western philosophy and political ideas. But he was nonetheless determined to help Muslim societies advance intellectually and scientifically, not least of all so that they would be able to rid themselves of the Western colonial powers.[97]

Several of his associates agitated for religious reform. These included a Catholic priest from North Mesopotamia – the Reverend John Louis Sabunji – and Yaqub Sanu (1839-1912), who went by the name of James Sanua, and who was Jewish. Sanua founded the journal *Abou Naddara*, which opposed the Khedive Ismail for his stoking religious fanaticism, and rejected the idea that religious differences were important, regarding all people as "brothers in humanity." Sabunji likewise published his own newspaper – the London-based *al-Nahlah*, (The Bee).[98]

Another of al-Afghani's associates was Mirza Malkam Khan (1833-1908). An Armenian and a nominal convert to Islam, Khan had founded a secret society called the *Faramushkhaneh* (House of Oblivion), which he modeled on Freemasonry, in Tehran in 1858. He had been initiated the preceding year, in a mass induction of Iranian ambassadors into the Grand Orient Lodge Sincere Amitie in Paris.[99] The purpose of the *Faramushkhaneh* was to formulate and spread a supposedly "purer doctrine" of Islam, which would advance modern, liberal ideas. In order to convince Muslims, Islam, it was claimed, had been the originator of the progressive worldview.[100] Some years after the dissolution of his society Malkam Khan told an audience in London that:

> I went to Europe and studied there the religious, social and political systems of the west. I learned the spirit of various sects of Christendom, and the organization of the secret societies and freemasonries, and I conceived a plan which should incorporate the political wisdom of Europe with the religious wisdom of Asia. I knew that it would be useless to attempt a remodeling of Persia in European forms, and I was determined to clothe my material reformation in a garb which my people would understand, the garb of [the Islamic] religion.[101]

The *Faramushkhaneh* provoked fierce objections from the 'ulama.[102] It also stood outside regular Freemasonry during its short lifespan, since it was neither Masonic in its character or intentions, nor had it been chartered or otherwise endorsed by any Masonic Grand Lodge. Nevertheless, interest in Freemasonry was growing among Persia's elite. In January 1864, the *American Freemasons' Magazine* claimed, on the authority of a Persian military officer, that Freemasonry enjoyed wide popularity among the members of the Court of Tehran.[103]

Al-Afghani's importance as a political agitator began only after his arrival in Egypt in March 1871, at the beginning of a turbulent decade for the country. Despite extortionate levels of taxation burdening the population, the Treasury declared bankruptcy in 1876. Under the Khedive Ismail, the influence of European nations had grown considerably and was growing still. As a consequence of the turmoil, creditor nations imposed financial controls on Egypt. Two years later Europeans were included in the cabinet.

On his arrival in Egypt, al-Afghani began teaching philosophy at the highly-respected mosque-university of al-Azhar, although the 'ulama quickly protested the introduction of the rational sciences, and he was forced to withdraw. Al-Afghani continued to lead a circle of disciples, however, and would go out at night to meet with them in a coffee shop, to drink tea, smoke, and talk. The occasional glass of brandy also passed his lips as he held court, before returning home at dawn. He was, Elie Kedourie says, "the centre of a group of intellectual malcontents and religious rebels, to whom he purveyed secret and subversive philosophical doctrines."[104]

Open agitation against the khedive was, of course, a risky business, and Lodges and other private groups potentially provided some cover. Al-Afghani applied to become a Freemason in May 1875, and was soon initiated and attending various Lodges, including three Italian Lodges in Cairo. A number of educated Egyptians were already Freemasons, and al-Afghani had no trouble in convincing members of his own circle to join. He evidently regarded Freemasonry as a fraternity bound by the bonds of liberty and dedicated to the destruction of tyranny. To his dismay, though, his powers of persuasion proved far less effective during Lodge meetings than he had hoped, with his attempts to discuss politics quickly quashed.

Political discussion had long been taboo in Freemasonry, at least in English-speaking countries, even if Lodges have sometimes indulged in such conversation, and even if some others have found themselves involved in revolutionary activity – such as was the case in the lead-up to, and during, the Mexican War of Independence (1810-1821).[105] For al-Afghani, unwillingness to even discuss politics exposed cowardice. He was further enraged by the reverence shown to the Grand Master for England, the Prince of Wales, who visited Cairo in both 1875 and 1876, and was addressed inside the Lodge as "Crown Prince."

Not long after this time, the radical thinker began to withdraw from Egypt's loose network of Lodges and formed a "National Lodge" of his own. It was formally affiliated with the Grand Orient of France, one of the most liberal Masonic jurisdictions, but al-Afghani may have viewed it as potentially the most revolutionary.

There is some suggestion that he had been accused of not believing in God, by one Lodge, not long after being initiated into Freemasonry, and this may also have been part of the reason for the rupture since it was a requirement of Masonic Lodges at that point. The Egyptian authorities would also later come to view him as an atheist, but al-Afghani must have at least claimed – for some considerable time – to have believed in God, to have been eligible to join the Masonic fraternity. It is more likely, then, that his views were unorthodox but not atheist per se. Nevertheless, it is interesting to note that, having already omitted references to "the Great Architect" in its Ritual, in 1877 the Grand Orient of France dropped belief in God as a requirement for membership.

Unlike others in Egypt, al-Afghani's National Lodge had clear social and political aims. To further them, it created several committees to approach Egypt's ministries, to agitate for better treatment of Egyptian civil servants, officers, and other government employees (who earned a fraction of Europeans employed in the same capacity). Not surprisingly, perhaps, besides al-Afghani's students, members of his National Lodge included intellectuals, journalists, army officers, members of the Assembly, and a number of clerics. However, his political agitation alarmed the authorities, just as his teaching philosophy had earlier unnerved some of the 'ulama at al-Azhar. On August 24, 1879, charged with heading a secret society that aimed at the "corruption of religion and the world" through violent means, al-Afghani was taken by the police and put on a ship bound for India.

Restless and energetic by nature, by 1883 al-Afghani had found his way to Paris. There he continued his political work, meeting with Egyptian exiles, and mingling with the city's cultural elite. He also began publishing a journal, in which he called for Muslims to unite under a caliph and rise up against Western imperialist powers, especially the British.[106] During this decade he also traveled to Persia at the invitation of the shah, who hoped that he would serve as an advisor. The radical activist traveled back and forth and was finally expelled in 1891, at which point he went to neighboring Iraq.

The following year, in 1892, Sultan Abdul Hamid II invited al-Afghani to Istanbul, and gave him an appointment to work with a number of Persians whose unorthodox religious and political views had caused them to flee their homeland (these included adherents of the schismatic faith of Babism, the forerunner to the Baha'i). This group was charged with writing letters to Iran's Shi'ite 'ulama, to appeal for their support for a caliphate under the Sultan.[107]

Although not as well known as al-Afghani, one of his students would go on to shape, to a greater degree, his countrymen's conception of Islam. Muhammad 'Abduh (1849-1905) was part of al-Afghani's immediate circle of disciples in Egypt from 1871, meeting in the home of the latter for informal classes, and spreading the ideas he absorbed. He would also later join al-Afghani in Paris, after being exiled from Egypt himself, "helping him [al-Afghani] to organize his secret society and publish [his journal] *al-'Urwa al-wuthqa.*"[108]Al-Afghani was not the only influence, however. 'Abduh read and communicated with some European thinkers, and throughout his life would periodically visit Europe "to renew himself."[109]

'Abduh had been born into a family of some local prestige in the Egyptian delta. At thirteen, he had been sent to the Ahmadi mosque at Tanta to be educated, but he soon ran away, despairing at the rote learning of commentaries on the classical Islamic texts. His uncle, a shaykh, freed the young 'Abduh "from the bonds of literalism to the freedom of true belief in God," and convinced him to return to complete his studies.

After graduating at Tanta, 'Abduh went on to al-Azhar university. He remained there from 1869 to 1877, studying logic and philosophy as well as esoteric theology, the latter of which became the focus of his studies. He graduated with the degree of *'alim* (Muslim scholar), and began both teaching at the university and holding informal classes in his home, shortly before taking a position with Dar al-'Ulum, a new college that aimed to provide a modern education for those aspiring to become judges or teachers in state schools.

Politically active during his period of exile, 'Abduh visited London in 1884 to raise the issue of Egypt and the Sudan, and then traveled to Tunis and Beirut, briefly entering Egypt again in disguise. He was formally allowed back into the country in 1888, partly due to an appeal by the British Agency. Although he had hoped to commence teaching, the khedive was unenthusiastic about the radical being in a position to influence young minds, and he was given the position of judge in the "native tribunals." The following year, however, 'Abduh had risen to become the Mufti of Egypt. Now as supreme head of religious law in his country of birth, 'Abduh began to reform the religious courts. Regarding public law, he also began to issue *fatwas* (religious opinions/rulings) reinterpreting Islamic doctrine to suit the needs of the time.

For 'Abduh, as for al-Afghani, the essential problem of the Arab world was an inner one. Egypt had, metaphysically, split into two with the establishment of two distinct types of education. Younger Egyptians had absorbed European thought and clamored for change and modernity.

They contrasted the other half of society, which represented Sunni Islam, and believed in tradition. While 'Abduh believed that individualism – and its emphasis on reason as the ultimate guide – threatened to undermine the moral basis of society, he also felt that it was undesirable to remain in the past. Change was already upon Egypt, and it was his duty to enable his countrymen to see that the transformation underway could occur within the limits of Islam. The religion could, he believed, be the voice of change while safeguarding morality.[110]

FOUR

Shaykh Abdullah Quilliam and the Ancient Order of Zuzimites

The man who founded Britain's first mosque was a multi-layered character. In what would surely lead to accusations of his being an Islamist today, William Henry Quilliam (1856-1932) sought to counter negative impressions of Islam, advocated pro-Ottoman and pan-Islamic positions, and was a vocal advocate of rights for Muslims. Writing in the journal of *Comparative Studies of South Asia, Africa and the Middle East* in 2007, Eric Germain describes Quilliam as one of a few Muslim activists of the Victorian period who "were staunch advocates of the mobilization of an international Muslim brotherhood." At the same time, however, the British convert to Islam was involved in a number of very secretive, marginal esoteric societies, the symbolism of which – derived from Christian mysticism, the Old Testament, Freemasonry, Pharaonic Egypt, and, to some extent, Hinduism seems, on face value, to contradict the image of the Muslim convert as an Islamic purist. But, as ever, political and cultural reality and concerns intervened to create a complex picture.

Quilliam converted to Islam in 1887, taking the name "Abdullah" – although he sometimes used this in conjunction with "William Henry," as if it were a middle name. He would later found the Liverpool Muslim Institute which, by the middle of the 1890's, was publishing an eight-page weekly called *The Crescent* and the monthly *Islamic World*, the latter of which focused on Muslim issues at home and abroad. Besides these, the institute put on regular lectures and published a number of pamphlets. One of these –

The Faith of Islam – caught the attention of the Ottoman government, which invited Quilliam to visit Constantinople. In 1894, the Ottoman sultan and the emir of Afghanistan appointed the British convert "Sheikh-ul-Islam of the British Isles." The following year the emir's son visited Liverpool and gave the institute £2,500, which enabled it to purchase premises, and to ready itself for teaching and lecturing.

Outreach to the Muslim diaspora played a large role in the Liverpool Muslim Institute's activism. Publications – especially *The Crescent* and *The Islamic World* – meant that it could reach Muslims around the globe, especially those communities that were part of the British Empire. Muslims in Johannesburg, Cape Town, New Zealand, New South Wales, and Western Australia regularly received the institute's publications. Staking its claim to be a major player in connecting Muslims globally, correspondents from Afghanistan, Turkey, Egypt, Sierra Leone, Morocco, Australia, and elsewhere were elected as honorary vice presidents for the society in 1895.[111]

Ron Geaves suggests in *Islam in Victorian Britain: The Life and Times of Abdullah Quilliam* that, being a "prominent Mason," Quilliam was able to capitalize on his membership of the fraternity, to make business and political connections.[112] However, although he was a member of mainstream or "regular" Masonic Lodges, Quilliam was also highly active in what is generally termed "fringe Masonry," i.e., spin-off, secret societies that, typically, focus their energies on exploring arcane, mystical knowledge, ritual initiations, and (though not in Quilliam's case) even occult practices.

Quilliam's fringe Masonic connections were clearly not of a business or political nature. Rather, the Liverpool shaykh rubbed shoulders with a few of the creators and founders of some of the most important occult and esoteric societies of the day, as we shall see.

It is true that he came into contact with these via regular Freemasonry, which was and still is generally seen as the prerequisite, but this itself indicates that Quilliam's interest in "the Craft" was its esotericism, spirituality, and ethics, not the often grossly exaggerated potential to meet business or political contacts. By their nature, esoteric societies want to stay out of the limelight, and fringe Masonic societies have tended to try to avoid the attention of regular Masonic governing bodies. Since most are, or could be, considered illegitimate or "irregular," membership in such an organization might provide grounds for expulsion from Freemasonry proper.

Quilliam's involvement with the Masonic fraternity began when he was still a young man. His father and grandfather had been Freemasons – though this was not unusual for the time – and, as such, the future shaykh must have come into contact with the fraternity, and to some degree with esotericism, in his formative years. This may well be significant for Quilliam's conversion to Islam, since many Freemasons, as we have seen, were curious about non-Western religions.

But Quilliam's interest in Freemasonry was to last well beyond his conversion. He was a member of a Lodge in Liverpool for a quarter of a century and was elected its Worshipful Master – or head of the Lodge – in August 1904, becoming the first Muslim in Britain to hold the position. In November, he was appointed Grand Deacon of the Grand Council of the Allied Masonic Degrees of Great Britain and its Dependencies Beyond the Seas, and ceremonially invested by the Earl of Euston.[113] By this time, though, Quilliam was already adventuring in the fringe Masonry that lay beneath all of this and that would have been frowned upon by the majority of regular Freemasons.

It all started after a trip to Morocco. Quilliam was then in his twenties. He was initiated into what Germain refers to as the "Masonic Royal Oriental Order of the Sat Bhai." The life of this secret society remains relatively obscure. How involved Quilliam was is unclear, but there is some suggestion that it was fairly significant. *The Freemason* for November 16, 1901, reports that, "According to a contemporary, Sheikh Abdullah Quilliam, who, we believe, is a Liverpool solicitor, has, under a mandate dated 12th October,

1901, from the Supreme Council '360 Degrees' of the Royal Oriental order of the Sat Bhai (Asiatic Masonic), been constituted one of the seven Arch Censors (the highest dignity in the Sat Bhai)."

Quilliam was now an active Muslim, both religiously and politically. Yet the symbolism of the Sat Bhai would appear to have been quite different to that of the faith of the Liverpool shaykh. *The Freemason* tells us that, according to rumor at least, the Sat Bhai "embraces the highest point of the Masonic fabric,"[114] creating a meeting point of Eastern and Western Freemasonry. Such flowery rhetoric is not unusual in Masonic periodicals of this time. In reality, the Order was neither Masonic nor royal. In his *Arcane Schools*, 1909, Yarker describes it as "a Hindu Society organized by the Pundit of an Anglo-Indian regiment, and brought to this country [Great Britain], about the year 1872, by Captain J. H. Lawrence Archer,"[115] though the truth probably lies somewhere between the accounts just cited.

The Order is also mentioned in Rudyard Kipling's *Kim*: "Sat Bhai—the Seven Brothers, [...] is Hindi and Tantric. It is popularly supposed to be [an] extinct Society, but I have written notes to show it is still extant. You see, it is all my invention. [...] Sat Bhai has many members." Kipling mentions the society again in his short story "Miss Youghal's Sais," where he describes his character Strickland as having been "initiated into the Sat Bhai at Allahabad." It is this, and Strickland's learning of native Indian song and dance that indicates that he has "gone deeper than the skin."

The Order was promoted early on by Captain James Henry Lawrence Archer, a gazetted Second-Lieutenant in the 39th Foot Regiment, who had joined a Masonic Lodge in India in 1851, though its creation has been accredited to a Pundit in the 43rd Rifles. Like many secretive, esoteric societies of the day the Sat Bhai ("Seven Brothers" – the name of a species of bird) was loosely based on Freemasonry, though apparently infused with unorthodox Hindu symbolism. Soon it became associated with John Yarker and Kenneth MacKenzie, both highly significant figures in the fringe Masonic world.

Conversations with Angels

Quilliam was certainly connected to Yarker. The latter was the head of the little-known Swedenborgian Rite of Phremasonry. *The Balustre* – a publication for the Rite – for May 1902, lists Quilliam as Grand Master for the Province of Lancashire, England, and as "V[ery] W[orshipful] Bro. W. H. Quilliam, P[ast] M[aster] 6, Supreme Grand Chaplain." As such, Quilliam was a member of the Rite's Supreme Council. A list of Lodges and Temples of the Order also credits to the shaykh – along with Henry B. Brown and Henry Hawley, both Past Masters – a Lodge and Temple called Royal Oscar, located in Liverpool. Warranted June 15 and August 13, 1877, respectively, these met "as a L[odge] and T[emple] of Instruction, at 128 A Mount Pleasant."[116]

The Swedenborgian was one of the more obscure fringe Masonic Rites of the English-speaking world of the late 19th and very early 20th century. Claiming to teach "philosophical explanations of Masonic Science of deep significance," the Rite was named after the Swedish scientist and Christian mystic Emanuel Swedenborg (1688-1772), and drew – in its extraordinarily lengthy rituals – from his *Arcana Cœlestia*.

In this work, Swedenborg offered an esoteric interpretation of each of the passages of the Bible, the nature of heaven and hell, and so on, obtained through gnostic experiences of conversing with supernatural beings. The works of the Christian mystic made some impact on esotericism in Britain after his death, including on the work of William Blake, who cites Swedenborg in his *Heaven and Hell*. There were other influences on the Swedenborgian Rite of Phremasonry, as well, however. Egyptian symbolism appears in the Grand Seal, which was formed from a sphinx and a Crux Ansata, the latter being comprised of a Tau – or "phallic cross" symbolizing "eternal life" – below a circle – "an emblem of eternity and activity."

One of the more mystical fringe Masonic Rites, Quilliam could count among his Swedenborgian Brothers William Wynn Westcott (Supreme

Grand Senior Warden for the Rite, and co-founder of the Hermetic Order of the Golden Dawn), Theodor Reuss (Supreme Grand Standard Bearer, and co-founder of the Ordo Templi Orientis) and Gerard Encausse (The Rite's Supreme Grand Marshal, and co-founder of the Martinist Supreme Council).

Why was the Liverpool shaykh involved in such an esoteric society? Members of the Swedenborgian Rite could only have viewed their circle as a spiritual elect, initiated into the Mysteries, and, as such, distinguished from both the general public and their ordinary Masonic Brothers. Quilliam's involvement is particularly interesting, though, since fringe Masonry was often pursued as an end in itself, i.e., as almost a religious calling. But Quilliam had adopted Islam.

Though regular Freemasonry already allowed Muslim men to join, and to take their initiatory "Obligation" on the Qur'an, fringe Masonry and esoteric societies drawing upon Hinduism and unorthodox Christian mysticism seem unlikely pursuits for a shaykh of Great Britain. However, there is another way of looking at it. Partly because the number of Muslims in Britain were small, and converts virtually unheard of, Quilliam almost certainly saw himself, as a Muslim, as a member of a spiritual and religious elite – a sense that he would have imbibed in his involvement with fringe Masonry. Support for his mission from the Ottomans and Persians would surely have reinforced this view. His activism, countering negative British press about Islam and Muslims, though unquestionably sincere, may well have been tinged with a sense that the public needed to be educated about spiritual matters perhaps more broadly.

The involvement of the shaykh in esoteric societies suggests, moreover, that he, and those with whom he was in contact, viewed Islam as part of the underground spiritual milieu that drew on ancient, and non-Western religions, and that sought to discover a secret common thread – either historical or theological – running through them. This movement would later form the basis of the "New Age" movement.

In this regard, we should note that Swedenborg's claim to have conversed with angels and to have received his esoteric knowledge of the Bible from them, is strikingly reminiscent of the founding claim of Islam, i.e., that the Prophet Muhammad had received the Qur'anic revelations via the Angel Gabriel. It is not impossible that, though a faithful Muslim, Quilliam was not only aware of such similarities, but perhaps saw himself as tapping into either a universal spiritual truth or Western approximations of Islam's worldview. In either case, it is clear that fringe Masons and similar spiritual seekers proved friendlier to Islam than the public at large.

The Ancient Order of Zuzimites

As Germain observes, Quilliam's links to "Freemason, spiritualist, and other temperance societies' networks" helped engender a positive response to the missionary work of the Liverpool Muslim Institute, at least among the spiritual underground. One Melbourne-based Muslim convert, T. M. Mitchell, wrote to Quilliam, as Germain notes, telling him that, "spiritualists are very friendly towards Islam." They took the faith to be a kindred spirit since it was consciously outside the mainstream. "Spiritualists," Mitchell communicated to Quilliam, "at any rate can deeply sympathize with Mahommedans, as each are bitterly opposed, ridiculed and misrepresented by Christians."[117]

As such, it is not surprising that we should find fringe Masonry and Islam overlapping in figures such as Shaykh Quilliam. What is more curious, perhaps, is the fact that Quilliam's Islamic credentials and work are mentioned in fringe Masonic journals, considering their specialist nature. It suggests a considerable sympathy for the shaykh. A brief description of *The Crescent* magazine was included in S. C. Gould's *Rosicrucian Brotherhood* in January 1908. The journal describes it as "A Weekly Record of Islam in England. The advocate of the Mohammedan Faith in Religion. Ably Edited by H. E. [*sic*] Sheikh Abdullah Quilliam Bey, Sheikh-ul-Islam of the British Isles," who is "well versed in all branches of knowledge."

Yet, again, normally dedicated, as the title suggests, to Islam, one of the most obscure of the fringe Masonic societies appears in Volume XXVIII, No. 721 of *The Crescent*.[118] This was the Ancient Order of Zuzimites. Limited to men over the age of 21 (or, in exceptional cases, 18), the aim of the AOZ was to cultivate "an international fraternity and universal brotherhood without distinction of race, colour, or creed." Its principles included friendship, fidelity, charity, humility, and justice. Its Ritual, as we shall see, embraced unconventional Hermetic-type symbolism.

Attesting to its marginal status even within the minuscule world of fringe Masonry, the AOZ is not mentioned in Ellic Howe's article "Fringe Masonry in England 1870-85," published in the *Ars Quatuor Coronatorum* in 1972, though he does discuss both the Sat Bhai and Swedenborgian Rite. Nor does the AOZ appear in the two-volume *New Encyclopedia of Freemasonry* by Freemason and prominent esotericist A. E. Waite. Its omission from the latter is especially interesting since Waite moved in circles that overlapped with Quilliam's.

Nevertheless, the British shaykh wrote an article on the Order for Yarker's *Kneph*, journal of the Antient and Primitive Rite of Masonry in England, one of several manifestations of the Rites of Memphis and Misraim, which fused Freemasonry with Hermeticism and Rosicrucianism to create complex hierarchies of initiatory Degrees numbering, usually, over 90.

Quilliam's account of the history of the AOZ, published in *The Kneph*, in June 1881, is, like those of many fringe Masonic organizations, little more than a mythology developed to suit its symbolism. Such "histories" were sometimes recited as part of initiation rituals and were meant to impress upon the new member that he had not joined a recently concocted Order (though that was often the case), but one with roots in antiquity. Since these societies were concerned with, and spoke to their initiates through, the language of symbolism, in some cases, at least, these "histories" were meant to be regarded more as allegories for the transmission of esoteric doctrines.

Published under the name W. H. Abdullah Quilliam, the shaykh informed readers that the term *Zuzimite* "in the original Hebrew signifies splendour and beauty." The AOZ "is supposed to have been founded in the early part of the 2nd century (Anno Mundi)." "Authentic chronicles," Quilliam suggests, "mention the Zuzimite in the year of the world 2097 (1918 years before the Christian era [...]) as being 'a people great and many'."

Throughout its long history, we are told, the Order absorbed a number of important initiation rituals. The "Celestine Zuzimite" Degrees were "the invention" of Pietro Di Murrone (1215-1296), who was made Pope Celestine V in 1294, though he abdicated the same year. According to Quilliam's mythology, the Order recognized the Degrees the following year, although Di Murrone was already the head, or M. W. G. M. (Most Worshipful Grand Master), of the AOZ before being elected pontiff. Following in the footsteps of the medieval Pope, at least of AOZ mythology, according to Gould's *Rosicrucian Brotherhood* journal, January 1908, Quilliam – "Sheikh-ul-Islam of the British Isles" – had himself ascended to the supreme position of "M. W. G. M of the Grand Tabernacle of [the Order in] England."[119]

In 1881, Quilliam had described the AOZ as "a secret society analogous but in nowise antagonistic to the Masonic Order, and the various rites in connection therewith." As in Freemasonry, the first three Degrees of the AOZ – Neophyte, Graduate, and Fellow – constituted the Order proper. Additional Degrees were available for those who wanted to take them. These included "Mark Zuzimitsm," (a term borrowed from "Mark Masonry") the "Arch Zuzimites" (the title probably taken from "Royal Arch Masonry") and the "Cabbalite," apparently related to the Cabala.[120] Parts of Quilliam's history of the Order appears – sometimes word-for-word and at other times only slightly differently – in the AOZ Ritual itself. That Quilliam wrote these elements seems beyond dispute, but it is likely that he wrote either most or all of the AOZ Ritual, basing it on the Masonic Degrees.

In parts, the initiation rituals of the two societies are almost the same, as is the ritual format for opening a Masonic Lodge and a Zuzimite "Tent," as formal gatherings of members were called. The AOZ obligation, in which the initiate swears not to reveal the esoteric secrets of the society, has been changed only very slightly from the Masonic. In both societies, too, the initiate enters from "darkness" seeking "light"; he is blindfolded, and will have had all "metallic substances" removed from his person. His breast will be exposed, and he will be either barefoot or wearing only one sandal. In both cases, the initiate is given a "password" (Freemasonry) or "watchword" (AOZ) that he will have to convey to officers of the society; he is taught grips and tokens (symbolic "handshakes" to be used during the Ritual), and presented with a small, rectangular, ceremonial apron.

Though adopting its Ritual structure more or less wholesale, the Masonic symbolism has been stripped out of the Zuzimite Degrees, and a much vaguer, or – probably from Quilliam's perspective – more universal symbolism and ethos prevail. "Friendship" is the focus of its first Degree. The AOZ's second Degree, though, is more esoteric, albeit somewhat unconventionally. During the proceedings, the initiate is instructed in the AOZ Mystery via somewhat adapted Pharaonic Egyptian mythology. Typhon has destroyed the "Virgin Truth, surnamed ISIS," he is told. The "friends of Truth" have been searching for the pieces of the body of ISIS, and the initiate must undertake the same search. The purpose of the Degree is revealed to be to prepare the initiate's mind for the reception of the Truth.

Now the initiate is described as, "A Brother from Goetia seeking Osiris," while Goetia – a term usually indicating the evocation of spirits in medieval, European occultism – is defined, more naturalistically, as "the magic that lies within nature as electricity within the cloud." The AOZ mythology explains that in the early days of the Order, the members of the "Tribe" left their tents, and convened a Grand Council to elect the "sage masters." Typhon, a young and arrogant member of the society was there also, but, unsurprisingly considering his personal shortcomings, was not elected.

He and his comrades took revenge on the Tribe, smashing the "Tables of the Law," and kidnapping Isis, a young virgin who had been appointed to attend the "altar fire." "Captain Osiris" alone went out to find Isis.

Discovering her almost dead in a well, he climbed down and managed to carry her out, restoring the "hidden gem of truth" to the Tribe.[121] The Third Degree of the AOZ reveals that Osiris was given Isis's hand in marriage as a reward for his bravery. The lesson of this Degree is "Love."

At first glance, the secularization of the ancient Egyptian pantheon is perplexing. Why make the god Osiris into Captain Osiris? Or the goddess Isis into "truth"? It is highly likely that, as a Muslim, Quilliam would have regarded the invocation of pharaonic deities as the sin of *shirk*, or idolatry. Still, whether or not this was intended, the AOZ Ritual seems to suggest that a universal Truth may prevail, even as the details differ. "No man has any right to erect his own opinions into an universal and infallible standard," the initiate is instructed in the AOZ First Degree, "and the more enlarged man's mind is, the more readily he will overlook differences in sentiments, so long as he is persuaded that the mind of his friend is upright, and that he follows the dictates of conscience and integrity."[122]

FIVE

René Guénon, Esotericism, and Islamic Traditionalism

As we have seen, by the end of the first quarter of the 20th century practitioners of underground forms of spirituality – often connected to esoteric Freemasonry – had appropriated aspects of Hinduism, Buddhism, paganism, and, to some extent, Sufism. Soon, René Guénon (1886-1951), a French esotericist, would prove a more significant bridge connecting Islam and a number of Western spiritual practitioners and intellectuals, some of whom would make important contributions to the scholarship of Islam in the Western world.

Guénon believed that the modern West could be positively influenced by the East, which would help "it to recover the lost meaning of its own [spiritual] tradition."[123] For Guénon, the modern Western world's faith in scientific, technological, and moral "progress," regardless of its consequences, negated "Tradition" and its eternal values, and consequently mired Western society in spiritual confusion and ignorance.

"Tradition," capitalized, we should note, is a technical term associated with Guénon. It does not indicate the conservative's reverence for the customs of a particular society. Rather, "Tradition" refers to the authentic, primordial revelation of Deity and way of life that was in accord with Divinity and cosmic law, and that preceded contemporary religions.

According to the Traditionalist doctrine, knowledge (gnosis) of Divinity is acquired through stages of esoteric learning, which is, necessarily, structured hierarchically, as is the case in initiatic organizations, whether

Sufism, Freemasonry, Hindu Tantra, etc. For Guénon, as for Islamic esotericists, it was the *haqiqa* (i.e., the inner, spiritual truth) that counted. The Qur'an had to be understood not by the procedures of the "doctors of the *shari'a*," the *'ulama az zahir* ("doctors of the outer") but by the inward truth.[124] Like the Naqshbandi Sufis, Guénon personally observed the *shari'a* but believed that the *raison d'être* of Islamic law could only be grasped through comprehending its *haqiqa*.

Born in Blois, France, Guénon had had an early interest in mathematics and philosophy and developed a curiosity about Freemasonry, the occult, and spiritualism while still a young man. However, despite later joining a number of esoteric societies, having a genuine interest in the Mysteries, and a certain degree of commitment, Guénon was skeptical. After a relatively short time, he had become openly hostile to France's spiritual underground. In the 1920s, he published two books in which he elaborated upon his critique of alternative spirituality, singling out Theosophy for particular criticism. Guénon also wrote for an anti-Masonic publication while still involved with fringe Masonry.

Traditionalism should be distinguished from Theosophy, not only because of Guénon's loathing of the latter, but because the former often steers close to orthodoxy in appearance, while the latter was shaped by the visions and personal revelations of Mme. Helena Blavatsky (1831-1891), who claimed to be in direct psychic contact with spiritual masters – "the Hidden Chiefs" – in the East. Traditionalism is an esoteric doctrine by which the faithful of one of the living religions can navigate difficult texts to penetrate their mysteries – coming in effect to the primordial Tradition.

As we have noted, viewed from an "inner" perspective, religion and religious teachings appear very different than if viewed from an outer, or literalist, perspective. For Guénon, for example, Islam's warrior symbolism is indicative of inner struggle, "the greater Jihad." The sword of the imam "symbolizes above all the power of the word." Its legitimacy can be demonstrated, according to the Traditionalist doctrines, not least of all by finding its equivalent in other authentic religions. Guénon thus informs his readers that it is comparable to the Vajra, or "thunderbolt," wielded by the Vedic Indian god Indra, and to the arrows that the Greek god Apollo uses to kill the serpent Python.[125]

In Guénon's opinion, the spiritual man should avoid becoming involved in politics, let alone politicizing religion and spirituality. Although not all of Guénon's associates have heeded his advice, he was especially critical of Theosophy and the spiritualist movement more broadly on this point. Notably, in his *Theosophy: History of a Pseudo-Religion*, Guénon suggests that "Most revolutionaries of that time [1830-1848] were 'mystics' in the worst sense of the word." For Guénon the "sole purpose" of "these socialists" was to explain the "inequalities of social conditions" by actions performed in previous lives.[126]

Aside from his many books, Guénon contributed to a number of journals, especially *Etudes Traditionelles*, which had originally been dedicated to the study of Theosophy. Guénon took it over and succeeded in turning into a venue for his Traditionalist worldview.[127] He was still writing during the latter part of his life, although he rarely addressed the subject of Islam, perhaps because he could not read classical Arabic, the language of the Qur'an, and because he did not forge extensive contacts with the 'ulama in Cairo. Historian Mark Sedgwick notes that at the time of his death Guénon's personal library contained 3,000 volumes, yet he had collected four times the number of volumes on Hinduism as he had on Islam, though his inability to read classical Arabic must have been a factor here, too. In Cairo, Sedgwick claims, "Guénon remained not only a universalist in his beliefs, but a Traditionalist rather than a Muslim in his writings."[128]

Swedenborgianism and Anti-Freemasonry

In 1908, Guénon helped organize a large spiritualist-Masonic conference, although he walked out on the proceedings almost at the very beginning.

The following year, he was consecrated a bishop in the Gnostic Church, and was planning to revive the fringe Masonic and faux chivalric Order of the Temple. Guénon came into contact with the Masonic *Loge Symbolique Humanidad* (under the jurisdiction of the *Rite National Espagnol*), into which he was initiated. Its head, Charles Détré (also known as Teder), was connected to John Yarker, and, like the latter, promoted a number of fringe, esoteric, Masonic Rites. Détré initiated Guénon into a French Swedenborgian Masonic Rite (under the jurisdiction of *La Grande Loge Swedenborgienne de France*) as well as into the elaborate Rite of Memphis and Misraim, the rituals of which, as mentioned, are steeped in Hermetic, Rosicrucian, and Pharaonic symbolism.[129]

These associations are particularly striking in light of Shaykh Abdullah Quilliam in England, who was likewise associated with Yarker, head of the Swedenborgian Rite of Phremasonry. Moreover, the shaykh, as we have seen, was a prominent member of the Rite, holding among other positions that of Grand Master for the Province of Lancashire, in 1902. In the same year, Yarker gave Theodor Reuss a charter to constitute "The Swedenborg Lodge of the Holy Grail No. 15 at Berlin." This was to have the power to charter Provincial Grand Lodges in Germany, though Yarker quickly resigned from the German branch after quarreling with some of the more prominent members of the Rite in Britain, of which he remained a member.[130]

No less curious, according to his friend and collaborator Paul Chacornac, Guénon was initiated by Reuss into the fringe Masonic Order of The Chapter and Temple INRI of the Primitive and Original Swedenborgian Rite,[131] who gave him the "black silk sash of the Kadosh."[132] It was not unusual for a fringe Masonic Rite to confer several Degrees at a time on an initiate if he was already a high-ranking member of another, comparable Order. Fringe Masonry and the occult Orders connected to it (such as the Hermetic Order of the Golden Dawn and the Ordo Templi Orientis) constituted a small and insular community. Moreover, the nature of these societies was fluid. Not only did membership overlap, but the symbols, and, sometimes, the rituals of one society were absorbed into another. Schisms complicated things still further, with competing, secret Orders emerging and claiming to be the legitimate heir to a particular Rite, and using its name, Degree system, etc.

Still, the fact that both Quilliam and Guénon had, in the first decade of the 20th century, been members of fringe Masonic Swedenborgian Rites, as well as colleagues of Yarker, the prominent British esoteric Freemason, is surely significant. We have noted the similarity of Emanuel Swedenborg's claim to have conversed with angels, who gave him an esoteric understanding of the Bible, to the Muslim belief that Muhammad was taught the Qur'an by the Angel Gabriel. More prosaically, as a re-Christianized, though esoteric, form of Freemasonry, from a certain perspective Swedenborgian Freemasonry could be construed as more conservative and more in sync with orthodox religion than regular Freemasonry in Britain or France, or with occult Orders like the Hermetic Order of the Golden Dawn.

Soon, though, Guénon would be a regular contributor to a Catholic anti-Masonic journal edited Abel Clarin de la Rive. While fringe Masonry remained steeped in esotericism, Freemasonry under the Grand Orient of France had become increasingly secular from the latter half of the 19th century, as we have seen. By this point, it had become immersed in anti-clericalism, motivated undoubtedly in part by a long history of Catholic anti-Masonry. For Guénon, though, this shift indicated a movement away from the transcendental, and, as such, something to be actively fought against.

Anti-Masonic hysteria had reached its height a little more than a decade earlier when Leo Taxil had claimed that he had proof that Freemasons indulged in Satanic rituals. In 1897, exposed as a fraud, Taxil confessed to fabricating the evidence behind his lurid allegations. Although Guénon dismissed the more paranoid conspiracy theories against Freemasonry as absurd, he did accept the idea that there existed clandestine, organized groups whose sole purpose was to subvert authentic initiation and overthrow religion. Yet, despite his interest in Catholic anti-Freemasonry, Guénon soon wearied of the Church as well, believing it, also, had become too modern and too liberal. Whether or not he had come to a similar conclusion, Clarin de la Rive was fascinated with Islam by the time Guénon was contributing to his anti-Masonic periodical – which also published a series of articles about North African Muslim secret societies. There was a rumor that the editor of *La France chrétienne antimaçonnique* might even have converted to Islam.[133]

Dismayed at both Christianity and the French esoteric underground, Guénon moved to Cairo in 1930. He adopted the practice of Sufism, being initiated into the order of Shadhilites and taking the name 'Abd al-Wahid Yahya. Although Cairo was already a modern, cosmopolitan city that had absorbed much modern Western culture, such as the movie theater and the department store, Guénon preferred to remain in the poorer areas of the city where foreigners did not venture. Abandoning Western dress – which was all the rage among younger, more affluent Egyptians – Guénon opted to wear the traditional *galabiyya* (a long shirt-like garment that reaches to the ankles, and is usually white, and made of light cotton). He did, however, have a few European acquaintances.

Guénon's existence was meager, although after a wealthy admirer traveled to Egypt and found him malnourished and living in a single room, his French disciples started sending him funds, pretending that these were royalties to spare him from embarrassment. Then, in 1939, John Levy, an English disciple and convert from Judaism to Islam purchased the house in which Guénon was residing, and gave it to him.

Disciples

Devotees of Guénon's Traditionalist school have made a significant, if generally unacknowledged, impact on the Western consciousness in regard to Islam. Traditionalists have often either been among the leading scholars of Islam of the day, in the West, or have presented Islam as an essentially spiritual and gnostic faith, with Islamic law and jurisprudence sometimes pushed to the periphery.

A journey to Morocco as a young man set the rest of Titus Burckhardt's life on the track of studying Islam. A German-Swiss scholar born in Florence, Italy, he had been a school friend of one of the most famous of the Traditionalists, Frithjof Schuon (1907-1998). Burckhardt's family was Protestant. His father was a sculptor by profession. Unsurprisingly, the future Traditionalist initially pursued the arts, studying in Switzerland and Italy, and leaning toward sculpture and illustration.

Burckhardt had already studied Eastern art and religion before setting foot in Morocco. There he studied Arabic language, Islamic jurisprudence, and Sufism. He later converted to the faith, taking the name Sidi Ibrahim Izz al-Din on his conversion. As a Muslim scholar, Burckhardt did much to introduce Sufi doctrines to the West, translating works by Ibn 'Arabi among others, and writing several books on Sufism. He also wrote about Islamic material culture such as architecture, art, and even clothing.[134]

The arts also played a role in the life of Frithjof Schuon. Born in Basel, Switzerland, Schuon's earlier years were likewise characterized by a somewhat artistic environment. He himself expected to become a painter or poet and did, in fact, produce a number of paintings during his life, many of them portraying – in rather a Gauguinesque style – native American religion and culture.

When Schuon was thirteen years old his life changed dramatically. His father died unexpectedly, and his mother took the young Frithjof and his elder brother Erich to live with their grandmother in Alsace, France. A few years later Erich entered a Cistercian monastery with the intention of becoming a monk, while Frithjof pursued an interest in Eastern philosophy and religion by himself, coming across Guénon's book *Orient et Occident* at the age of sixteen.

Later, in 1931, while performing military service, Schuon wrote to Guénon, asking for advice. He was unimpressed with the latter's suggestion that he adopt Sufi Islam since he had already developed a love for Christianity and Hinduism. Indeed, for Schuon, Hindu *Advaita Vedanta* was the perfect expression of metaphysics. However, soon, unable to find a teacher in this school – and hoping to find the Islamic equivalent of the Hindu practice of reciting mantras to Deity – Schuon would begin to search for a Sufi master to initiate him.[135] Or perhaps it is more accurate to say that he was drawn, almost unconsciously, to the master.

During this year, Schuon visited the International Exhibition at Vincennes, and there, as if it had occurred involuntarily, he found himself repeating the name of "Shaykh Nur ad-Din" – a Sufi master of which Schuon claimed to have been previously unaware. The following year, the spiritual seeker had another such experience. Schuon was in Paris's Luxembourg Gardens when he wondered to himself whether he should adopt Islam. It occurred to him that he would if he saw a *burnous* – a type of cloak worn by Arabs and Berbers – before midday. After this, Schuon went walking through the city as usual and forgot about the deal he had struck with himself until, at five minutes before twelve, "a parade of Algerian troopers, every one in a burnous" passed before him. Shortly afterward, Schuon returned to Switzerland, and found an Iranian mullah to teach him *al-Fatiha* (the opening chapter of the Qur'an, used in daily prayers). Schuon had not, however, relinquished his interest in other religions.

He wrote again to Guénon, now hoping that he would be able to recommend a shaykh that would be able to instruct him in Sufism. However, in 1932, before receiving a reply Schuon traveled to the port of Marseille. After meeting some Algerian or possibly Yemeni sailors who talked to him about Shaykh Ahmad al-Alawi, he was given passage to Mostaganem in French Algeria, to study under the shaykh. There, Schuon lived in the mosque complex, and was able to converse with other disciples, although his contact with al-Alawi was limited since the shaykh's health was failing.

The young spiritual seeker stayed only three months, partly because the French authorities were becoming suspicious at his presence since Sufism was bound up with anti-colonial activity. Al-Alawi had managed to remain on friendly terms with the French authorities by emphasizing the similarities between Sufism and Christianity, and by carefully avoiding the differences. This position would also have appealed to Schuon, although the ecumenism was not shared by all of the shaykh's disciples. During his stay at the mosque complex, Schuon had argued with a fellow disciple who suggested that Christians could not enter heaven. Nevertheless, in early 1933, before leaving Mostaganem and the mosque, Schuon was formerly received into the Alawiyya Sufi Order and given the initiate name 'Isa (Jesus). As Schuon recollected,

> "[W]e reach the half-darkened room of the Shaykh. [...] In the room nothing stirs; only the barely audible words of the Koran, uttered by the Shaykh beside me, vibrate in the semi-darkness. He says prayers; the moments that go by while he prays are holy; something passes over into me from these waxen, other-worldly hands, like a current even into the heart. I am spiritually joined with him for life."[136]

It was not long before Schuon had once again departed Europe for Mostaganem, this time prompted by the death of al-Alawi. The new head of the Order sent him on retreat, and, later, gave him an *ijaza* (certificate of authorization) to spread Islam. Schuon believed that this empowered him to act as an emissary of the Alawiyya Order, and to establish and run a branch in Europe. In reality, Schuon was authorized only to accept converts to Islam by witnessing their conversion (which is permitted for all Muslims), but, back in Switzerland, he soon began conducting initiations into the Sufi Order anyway.

One of those who studied under Schuon was the British-born Traditionalist Martin Lings. Like Guénon, he concluded that Christianity could no longer offer authentic initiation, and, like Schuon, he had initially sought to find this, instead, in Hinduism. What he wanted more than anything, though, was a spiritual guide who could lead him along the initiatic path. On hearing of Schuon's group, Lings traveled to meet him. Despite having no great interest in Sufism originally, he was convinced that Schuon was a both a spiritual master and a "true saint." He accepted Islam within only a few weeks of their first meeting, whence he was initiated into the Shadhili-Darqawi Sufi Order, and took the name Abu Bakr Siraj al-Din. Later, as a scholar of Islam, Lings wrote a highly acclaimed account of Muhammad, as well as works on Sufism and Islamic spirituality.[137]

An eccentric, artistic, and independent thinker, Schuon was always bound to be unconventional in his steering of his Sufi group, and over time it became increasingly unorthodox. He focused his group on the practice of *dhikr*, during which Names of God are recited and the upper body sways rhythmically in sync with the recitation. For Schuon, *dhikr* held out the promise of a mystical union with God, and, as such, he considered it the essence of Sufism. Other practices could be safely ignored, he believed. Although he instructed disciples to follow the obligatory practices of Islam, he told them to disregard the recommended practices, even allowing his disciples to drink alcohol when they met with family or during business meetings.[138]

During his retreat in Algeria, he had had a vision of the Japanese golden Buddha as well as some of Islam's prophets. Even as he led his Sufi group, Schuon remained a Traditionalist. He broke with the Algerian Alawiyya Order in 1937, after introducing his own teaching on the "Six Themes of Meditation" (Death and Life, Repose and Action, and Knowledge and Being).

De-Islamizing his Sufi group, Schuon began seeing his disciples drifting away in the 1950s.[139] He came to have serious disagreements with Guénon, who insisted on following the traditional Islamic prescriptions. From the 1970s Schuon was increasingly abandoning Islamic orthodoxy in favor of a universalist, esoteric religiosity. In 1981, though an old man by this time, Schuon Left Switzerland for Indiana in the USA so that he could be close to practitioners of the native American faith, which he revered as a "primordial religion" like Hinduism, based on nature itself.[140]

SIX

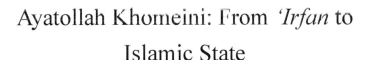

Ayatollah Khomeini: From *'Irfan* to Islamic State

Ruhollah Musavi Khomeini – the man that would one day rise to become Supreme Leader of the Islamic Republic of Iran – was born on September 24, 1902, in the small town of Khomein in central Persia. His father, a minor landowner and cleric who had studied in Najaf – the Shi'ite holy city of Iraq – was killed by local bandits when Khomeini was just a few months old, in early 1903. The family was moderately wealthy, and though the responsibility of caring for him fell to his mother and her sister-in-law, Khomeini's childhood was relatively idyllic.

The house in which his family lived was a spacious two-story building with balconies, two watchtowers, a large garden and three courtyards. Khomeini attended a local elementary school until the age of seven, where he was taught the foundations of Islam and learned to recite the Qur'an. After this, he began attending a school built by the constitutional government of the region. Part of Iran's modernizing project, it taught Persian language and literature, as well as arithmetic, geography, history, and basic science. The young Khomeini also had private tutors who taught him Arabic grammar and calligraphy.[141] Charismatic, a natural leader even as a youth, outside of his studies Khomeini nearly always played the leading role, such as vizier or shah, in games with local boys.[142] A few years later – physically strong and energetic – he would have little problem beating his friends at wrestling.

Then in 1918, a cholera epidemic swept across the country. Both Khomeini's mother and aunt died after catching the disease. His childhood was over. He stayed with his family until the age of nineteen and then went to Arak, one of the major centers of religious learning, where he was taught by the well-known and well-respected cleric Shaykh 'Abd al-Karim Ha'iri Yazdi (1860-1936). Khomeini was a dedicated and serious student, who, according to his son, once politely but firmly admonished his teacher for speaking too loudly and disturbing his studying, which he was undertaking in the courtyard of the school. But Khomeini's devotion to the study of Islam paid off. And Ha'iri Yazdi, though certainly surprised at being rebuked by a student, was not, it seems, offended by Khomeini's behavior.

In 1922, when Ha'iri Yazdi traveled to Qom, to found what would become the most important seminary in Iran, Khomeini followed. By this time he had already taken the formal initiation into the clergy, exchanging the skullcap and short jacket of a religious student (*talebeh*) for the long coat and cloak of the religious cleric. As a descendant of the family of the Prophet, Khomeini also received a black turban (*'imamah*), and was from then on addressed with the honorific title of "seyyed" – the equivalent of "shaykh," used by clerics who could not claim descent from the family of the Prophet (the latter received white turbans during their initiations). At Qom, Khomeini undertook advanced religious studies, including in Islamic gnosticism and its related philosophical tradition (*hikmat*).

'Irfan

Sufi Orders had proliferated in Iran during the early Safavid period (1502-1736), which saw the rise of Shi'a Islam. By the end, though, opposition to the Sufi lineages had grown and Shi'ite scholars had begun to talk of *'irfan* rather than *tasawwuf*. But Sunni mysticism had already come to establish itself within Persian culture. Before the rule of the Safavids, Nur ad-Din 'Abd al-Rahman Jami (1414-1492) – known as the Seal of the Persian Poets – had married the teachings of Rumi and Ibn 'Arabi in his own writings. The latter's influence would be most keenly felt in the works of Mulla Sadra (1571-1640). While it had stagnated to a certain degree after the Safavid period, it was the revival of interest in Sadra during the 19th century that revivified *'irfan* in Iran.[143] This background had influenced Khomeini's own teachers,[144] and would influence the future Supreme Leader himself.

Because of its central thesis, of the unity of the Creator and His creation, and, moreover, the possibility that the devotee might achieve union with God, *'irfan* was sometimes seen as a descent into pantheism, and, as such, an abandonment of the monotheism of Islam. It had also come to be associated with radical anti-authority movements, causing both clerical and secular elites to view the subject with skepticism, if not hostility.

Khomeini studied Islamic gnosticism with three tutors, typically at their private homes, though Ayatollah Muhammad 'Ali Shahabadi would prove to be his main teacher in this field, guiding Khomeini through *Fusus al-Hikam* (The Bezels of Wisdom) of Ibn 'Arabi. By Khomeini's own account, he met Shahabadi at the Feiziyeh seminary in Qom. An impressive building with courtyards, gardens, pool, and blue and turquoise mosaics, it was built during the 13th century, and originally called the Astaneh School. It was later renamed after Feiz Kashani, one of its most respected and well-known teachers. Later still, it would become associated with agitation against the secular dictatorship of the shah, and with the Islamic Revolution itself.[145]

At the Feiziyeh seminary Khomeini questioned Shahabadi about *'irfan*. On hearing him talk, the young seeker believed he had found what he had been looking for in a teacher. He asked Shahabadi to accept him as a student, and though his request was initially refused, Khomeini persisted until the cleric relinquished, and agreed to teach him. Shahabadi had thought that Khomeini was interested in learning philosophy, but the future Supreme Leader made it clear that he had already studied, and was well versed in, the subject. What he wanted to explore was gnosticism. In particular, he had set his sights on the *Sharh-i Fusus*, a commentary by Sharaf al-Din Davud Qeisari (d. 1350) on Ibn 'Arabi's *Fusus al-Hikam*.[146] To anyone wishing to study *'irfan* in Iran, these texts were of primary importance. But Khomeini's education in Islamic mysticism, under Shahabadi, was extensive, and he would eventually become known as one of only a few who were learned in the work of Mulla Sadr, which he had studied as Shahabadi's student.

Although, as a young cleric, Khomeini was reserved when it came to letting others know about his interest in the gnostic, it was far from a passing interest. Khomeini wrote mystical poetry, and *'Irfan* was the focus of his books from 1925 to 1937. Having already taught ethics, he also instructed a few select students in *'irfan* during the 1940s. Khomeini's early reserve was, at least in part, a response to the hostility toward mysticism and even philosophy among members of the clergy at Qom. Shahabadi had attempted to dispel the fears of the clerical elite and to make them see that the doctrines of the mystics did not contradict the teachings of Islam.[147] It was a cause that Khomeini himself would take up publicly after the Revolution. Like his teacher, the younger cleric would come to believe that the people had the potential to understand mysticism and that they should even be introduced to its doctrines, no matter how subtle, abstract or complex they might be.

A group of merchants had approached his teacher one day, Khomeini would later recall. Shahabadi began talking to them about mysticism. No one was excluded from his conversation. Khomeini asked if it was appropriate to teach those who had no background in the foundation of clerical learning. "Let them be exposed just once to these heretical teachings!" Shahabadi responded, adding, "I too now find it incorrect to divide people into categories and pronounce some incapable of understanding these matters."[148]

Khomeini recalled the event during one of his lectures on Surah *al-Fatihah* (the first chapter of the Qur'an). At this point, he was Supreme Leader of the Islamic Republic of Iran, and his address was to the nation. Khomeini's aim was to reintroduce Islam – which had been increasingly marginalized under the modernization programs of the shah – to all aspects public life. While this certainly meant *shari'a* and *fiqh*, it was based on an understanding of *'irfan* – the idea of union with God. "The revolutionary Islamic movement led by Imam Khomeini," Dr. Muhammad G. Legenhausen wrote in 1991, "may even be viewed as the exoteric dimension of the impetus to reveal Islamic mysticism to the public."[149]

After the Revolution, Ayatollah Taleqani gave a series of televised lectures on the interpretation of the Qur'an. He passed away on September 10, 1979, and a younger scholar took over, though Khomeini wanted to see a more senior cleric in the role. After reflecting on the Supreme Leader's request, those behind the broadcast suggested that Khomeini himself should be the one to present future lectures. He agreed on condition that the filming would take place at his home. It was in this context that Khomeini wrote and delivered his lectures on Surah *al-Fatihah*.

Known to much of the world as the man who issued a fatwa calling for the death of Salman Rushdie – author of *The Satanic Verses* – for blasphemy, and as the leader of Iran during the American hostage crisis, Khomeini has become a symbol of intolerance and ultraconservative Islamic values in the West. His lectures, however, reveal a different kind of man. Khomeini had surely reflected, over the years, on the lack of sympathy for Islamic mysticism and even philosophy – an only slightly less taboo subject – among the clerical establishment. So fearful were some seminarians that, on one occasion at Qom, a group had even performed a cleansing ritual on a cup that Khomeini's young son had drunk from since they feared that teaching philosophy indicated impurity and believed that they themselves might somehow become contaminated.

"[N]o one should be denounced as an unbeliever merely because he uses the language of the [Muslim] mystics,"[150] Khomeini told the fledgling Islamic Republic. In his lectures from 1979 to 1980, the Supreme Leader sought to expound a mystical interpretation of the opening lines of the Qur'an, and to convince his audience that the philosophers, jurists, mystics, and poets were all in agreement. Division and dissent had occurred, he believed, because of their "failure to understand each other's languages."[151] The Supreme Leader wanted to "reconcile" the branches of Islamic knowledge.

Secularism by Force

The ayatollah's road to political power had been paved before him, by a century of government corruption, coups, reforms and counter measures. With the blessings of foreign powers, the shahs had tried to play the religious and the Left against each other. Appeasing modernizers one year and, then, to check their growth, promoting the 'ulama the next, official policy swung wildly in reaction to popular opposition. Anti-Islamic policies thus sometimes preceded and at other times succeeded outreach and concessions to the clerical elite and the country's Shi'ite majority. It would prove a failed policy.

The roots of anti-government agitation – though not exactly a unified movement – can be traced back to 1888-1889, when Britain won a number of concessions from Nasir al-Din Shah's government, including navigation rights over the Karun River, the creation of the British-owned Imperial Bank of Persia, and the tobacco concession, which surrendered the right to produce, sell, and export the country's entire tobacco crop for a period of fifty years. The shah, in return, was promised a quarter of the profit annually, plus a five percent dividend.[152] But the concession adversely affected small traders and merchants, as well as the 'ulama, who were closely connected to the merchant class, and often controlled the land on which tobacco crops were grown.

The concession also attracted the attention of such radicals as Sayyid Jamal ad-Din al-Afghani,[153] who realized that the grievance could be used to agitate for broader reforms. He had been expelled from Persia 1891 after publishing a pamphlet condemning the shah for selling the country to the "infidel."[154] Settling temporarily in Iraq, al-Afghani corresponded with Hajji Mirza Hasan Shirazi at Karbala. Later that year he signed his name to a fatwa calling for tobacco to be boycotted in Iran. News of the fatwa soon spread, and by November, the boycott was widespread in Tehran. In December it went nationwide. Bowing to pressure, in January, Nasir al-Din Shah canceled the concession. The British tobacco company had to be compensated, and the shah was forced to borrow money from the Imperial Bank of Persia. The debacle provoked the Iranian head of state to change his approach to foreign and internal affairs. He now put limits on both foreign loans and the sale of concessions and turned his back on foreign institutions inside Iran. When a modern school building was burned down by 'ulama in Tabriz, the shah decided not to make a fuss.

Britain was no longer in favor with Nasir al-Din Shah, who now aligned his country with Tsarist Russia.[155] This change of alliances provoked the reformist movement to seek support from London, and soon the shah's former ally was theirs. By this time, al-Afghani had taken up residence in Istanbul. A secret society in Tehran, answerable to him, and ostensibly adhering to his pan-Islamic ideology, continued his work, agitating for reforms. The group attracted a number of government officials, wealthy merchants, and reformers. One of its number was Mirza Riza Kermani. He, along with another member of the group, was charged with sedition and given an eighteenth-month sentence. On his release, he visited al-Afghani in Istanbul, before returning to his home country in disguise.[156]

Nasir al-Din Shah was shot and killed in 1896, while on a visit to the shrine of Shah 'Abd al-'Azim. He was buried at the site soon after. Kermani was the assassin. Both he and al-Afghani died the following year, the former being hung for his crime, and the latter succumbing to cancer.[157]

The assassination of the shah brought his son Muzaffar to power. Although opposed by the 'ulama, he instituted a number of reforms, including in education. Then, between 1900 and 1902, Persia obtained more Russian loans, two of which were spent on the shah's European trips between 1900 and 1905. The opposition movement reemerged in response to his excesses, and, in 1906, partly influenced by the 1905 Russian Revolution, numerous groups joined together. The opposition has often been regarded as being comprised of merchants and clerics, but as Janet Afary notes, "many leaders of the revolution who seemed to be conventional clerics […] were in fact

Azali Babis, pan-Islamists, Freemasons, and freethinkers."[158] Drawing from different sectors of society, from students and craftsmen to the 'ulama, the opposition won the right to a Parliament (*Majles*) and a secular constitution representing the clerical class, trade guilds, landowners, merchants, and nobility.

In 1925, Reza Shah Pahlavi (1878-1944) effectively ousted the last of the Qajar dynasty, Ahmad Shah Qajar (who was away in Europe, ostensibly for medical treatment), to become absolute ruler of Persia. The Democratic Party of Iran, which had been created during the protests that led to the Constitutional Revolution of 1906, was brutally suppressed.[159] Although the 'ulama had placed some hope in the new ruler, his reforms soon weakened their positions in society. As education and law were secularized and brought under the jurisdiction of the government, the madrasa was outshone in the eyes of parents who had more worldly ambitions for their children. For the 'ulama, though, worse was to come. In 1934, Reza Shah Pahlavi visited Turkey, and inspired by the sweeping reforms of Mustafa Kemal Ataturk – who had abolished the sultanate and caliphate, and had begun to transform his country into a modern, Western-oriented nation state – stepped up his campaign to modernize Persia.

The following year, foreigners were officially requested to refrain from using the name "Persia" (land of the Parsa) and to use only the name "Iran" (land of the Aryans) instead. Both terms had been used, to describe the nation, since antiquity. It had been known as "Persia" to outsiders since the ancient Greeks had first used it, and the name had come to evoke a mysterious and alluring culture of Persian rugs, mystical poetry, and ornate gardens. "Iran", derived from *Iranshahr* (Empire of the Aryans), was a term invoked by the Sasanians of the 3rd century C.E., as a way of claiming descent from earlier dynasties (including the Achaemenids, whose rulers Darius and Xerxes had stressed their "Aryan" origin). The term "Aryan" (noble) was also strongly associated with the pre-Islamic faith of Persia, Zoroastrianism, established by the prophet Zarathustra.[160]

In Europe, the notion of a superior "Aryan" race had begun to take hold only during the last part of the 19th century, when Mme Blavatsky, founder of the Theosophical Society, had set out her vision of the progress of man as a spiritual being. It was not based on biological notions of race as such, but many of her ideas were, nonetheless, absorbed into pan-Germanic nationalist circles, who reinterpreted them. Later still, this milieu was absorbed into the national socialism (or "Nazism") of Adolf Hitler and the NSDAP.

Reza Shah Pahlavi saw a potential ally in Germany that, he believed, would help him to withstand the advances of Great Britain. He may not have entirely appreciated that, for Hitler, the Aryan was blond-haired and blue-eyed, and did not possess Persian characteristics or history.[161] Nevertheless, national socialist glorification of ancient Germany had gone hand in hand with re-industrialization, and no doubt Reza Shah Pahlavi saw a similar possibility for Iran, with the added benefit that a mythology that replaced God with the land itself, and the people's ancient connection to it, would aid in sweeping aside the mullahs and religion.

Although not fascist *per se*, Reza Shah Pahlavi's modernizing secularism and Westernization was imposed by legislation and force, against the popular will, and, more especially, against the convictions of the clerical class. Women were made to unveil. Men had to wear Western-style hats in public. And any mullah who had yet to become a *mojtahed*, qualified to rule on matters of religion, was forced to wear secular clothing. Strictly enforcing the law, police fined anyone who disobeyed. If they caught a woman wearing a veil, they would tear it from her, forcibly uncovering her head and face.[162]

Officials also had to play their part in promoting secularism and were instructed to attend functions, once a week, with their unveiled wives, either at the ministries or at the socially elite Iran Club. On an official visit to Shiraz in 1935, after the Minister of Education Ali-Asghar Hekmat had given the customary speeches, a group of schoolgirls appeared on stage. They threw off their veils and began performing gymnastic exercises in time to music. Some members of the audience were shocked enough to walk out. One cleric who complained the following day was imprisoned. Two more were exiled from the city.[163]

The mullahs had reluctantly tolerated the shah's earlier educational reforms and displayed little dissent in public, but the new reforms stoked their passions and resentment. Ayatollah Hossein Qomi visited Tehran to plead with the shah, but he was ignored, and then sent into exile in neighboring Iraq. By July 1935, the regime's treatment of Qomi and the ayatollah's anti-government sentiments were well known in his hometown of Mashhad, and protests erupted in the city's Gowharshad mosque. Many of the protesters were shot dead. In Qom, the clergy decided to refrain from attacking the shah, believing it would provoke him to order the seminary destroyed.[164]

The pro-German sympathies of the shah became ever more conspicuous throughout the late 1930s, and his policies eventually attracted a number of technicians and businessmen from the Third Reich. Needing to secure a supply route from the Persian Gulf to Russia, the Allies used their presence as a pretext to invade and finally entered the country in the autumn of 1941. Reza Shah Pahlavi was forced to abdicate only a few days later, on September 17, and the Crown Prince Mohammad Reza Pahlavi ascended to the throne in his father's place.

Encouraged by the Allied presence, the new shah abandoned his father's reform program and autocratic behavior. Political prisoners were released. Muslim men began wearing turbans, and women began veiling again. Intellectuals, tribe leaders, clergy, and others became more politically active. But, as Marxism began to spread among the educated youth, the Western powers felt uneasy. To check the burgeoning movement – which had already founded its own political party, Tudeh, with the blessings of Moscow – Mohammad Reza Pahlavi turned to the clerical establishment, meeting their demands, in the hope of using religion as a counterweight.

The previous shah's policies had affected Iran, however. A section of society was now secular, and largely Westernized. For this group, religion was an outmoded institution at best. The reimposition of the veil and the banning of theater and other forms of popular entertainment by the clerics came as an unwelcome shock. After World War II, Muhammad Mosaddeq drew together the small and isolated groups that had emerged from the ashes of the crackdown on the Democratic Party of Iran, creating the National Front. "He sometimes referred to the thought of the founders of the Iranian Masonic tradition," says Yann Richard, "although this was far from being his only source of inspiration."[165] A secularist, Mosaddeq believed the 'ulama should not involve themselves in politics, though his National Front included a number of nationalist-leaning clerics.

In 1951, with the support of the Majles and the public, the National Front embarked on a campaign that ended, as they had hoped it would, in the seizure of the Anglo-Iranian Oil Company facilities. Mosaddeq became Prime Minister, and, with Iran's oil industry nationalized, he now turned his attention to the monarchy, agitating against it. Mohammad Reza Pahlavi was forced to flee the country in 1953 as a result. However, enraged at Mosaddeq's behavior, Britain and the USA soon intervened, using the CIA to instigate a coup against the Iranian Parliament and to restore the shah to absolute power. In the aftermath, Mosaddeq was arrested and forbidden to involve himself with politics, while the National Front was accused of being a front for the Marxist Tudeh party, and disbanded.[166]

Ayatollah Khomeini: Emergence and Exile

For a decade the monarchy and the clerical class had been able to avoid serious clashes. Ayatollah Muhammad Hossein Borujerdi, the leading *marja'* (religious leader and spiritual guide) had tolerated and perhaps even tacitly supported the government, believing that he could serve Shi'a Islam under the rule of the shah.[167] Borujerdi died in 1961. By late the following year, tensions between the camps of the monarchy and clerics were rising precipitously. In October 1962, under pressure from President Kennedy and the International Monetary Fund, the shah of Iran pushed forward with new reforms. These were intended to stave off any possibility of a re-emerging Leftist opposition. For the first time, non-Muslims – including Jews and Baha'is – were to be allowed to run in local council elections, and to swear on their own holy book if they were elected to office. Women were also to be given the vote.

For Khomeini, as well as other members of the clergy and faithful, this was nothing other than a brazen attack on the religion of Islam and its prerogatives and responsibilities. The bill was announced on October 8. That evening Khomeini met Ayatollahs Shari'atmadari and Golpayegani to discuss the situation. They decided to actively oppose the shah. Khomeini wanted the group to send a joint letter of complaint, but the three had to settle for sending individual letters since they were not in complete agreement with each other. For his part, the shah did not take the protest seriously, and responded by letter, suggesting that the clerics stick to religious matters and avoid meddling in politics. The government press also began attacking the mullahs for wanting to keep Iran in the "Dark Ages."

The clerics rallied the faithful through *Maktab-i Islam*, a widely-read, monthly circular. Sermons – which, until then, had been restricted to religious matters – now took on an overtly political character, and focused on attacking the Iranian government under Prime Minister Amir Asadollah Alam, a puppet of the shah. Having ignored their pleas to promote him as a candidate for *marja'*, on the death of Ayatollah Borujerdi in 1961,[168] Khomeini now encouraged his students to forge links with other groups espousing his opinions, widening his circle of supporters – many of which were members of the bazaars, a powerful, religiously conservative merchant class within Iran.[169]

This was not the first time that Khomeini had entered into the political arena. The reforms pertaining to local elections – which were generally corrupt, and which conferred on elected councilors no real power anyway – had merely provided the ayatollah with a pretext to enter into the political fray publicly, and to push back against secularism and its forces inside Iran.

Though most of Khomeini's early books were concerned with the nature of *'irfan*, he did not view Islamic mysticism necessarily as a path of introversion. Rather, the spiritual and esoteric provided the basis for his social and political action. (Written in response to the reforms of the shah that were underway at that time, as well as to attacks on the 'ulama and Islam, his first political work, *Kashf-i Asrar* (The Unveiling of Secrets), published in 1943/44, cites Islamic mystics Ibn 'Arabi and Mulla Sadra as well as Plato's *Timaeus*.[170] The ancient Greek philosopher would prove influential on the ayatollah, shaping, to an extent, his notion of the *vilayat-i faqih* (governance of the jurist), which he would install, to govern Iran, after the Islamic Revolution.)

Under pressure, on December 1, Alam announced that the local council legislation had been suspended. The shah was, nonetheless, determined to see reforms enacted, and, on January 9, he announced a new six-point program that would form the basis of the so-called "White Revolution." These included land reform, the sale of state-owned factories, the nationalization of forests, and electoral power for women. For different reasons, many segments of Iranian society, from the aristocracy and clergy to middle-class professionals, were unhappy with the reforms. Intellectuals derided it as a revolution against the people.[171]

Khomeini denounced the entire program and appealed to his supporters to boycott the referendum on the shah's White Revolution. Unsurprisingly, the results supported the reforms, but Khomeini kept up his attacks, preaching a number of inflammatory sermons from Feiziyeh madrasa in Qom, accusing the government of doing the bidding of the USA and Israel. The shah was growing impatient, not least of all with the ayatollah and his growing support. Speaking to an audience of the Lions Club on March 16, he declared that his revolution would require nothing less than brute force. It would mean spilling "the blood of innocent people... and of wretched, misguided people."[172] On March 22, the shah sent paratroopers into the madrasa. A number of students were killed in the assault. Others were beaten and arrested, while the building itself was ransacked.[173]

Shocked by the attack on the religious establishment, Khomeini now decided that not just the reform program but the regime itself had to be abolished. He continued his fiery sermons as 'Ashura – the Shi'a commemoration of the martyrdom of Imam Husayn, which falls on the tenth day of Muharram (the first month of the Islamic calendar) – drew nearer. Khomeini understood that the public rituals of mourning and remembrance would bring to life the metaphysical basis of his political positions. Husayn, the second son of Imam 'Ali, had refused to swear allegiance to the Caliph Yazid (whom many Muslims regarded as corrupt) and, as a consequence, had been slaughtered on the orders of the caliph, during the battle of Karbala. Now the ayatollah presented Iran's secular dictator and government as being, metaphysically, in the fold of Yazid, and the people as akin to the martyrs that had fallen with Husayn.[174] Khomeini's status among the shah's opposition was growing unchecked.

On June 3, the day of 'Ashura, Khomeini gave another address, denouncing the shah, and telling Iran's leader to change course. If he did not, the ayatollah warned, the shah would one day be exiled from Iran. It was a bold move. Khomeini was arrested two days later, and taken to Tehran, where he was jailed for several months. Shocked and angered at his arrest, demonstrators took to the streets of several Iranian cities,[175] including Qom, Tehran, Shiraz, and Isfahan. Alam declared martial law and sent the troops to the streets. By the time the demonstrations had come to an end, three days later, hundreds – possibly thousands – had been killed by the Iranian soldiers. The fallen became the martyrs of the opposition movement.

After his release, Khomeini was placed under house arrest for another eighteen months. A government-run newspaper announced that he had agreed to refrain from attacking the establishment, but Khomeini promptly denied he had said any such thing, and resumed lambasting the shah. The following year, linked to a loan from the US, intended to help Iran on the road to modernity, a new law was enacted, granting American personnel working in the country immunity from prosecution. Unsurprisingly, the Iranian public detested the new law. Khomeini spoke out against it, lamenting this serious intrusion on Iranian sovereignty. He was arrested again. Only, this time, he was exiled to Turkey.[176]

Sending an Earthquake

Contrary to the Iranian regime's expectations, Turkey proved hospitable to the ayatollah. His Persian-speaking minder portrayed the country as a developed Islamic state, impressing Khomeini with visits to its cities. The shah, though, was unimpressed and sensed that Turkey, neighboring Iran, might be tempted to use Khomeini against them in any geopolitical struggle. Since it was paying for the ayatollah's life in exile, and believing that he would be overshadowed at the ancient center of Shi'a learning, the following year the Iranian regime facilitated Khomeini's travel to Najaf, Iraq.[177]

While Leftists and Shi'ite activists had come together before, after the 1963 protests they were drawn closer together. If they did not meet in intellectual circles opposed to the regime, then they met in prison, sentenced for campaigning against the shah. But the clerical class also sought to compete against the Marxists and to portray their worldview as the sole legitimate one in their struggle against Iran's leader. Nevertheless, Marxist and other Western ideas seeped into the activist religious milieu. Muslim intellectual Ali Shariati – whose books and speeches did much to prepare the way for the Islamic Revolution – presented Shi'ism as a revolutionary creed. For Shariati – who died in 1977, not long before the outbreak of the Revolution – Husayn was an archetype of such guerilla fighters as Che Guevara, while the history of Shi'a Islam embodied the dialectic of class struggle.

During the 1970s, Khomeini's organization, Nahzat, distanced itself from both the Marxists and the *mujahidin* (armed militias). Taken from the ayatollah's reference to the "Islamic movement" (*nahzat i-Islami*) after the defeat of the local election legislation, Nahzat had neither explicitly condemned nor condoned armed rebellion, though Khomeini believed that it would not work as a tactic. He recognized that the power of the anti-shah movement was rooted in the culture of Iranian, Shi'a Islam, with its sense of martyrdom and opposition to oppression, its religious fervor, and its ability to make sense of the believer's place and purpose in this world and the next.

Through his ever-widening network, the ayatollah was able to remain both in contact and involved with the anti-shah struggle in Iran. By the late 1970s, such was Khomeini's profile that he had gone from being a symbol of the movement – including for many Leftists and middle-class opponents of the regime – to being regarded as the *marja'* of the burgeoning revolution. To America, however, it was unthinkable that the shah could be threatened, let alone deposed, by an elderly mullah residing in neighboring Iraq. "Iran," Jimmy Carter declared on December 31, 1977, on a visit to the country, "because of the great leadership of the shah, is an island of stability in one of the more troubled areas of the world."[178]

Unwittingly reflecting the suspicions of many Iranians, who had come to view the USA as a colonizer, Carter went on to laud the "30,000 Americans here who work in close harmony with the people of Iran to carve out a better future for you, which," he added, "also helps to ensure [...] a better future for ourselves." The first stirrings of the Islamic Revolution had already occurred. Less than two years after Carter lauded the shah's leadership, his regime had collapsed, and the "king of kings" had been exiled, as Khomeini had predicted over a decade earlier.

In 1978, demonstrations and strikes brought the shah's Iran to a near halt. Although they had no love for the shah, with his regime in serious trouble, Iraq's secular Ba'athists began to fear that, unless action was taken, something similar might occur closer to home to take them down as well. After all, Iraq, like its neighbor Iran, was majority Shi'ite. For his part, the shah now wanted Khomeini exiled from Iraq and appealed to its secular dictator Saddam Hussein to have the ayatollah sent out of the country. By having him removed from the Shi'ite holy city of Najaf, in particular, the shah reckoned now, Khomeini's aura as a religious scholar and *marja'* would quickly evaporate.[179]

Saddam sent his half-brother Barzan al-Tikriti to Tehran to meet with the shah to discuss the issue.[180] What he found was a palace in darkness, affected like much of the rest of the city by power cuts. Al-Tikriti suggested that Iraq would be prepared to arrange an "accident" for the ayatollah, to put an end to the problem once and for all, but the shah was afraid that if Khomeini were assassinated he would become a martyr, and that his memory would inspire even greater dedication and resolve among the rebels to fulfill his ambitions.

The ayatollah departed Iraq on October 3. His intended destination was Kuwait, but Khomeini and his entourage were refused entry at the border. Algeria, Lebanon, and Syria were considered, but his second son, Hajj Sayyid Ahmad Khomeini, suggested that he travel to France. Conspicuous in his desire to avoid things un-Islamic – though taking up residence in the Parisian suburb of Neauphle-le-Chateau, in a house rented by a number of his Iranian devotees in France – Khomeini never ventured into the city of Paris.[181]

Able to communicate his beliefs and instructions with relative ease, the move to France turned out to be an enormous boon for Khomeini. Journalists, as well as religious and political leaders, visited his chateau each day. During his four-month stay, the ayatollah gave 132 press, television, and radio interviews. But his message was spread by more direct means as well. Not long after his arrival, a local recording studio was drafted by Khomeini's team, and set to work making thousands of cassette tapes of his talks to be distributed in Iran.[182] His campaign won over religious conservatives and Marxists. The former wanted the shah's reforms abolished, and the latter were enthralled by Khomeini's talk of "justice and equity." It tipped the balance firmly in his favor.

As lines of disciples spilled along the streets of the Paris suburb, each one waiting to see the ayatollah, wealthy Iranians – supporters of the shah for the most part – were fleeing the country, fearing for their future. The regime was unraveling. Rioting continued to rage throughout the cities. The army, increasingly ineffectual and unwilling to deal with the rioters, saw its first major internal challenge as conscripts began to desert in droves. In a demonstration of his grip on power, Khomeini ordered workers across the country to strike. With the help of Left-wing activists, the oil industry was brought to a complete halt. Power cuts plunged Tehran into near total darkness. The shah sat by, unable to exert any influence as the Iranian economy crashed around him.

Then the ayatollah ordered workers to produce enough oil for domestic needs. With the oil flowing again it was apparent that Iran had a new authority. Britain and the USA had already advised the "king of kings" to leave the country. Now the end of the regime was a mere formality. On January 16, 1979, the shah, along with Empress Farah Pahlavi, left the country. Statues of the shah were smashed, and his photos burned. Streets were renamed, wiping the old regime from history. Khomeini returned to Iran on February 30. A month later he declared the country an "Islamic state."

After the Iranian Revolution

Considering the shooting of Nasir al-Din Shah in 1896 by a follower of Sayyid Jamal ad-Din al-Afghani it is an irony of history that from the beginning of the Islamic Revolution of 1978-79, Iran's Freemasons were denounced by the main protagonists – the Islamists, Leftists, and neo-liberal-nationalists – as Anglo-American and Anglo-Zionist agents. Al-Afghani, as we have seen, was one of several radicals who had joined the fraternity, and had hoped that it could be used in aid of the anti-colonial cause.

Less than a century on, articles and books accusing the fraternity of conspiring against Iran and Islam were being widely published, fomenting hostility. Yet of more direct consequence for the Freemasons of Iran, a roster was soon discovered at the home of Ja'far Sharif-Emami – the Prime Minister, and Grand Master of the Grand Lodge of Iran – and used by the revolutionary committees to initiate a campaign of persecution. Membership in Freemasonry was made a crime, and, under the newly established Islamic Republic, Freemasons were purged from the government and universities. Many were imprisoned, and a number were also executed.[183] Others fled abroad, to the West.

Freemasonry had had a difficult time in Iran, throughout the 20th century. In 1908 Lodge Reveil de l'Iran was founded in Tehran with the permission of the monarch, Muhammad Ali Shah,[184] although he ordered its closure not long after, due to his suspicion of the fraternity. British and French Grand Lodges chartered new, subordinate Lodges later on. The Grand Lodge of Iran was founded in 1969. Like the clergy, the Pahlavis were suspicious of Freemasonry, though Mohammad Reza may have hoped to use the fraternal network for political ends.[185] Yet, despite hostility toward Freemasonry and secret societies more broadly, Sharif-Emami was not the only well-placed Freemason in the shah's government. Seyyed 'Abdollah Entezam (1895-1983) served in a number of prominent official positions. Known as a man of integrity, Entezam refused to kiss the hand of the shah during audiences with him. As a Sufi and mystic, Entezam answered to God, not worldly powers.

Like his father before him, he belonged to the Society (*Anjoman-e Okhovvat*) of the *Safi 'Ali Shahi* branch of the *Ne'matollahi* Sufi Order, which mixed the "organization and symbolism of Sufism and Freemasonry." Entezam was active in the Brotherhood since at least the 1960s and served as its leader in 1974.[186] He was also the nation's Foreign Minister between 1953 and 1956. He served as a diplomat, and was the director of the National Iranian Oil Company between 1957 and 1963, when he was relieved of his position for upsetting the shah. Entezam had been one of several Iranian officials to warn Iran's secular dictator about his harsh response to the June 1963 uprising.

Freemasons were far from the only ones that found themselves in trouble with the Islamic state, however. Ostensibly under the control of clerics, ad hoc Islamic revolutionary councils formed across Iran to try suspected sympathizers of the shah, or anyone not in step ideologically with the revolution. Before the beginning of April, there were an estimated 20,000 political prisoners. Six hundred executions were ordered by the end of the month.[187]

Besides the destruction of political enemies, the new regime set out to "Islamize" the public space. First and foremost, this meant new restrictions for women. The Family Protection laws of 1967 were overturned only a few months after the end of the revolution, stripping women of the right to seek a divorce, child custody, or to travel abroad without the consent of a male guardian.[188] Whether they were Muslim or not, women now also had to wear conservative clothes to cover their bodies and the hijab (usually black) to cover their hair. Single men and women were prohibited from meeting in public.

"Occasionally, after the 1979 Revolution, when officials came to see him with great problems or a major crisis," says Baqer Moin, "he would talk about God as if nothing else existed, oblivious to the great political, social and economic forces he had unleashed."[189] But the man who had fomented revolution from exile on the edge of another continent was far from a naïve dreamer. Despite, or perhaps partly because of, his interest early in mysticism, Khomeini was a man of sharp intellect and a shrewd political strategist. Indeed, because of his desire to unify the various interpretations of Islam – from the social to the esoteric – the ayatollah had manifested the mystic's aspiration for union with God as a social, political, and legal program.

Later, during the eight-year-long Iran-Iraq War, one of Khomeini's former students in 'irfan, Mehdi Ha'iri Yazdi, visited him at his home. There he found the Supreme Leader sitting on a rug, before a pool in his garden. His former student implored Khomeini to end the war, talking of its senseless killing. Khomeini responded rhetorically, asking, "Do you criticize God when he sends an earthquake?"[190] Mehdi Ha'iri regarded the remark as implicitly identifying Khomeini with God Himself. He later came to believe that the Supreme Leader of Iran had come to see himself as having moved so close to God that he was functioning as a virtually divine lawgiver. If this was how Khomeini saw things, then his understanding was certainly rooted in Islamic gnosticism.

But if, even on a pious religious level, Khomeini saw the hand of God in his own work, it would not be entirely surprising. He had gone from political exile to the man that had brought down the shah of Iran, the latter of which had enacted reforms that appeared to the clergy and many ordinary Iranians to contravene Islam. And, it was the figure of Khomeini – a former student and teacher of *'irfan* – that unified the Iranian masses. That many initially did not understand his message is clear. But with remarkable speed, the man who believed himself to be doing the will of Allah had come to sweep the "king of kings" and his regime into history. Elevating him far above other clerics, Khomeini's followers now referred to him as "the Imam."

SEVEN

Birth of a Conspiracy Theory

The Ottoman census of 1878 had recorded an Arab Palestinian population (both Muslim Christian) of 447,454, as well as a small Jewish community of 15,011 comprising less than four percent of the entire population.[191] Growing concern at state-sponsored anti-Semitism and pogroms in Tsarist Russia meant that about another 25,000 Jews had arrived in Palestine by 1891, with a further 35,000 to 40,000 arriving by the outbreak of World War I. Then, with the Ottoman Empire allied to the Germans, and their defeat predicted, Britain, France, and Russia began negotiating territorial ambitions regarding the Holy Land, which was then Ottoman territory. In 1917, Britain effectively expressed its support for "the establishment in Palestine of a national home for the Jewish people" via the Balfour Declaration. The "civil and religious rights of existing non-Jewish communities in Palestine," which still accounted for 89 percent of the population, were also to be guaranteed. But fears were growing, not least of all as the declaration made no obligation about their political rights.[192]

Arab hostility to Jews in the Middle East long pre-dated the arrival of increasing numbers from Europe, however. In 1840, Arab Christians in Damascus accused Jews of kidnapping and murdering a monk and a servant, to use their blood for *matzah* bread. Mob violence, forced conversions of Jews, arrests and torture quickly followed, provoking Western powers to complain, and the Ottoman Sultan to denounce the libel as a complete fabrication.

But the suspicion and hostility was not all one-way. Zionists themselves hoped for the "practically complete dispossession of the present non-Jewish inhabitants of Palestine," the 1919 King-Crane Commission reported after interviewing representatives of the Jewish community. Purchasing land from absentee Arab landlords, and evicting the peasants living there, was one method used to gain a larger foothold in Palestine. Discriminating against Arabs, Keren Hayesod employment agreements required settlers to hire only Jewish workers. Consequently, as antagonism toward the Zionist movement in Palestine grew exponentially, episodes of violence erupted between the Jewish and Arab communities throughout the 1920s.[193]

Portending the impact of European anti-Semitic literature in the Middle East, an Arabic translation of August Rohling's *The Talmud Jew* had already been published in Egypt in 1899. Later, in the latter half of the 1920s, Arab nationalists in Palestine and Iraq were citing *The Protocols of the Elders of Zion* approvingly. Translated from a French copy by a Lebanese Maronite Christian priest, the first Arabic version was published in Egypt in 1925.[194] Though the text itself would have an enormous influence on twentieth- and early twenty-first-century Islamist politics, the roots of *The Protocols* lead back to 18th century Europe.

Then, long-held assumptions were being overturned at an astounding rate. The scientific revolution was underway, and the ideas of the Enlightenment philosophers were winning ever more converts. The authority of the monarchy, the aristocracy, the Papacy, and religion was being called increasingly in question, or simply outright denied.

Colonial America had decried King George IV for establishing an "absolute tyranny" over the colonies and had declared independence from Britain in 1776. Less than a decade later, France would be in economic turmoil, with mass unemployment in Paris and poor harvests sending the price of wheat to an all-time high. The following year the situation had worsened, and bread riots broke out across the country. Bakeries, granaries, and mills were attacked by mobs, demanding that bread be sold at "the just price."

With such a wide gulf between the rich and the poor, the monarchy was the most obvious target of people's rage. But the flames of discontentment were fanned by pornographic pamphlets that depicted the queen, Marie Antoinette, in all kinds of lurid, sexual scenes. She had been only 14-years-old when she married Louis Auguste, who was only a year older, in May 1770. Four years later, in 1774, the first of the pornographic pamphlets had appeared. The royal couple had not yet had children, and this was enough for gossipers to conclude that the king was impotent. The pamphlets, too, claimed that this had driven the young queen into the arms of the king's brother, as well as other relatives, into lesbianism, and into other sexual liaisons with her servants and palace guards.

By 1789, the French Revolution was underway, and France found itself in the grips of "The Terror" as thousands of "enemies of the revolution" were rounded up and executed. In January 1793, King Louis XVI was publicly decapitated with the newly invented guillotine. In October, Marie Antoinette stood trial before an all-male jury of the Revolutionary Criminal Tribunal. Many of the accusations against her were ripped straight from the pages of the pornographic pamphlets that had attacked her, and that ultimately helped to seal her fate. The "tribunal" accused her of engaging in orgies at Versailles and of corrupting the regime with her sexuality. Marie Antoinette was executed later in the same month as her "trial."

In the Vendée, a coastal region in West central France, revolutionary forces put down a popular uprising with particular ruthlessness. The peasants of the region, who were fighting for God and king, managed to hold out for a decade. By the end, at least 80,000 had been killed by the revolutionaries. For Jean-Baptiste Carrier, a representative of the Revolution in the region, no slaughter was too large. He vowed that the Revolution would "turn France into a cemetery rather than fail in her regeneration," and ordered hundreds of counter-revolutionaries drowned in the Loire River at a time.[195]

Who could explain the ripping apart of society? The madness of the crowd? The slaughter? The attacks on the Church, religion, and even on God Himself? The situation was chaotic, but Augustin Barruel, a French

Jesuit priest in exile in Britain, saw only a meticulous and calculated plot. In 1798 he published his *Memoirs Illustrating the History of Jacobinism*, blaming the Lodges of Freemasonry for fomenting revolution. The following year, inspired by Barruel, John Robison, a professor of Natural Philosophy at Edinburgh University, published his book on the same subject, neatly summing up his paranoid thesis in the title: *Proofs of a Conspiracy against all the Religions and Governments of Europe, carried on in the secret meetings of Freemasons, Illuminati, and Reading Societies.*

Making and Disseminating *The Protocols of the Elders of Zion*

Although the French Revolution (1789-1799) had championed "the rights of man" revolutionaries and their supporters had overwhelmingly assumed that their values would not be extended to Jews. An attempt to debate the issue in the National Assembly, in December 1789, had to be tabled due to a lack of support. Nevertheless, complete emancipation was passed into law in 1791, after Portuguese, Spanish, and Avignonese Jews were emancipated the preceding year.[196] Later, from 1806, Napoleon passed further measures, easing restrictions on Jews, and releasing them from the ghettos in French territories. In the same year, the great French military and political leader summoned an assembly of respected French Jewish scholars and rabbis, dubbing it "the Great Sanhedrin" after the ancient Jewish court.

The idea of an ancient lineage of secret societies – all subversive – had already been floated by Barruel in his wildly popular *Memoirs*. For the priest and his followers, the Freemasons were the descendants of the medieval Crusader order of the Knights Templar. Having already attacked Freemasonry, not surprisingly, that a Great Sanhedrin was convening in France was all the proof they needed of a Jewish plot against Christendom.

In 1806 Barruel received a letter from Florence. Its author was supposedly a renegade army officer by the name of J. B. Simonini, although it appears to have been the work of French political police. Their intention was to propagate the idea that Jews were a potent threat to society that needed to be constrained, not liberated. The letter congratulated Barruel on exposing subversive sects that were busy paving the way for the Antichrist, but remarked that he had omitted mention of "the most formidable power" – "the Judaic sect." It went on to claim that Simonini had pretended to some Piedmontese Jews that he himself was of Jewish origin, but had been separated from the community as a child. Convinced, it was claimed, they, in turn, asked him to become a Freemason, promising that he would be made a general if he did so. He was also shown a store of gold and silver – apparently dished out to those who joined with them – and told various secrets, including that Freemasonry had been established by a Jew, and that no less than 800 of the clergy in Italy were also secretly Jews.

Barruel was convinced, and, hoping to forestall the Sanhedrin, made sure that those influential in French society heard of the plot. The letter was the first fake to link the Jews and Freemasons in a conspiracy against religions and governments, but it would not be the last. It might have been forgotten were it not for Russia undergoing a similar societal upheaval during the late 19th and early 20th centuries. An agrarian country unable to compete with the industrialized West, between 1898-1902, Russian farmers produced a meager 8.8 bushels of wheat per acre in contrast to British farmers, who produced more than 35 bushels for each acre. Wooden plows were still the norm, and by 1912, there were only 166 tractors in the whole country.

Russia had begun to modernize, slowly, under Count Sergei Witte, appointed Minister of Finance by Tsar Alexander III in 1892, and, later, the prime minister. Concerned that discriminatory laws against Jews in Russia were damaging the economy – though not particularly concerned with the plight of Jews themselves – Witte pleaded with the tsar for their emancipation, although to no avail. He did, however, introduce a number of reforms. To help facilitate foreign loans the ruble was put on the gold standard. A national railroad system was created, a national bank was founded, and industry was provided with state loans.

With Russia already experiencing episodes of political violence, modernization – far from a painless process – only increased discontent. Socialism began to make its appearance. Georgi Plekhanov spread Marxist ideas in Russia, publishing Karl Marx's *Das Kapital*. After being sent to Siberia for propagandizing, Vladimir Lenin traveled to Switzerland in 1900. There he published the revolutionary newspaper *Iskra*, and had it smuggled back into Russia. In 1903, still in exile, Lenin entered the Russian political arena as the head of the tiny Bolshevik ("Majority") party.

In the same year, the anti-Semitic forgery, *The Protocols of the Elders of Zion*, was published in serial form in *Znamya* (Banner), the newspaper of the pro-Tsarist, counter-revolutionary movement known as the Black Hundreds. The newspaper was edited by P. A. Krushevan, a militant anti-Semite, who had already instigated a pogrom against Jews at Kishinev. Forty-five were killed, several hundred injured, and more than a thousand Jewish homes and businesses destroyed.

Consisting of twenty-four chapters, the *Protocols* purports to be the minutes of a secret meeting of Zionists – early believers in the text ascribed its creation to the first Zionist Congress in Basel, Switzerland, in 1897. Two European Rabbis – Judah Alkalai and Zvi Hirsh Kalischer – had proclaimed from the 1830s that Jews should return to the Holy Land in preparation for the return of the Messiah. Although the idea did not win popular support, societies known as *Chovevei Zion* ("Lovers of Zion") were established throughout Russia by the 1870s. Following the assassination of Tsar Alexander II in March 1881, pogroms against Jews in Russia caused up to two million to leave. Most sought refuge in the US. Others went to Palestine.

Russia was not the only Western nation hostile to its Jewish citizens, however. In 1894, Captain Alfred Dreyfus, a Jewish officer in the French army, was falsely accused of passing military secrets to the Germans. Tried, convicted, and sentenced to solitary confinement on Devil's Island, Dreyfus was pardoned in 1899, but in the aftermath of the trial, mobs roamed the streets, calling for "death to the Jews." The trial was witnessed by Theodor

Herzl, a Jewish-Austrian journalist for the liberal *Neue Freie Presse*. Alarmed by the rise in anti-Semitic incidents in Europe, in 1896, in *The Jewish State*, Herzl advocated for a sovereign state for Jews. It was to work toward this end that he had called the first Zionist Congress. However, fed on the propaganda of the *Protocols*, anti-Zionists and anti-Semites saw things differently. For them, Jews and Zionists constituted a powerful cabal, secretly instigating revolutions, controlling the press, using the Freemasons to spread their influence, and destroying long-held traditions in all of the world's nations. They had not met to work toward a Jewish state, but, rather, it was claimed, for world domination.

The *Protocols* was exposed as a forgery by *The Times* of London in 1921, in a series of articles written by Philip Graves, the newspaper's Istanbul correspondent. Graves demonstrated that two-thirds of the text had been plagiarized from *The Dialogue in Hell Between Machiavelli and Montesquieu*, written by a French lawyer by the name of Maurice Joly, and published in Brussels in 1864. Though one chapter claims that Zionists are employing, and manipulating, "the Freemasons" in their bid for world domination, this theme ultimately derives from the letter Barruel had received.

Joly's work was a satirical attack on the government of Napoleon III and made no reference to Jews. Nevertheless, Hermann Goedsche (1815-1878) adapted Joly's theme of a dialogue in Hell for a chapter in his fictional work *Biarritz* (1868). The chapter was titled *The Jewish Cemetery in Prague and the Council of Representatives of the Twelve Tribes of Israel*, and it supposedly described a gathering of twelve Jewish elders – representing the twelve tribes of Israel, including the ten lost tribes – plotting world domination with the aid of Satanic forces. In the novel, the elders take turns in delivering speeches describing how they will take over control of Christendom. They will control the press, infiltrate governments, foment revolution, and corrupt Christian women. A lurid portrayal of Jews, the chapter was a gift to anti-Semites, and consequently reproduced in pamphlet form in Russia from 1872. In 1881, the speeches of the fictional elders were merged into a single work called *The*

Rabbi's Speech.

The *Protocols* was created using this textual tradition – mostly from Joly's *Dialogue* – by Matvei Vasilyevich Golovinski (1865-1920), the assistant to Pyotr Rachovsky, the chief of the foreign branch of the Russian secret police, *Okhrana*, in Paris. The intention was to shift the blame for Russia's troubles onto the Jews and to keep its population from embracing the possibility of a more egalitarian society.

In 1905, as revolution was erupting, a mystic by the name of Sergei Aleksandrovich Nilus published a second edition of his autobiography, *The Great in the Small: The Antichrist considered as an imminent political possibility*, which included the *Protocols* as an appendix. This was the first time the text had been printed in book form, and it is this version that has been used for all later editions, including those in other languages. In the 1911 edition, Nilus claimed to have acquired this text of a "secret Jewish Freemasonic conspiracy," from an acquaintance. He suggested that it was a translation from a French original stolen from a high-ranking Freemason at a meeting in France. In his 1917 edition, however, Nilus claimed that the *Protocols* had been read first at the first congress of the Jewish nationalist movement[197] at Basel, Switzerland in 1897.[198]

The *Protocols* attempts to convince its readers that liberal democracy is a trap set by Zionists. Their intention is to rid the world of autocrats and aristocracy, which, the *Protocols* suggests, are the only safeguard against a one-world Zionist government that would turn out to be far more brutal and oppressive. Some European countries had already taken the bait:

The people under our guidance have annihilated the aristocracy, who were their one and only defence and foster-mother for the sake of their own advantage which is inseparably bound up with the well-being of the people. Nowadays, with the destruction of the aristocracy, the people have fallen into the grips of merciless money-grinding scoundrels who have laid a pitiless and cruel yoke upon the necks of the workers.

We appear on the scene as alleged saviours of the worker from this oppression when we propose to him to enter the ranks of our fighting forces – Socialists, Anarchists, Communists to whom we always give support in accordance with an alleged brotherly rule (of the solidarity of all humanity) of our social [Free] masonry.[199]

The leaders of secular countries, the reader is informed, are more oppressive and brutal than the old monarchs. The populace does not rebel because it is convinced that it has rights and free speech, but these are illusions. Rights exist only in theory. "The triumph of free speech rests in the press, [...] and it has fallen into our hands. Through it, we have attained influence while remaining in the shadow," reads the *Protocols*.[200] With the onset of the Bolshevik Revolution in late 1917, the counter-revolutionary White Army distributed copies of the *Protocols* in the hope of convincing the populace that they were being ensnared by promises of equality. The text was dispersed throughout Western Europe as non-Jewish Russians fled their motherland to seek refuge from the Revolution. German, Polish, French, British, and American editions were published in 1920.

With a history of suffering discrimination and violence in Russia and elsewhere, yet still lacking "a strong ethnic nationalism of their own," younger, idealistic Jews had unsurprisingly sought refuge, instead, in internationalism. However, this commitment demanded not just the rejection of the state, and its discriminations, but "the repudiation of tradition, religion, Jewish family attachments" and identity. Wishing to be absorbed into the broader population, if not into a universal brotherhood of the Proletariat, these new internationalists opposed even Zionism. By the late 1800s, Jews made up around twenty percent of the activists of the Populist (People's Will) movement. When the Bolshevik Central Committee met on October 23, 1917, voting for an armed uprising, five of the twelve members present were Jews, as were three of the seven Politburo members who initiated the decision.[201]

Despite the repudiation of Jewish tradition and separate ethnic identity by young Bolshevik and Marxist Jews, their overrepresentation in leadership roles had led to the new stereotype of the "Jew-Bolshevik" and "Yid-traitor." But this would be only one of many. Despite contradicting each other, the entire range of Jewish stereotypes – from the "Jew-Banker" to the "Jew-Bolshevik" – would be incorporated, with ease, into the anti-Semitic and radical racialist worldview.

In Germany, the *Protocols*, and the notion of a Jewish-Masonic conspiracy, took root in the burgeoning, mystical, ultra-nationalist movement. Until then he had been best known for founding an anti-Semitic periodical called the *Hammer* in 1902, but in 1924 ardent German nationalist Theodor Fritsch (1852-1933) published a new edition of the *Protocols*.[202] Despite his journal having a readership in the low thousands, only a few years after its founding local "Hammer groups" had formed across the country, and in 1910 Fritsch was presiding as Grand Master of a newly formed organization – later called the Germanic Order – dedicated to preserving the racial purity of the German people. Suitable candidates were initiated into the organization in a theatrical and mystical ceremony that drew from pagan mythology.[203]

The Germanic Order also began recruiting assassins to target political enemies,[204] and its Bavarian branch, the Thule Society – established by Rudolf von Sebottendorf – had some influence on the *Deutsche Arbeiterpartei* before it became the *Nationalsozialistische Deutsche Arbeiterpartei* (the NSDAP, "German National Socialist Workers Party," or, as it is more usually called, the Nazi Party) under Adolf Hitler.[205] The future Führer also believed in the mythology of the *Protocols* and wrote in his autobiography, *Mein Kampf*, of the "shackles of Jewish Freemasonry" supposedly constraining Germany:

While the international World-Jew is slowly but surely strangling us, our so-called patriots vociferate against a man [Benito Mussolini] and his system which have had the courage to liberate themselves from the shackles of Jewish Freemasonry at least in one quarter of the globe and to set the forces of national resistance against the international world-poison.

Later he says that the proof that Jewry is drawing its "poison fangs" (a reference to a description of Jews as a "symbolic snake" in the *Protocols*[206]), although "in an indirect way," is implied in Fascist Italy's attacks on its alleged three principal weapons. Italy has embarked on:

The prohibition of Freemasonry and secret societies, the suppression of the supranational Press and the definite abolition of Marxism…

Not every Nazi Party official believed the *Protocols* to be true. Yet, rather than diminishing the power of the text, the recognition of its spuriousness only enhanced its authority. Propaganda minister for the Third Reich, Joseph Goebbels, exclaimed that "I believe that the *Protocols of the Elders of Zion* are a forgery [however] I believe in the intrinsic but not the factual truth of the *Protocols*."[207] The considerable power of the text – as a kind of modernist mythology – is based on its keen dissection of the vulnerability of liberal democracy to exploitation by self-serving organizations or individuals, and, consequently – and more essentially – to the frailty of the human character. It illuminates the unpleasant, self-serving, dark side of humanity – a side most people would prefer to imagine is alien to their nature – and ascribes it to the Jews and their alleged lackeys alone.

Militias in the Middle East

The *Protocols* and other European anti-Semitic texts appealed to the religious in the Middle East – both to Arab Christians and, later, to Muslims – as we have seen. But they also proved equally attractive to Arab socialists and the region's secular nationalists. The Syrian National Party – later renamed the Syrian Social National Party (SSNP) – excluded Jews, although, like other Arab nationalist movements, it accepted members of various ethnicities. Although largely unknown today, the party was behind what is believed to have been the first ever female suicide bombing, carried out by Sana'a Mehaidli, a 16-year-old member of the SSNP, who attacked an Israeli Defense Force convoy in April 1985.[208]

Founded by Antoun Saadeh – a Greek Orthodox Lebanese national – in 1932, the SSNP believed it could bridge the gap between Muslims and Christians by claiming a Canaanite origin for the homeland of its people (which included Cyprus). This was in some respects reminiscent of the Aryan myth of the Nazis, to whom the SSNP owed much, especially in regard to symbolism. It adopted a type of swastika, after the Nazi Party, and even sang its anthem to the tune of *Deutschland über Alles*.

Historian Michael Johnson claims, however, that "[t]he SSNP was unusual in its espousal of racist doctrines," which excluded even anti-Zionist Jews. Moreover, Johnson suggests that, while the Nazi influence on the SSNP is evident since Indian anti-colonial politics was known to the Middle East, that some of the region's militias or "shirts" may have been influenced by India's *Rashtriya Swayamsevak Sangh* (National Volunteer Organization). In contrast to the inclusive anti-colonialism and Indian nationalism of Congress, the RSS viewed India as an exclusively Hindu nation, and believed that Muslims were essentially alien to it, and should leave or accept a second-class status. As Johnson notes, "[f]ounded in 1925, the RSS was perhaps the first group in the colonized world to adopt the militia as a principle of organization," however, most Middle Eastern militant groups, he says, only wished to exclude the British and French, and otherwise accepted members of the nation state regardless of their ethnicity or religion.[209]

In late April 1939, a new radio program was heard in the Arab street. Broadcast from Zeesen, a small town to the south of Berlin, it was soon a popular choice of entertainment in the bazaars and coffee houses and remained so until it ceased broadcasting in 1945. The German national socialist regime was keen to win over the Arab Middle East, which it regarded as strategically important for its war on the Jews, and its Oriental Service was given "absolute priority" over its other foreign language services. The broadcasts mixed religion with current events, portraying the Jews as puppet masters engineering world events. The United Nations and the Allies alike were presented as being controlled by the Jews. In short, it was suggested, Jews were the eternal enemy of Islam, and their designs for world-domination were an existential threat to the faith.

From 1941, Haj Amin al-Husseini oversaw the broadcasting of Arabic-language programs from Zeesen, Athens, and Rome. Al-Husseini was the Grand Mufti of Jerusalem and a Palestinian nationalist possessed by a burning hatred of Jews. It was they, he believed, who had introduced decadent European culture to the Middle East. To halt the trend toward liberalization in the lands of Islam – which was well underway – and to reestablish the *shari'a*, the Jews would have to be destroyed. Signs of decay were everywhere, not only in the appearance of the cinema or the European styles of dress that many women had adopted, but, most of all, in the abolishment of the Caliphate by the young Mustafa Kemal Ataturk.

Al-Husseini had admired Germany's national socialism since the early 1930s. In a world that appeared increasingly decadent, it demanded discipline and obedience, glorified death in battle, and the struggle against Jewry. Illustrative of his admiration, the Grand Mufti formed a youth organization in 1933 that was initially known as the "Nazi Scouts." During the Palestinian uprising of 1936-39 against British rule and Jewish immigration, the swastika was adopted as an identity mark and used to decorate Arab-language propaganda leaflets.

Wherever the British power was defeated, and the Jews expelled, men and women were intimidated into adopting traditional dress – including the veil for women – and the Muslim leaders who opposed the Grand Mufti or who were willing to negotiate with the Jewish and British leaders were tortured and executed.

The Third Reich took little interest in the affairs of al-Husseini and pro-Nazi Arabs until 1937, however, when the British Peel Commission proposed that the British Mandate territory of Palestine be divided into a small Jewish state and a larger Arab state. Britain had come to control

Palestine after World War I (1914-18), and the British Mandate for Palestine was ratified by the League of Nations in 1922, article four of which sought to recognize an appropriate public Jewish body to advise and cooperate with the administration of Palestine, in the interests of establishing a "Jewish National Home" within it.[210] The Third Reich had wanted to avoid angering Britain, believing that it could be appeased, and conflict between the two nations avoided. But the report of the Peel Commission made this impossible, and Germany's national socialist regime soon began collaborating with Arabs sympathetic to it.

Al-Husseini is often credited as one of the leaders of the Arab revolt, though Philip Mattar claims that the mufti attempted to prevent the strikes, which initiated that period of unrest, from becoming too large or violent. He notes, also, that al-Husseini wrote to the colonial secretary at the time, asserting that passions had become too heated for Arab leaders to have any control over the strikers, who were demanding a complete end to immigration.[211]

By the end of the revolt, Zionist paramilitary groups had launched a number of attacks on Arabs, killing over a hundred in July 1938 alone, when six bombs were planted in Arab areas. Although the Irgun had attacked British targets before the outbreak of World War II, in 1946, the pressure was ramped up as Zionist paramilitary groups joined with the Haganah – the main Zionist military force. The King David Hotel – the site of the British administration's headquarters – was blown up. Lord Moyne was assassinated, and British soldiers were kidnapped, beaten and executed by the militant Stern Gang.

Wearying of the rapidly unraveling situation, the British evacuated all non-essential personnel during 1947. By December, as violence between Jews and Arabs had intensified into civil war, Britain announced that it would bring the Mandate to a close. The date of departure was set for May 15, 1948. Then, the day before, on May 14, Israel declared independence. Only eleven minutes later, over the objections of diplomatic staff and the State Department, the USA officially recognized the fledgling nation.[212]

EIGHT

Islamists Against the "Masonic" West

"Islamist extremists see the [Free]Masons as part of a Western crusade against Islam," the Canadian Security Intelligence Service (CSIS) concluded in a secret 2009 report, "Freemasonry is seen as a direct threat to Islam."[213] Islamist hatred of "Freemasonry" is a global phenomenon. However, just as some young, secular, politicized American men have an obsession with the "Illuminati," which they identify as the root or cause of political oppression,[214] so anti-Freemasonry may appeal especially to many young Muslim men, living in the West, cut off from authentic Islamic tradition, and more political than religious.

What is the meaning of "Freemasonry" in this worldview? In the Nazism of the 1930s and '40s, Freemasonry represented the traitorous gentile, working for the Jew against the Aryan. For the contemporary Islamist and Jihadist, the Western nation *is* "Freemasonic" in its nature – i.e., in its religious and sexual freedoms, its democracy, and so on. Amin Omar encapsulated this worldview neatly in his 1991 *New Straits Times* book review of Lukman Thaib's *Notion of State in Islam*. Omar objected even to the use of the word "state" in an Islamic context, "since in its strict sense, it is a Western-Jewish concept. State is structured in technique, it is system-controlled and influenced by international freemasonry."[215]

The Islamist use of the term, "Freemasonry," in anti-Western propaganda has gone almost unnoticed by analysts and media pundits. CSIS is a notable exception. The Canadian intelligence agency's assessment was largely correct, although it believed that this was a relatively new phenomenon. In fact, it has been a significant motif within extreme Islamism for several decades, and can ultimately be traced back to the importation of *The Protocols of the Elders of Zion* by Arab Christians during the early 20th century. Nevertheless, as CSIS observed,

Islamist extremists believe in what has been described as a "common narrative": Islam is under concerted attack by an entity vaguely called "the West" and all true Muslims have a religious obligation to defend their faith. The usual enemies cited on the internet and in communiqués are the US, UK and Israel, but many other countries have been named on occasion, including Canada. While the general enemy consists of Christians (Crusaders) and Jews (Zionists), there have been references to Freemasons as well.

Islamists use these terms in different ways, however. Although "Crusaders" can refer to Christians it is also used to signify the US and the West. "Freemasonry," likewise, often refers specifically to the USA, and occasionally to other Western powers, just as the term "Zionist entity" or "Zionist enemy" is used to refer to Israel. However, if "Crusader" denotes US or Western military "aggression," "Freemasonry" is generally seen as an attack on, and the active subversion of, Islamic culture.

It "undermines" all religions, the Islamic Fiqh Council, proclaimed in a lengthy fatwa,[216] issued in Saudi Arabia in 1978, "and aims at tarnishing the religion of Islam in particular in the eyes of its followers." Echoing the *Protocols*, the fatwa claims, wrongly, that Freemasonry has Jewish origins and is secretly controlled by a "worldwide Jewish management." It is also alleged that Freemasonry is in league with international Zionism, has been "overtly or covertly" involved with various military coups, and has influenced Arab and non-Arab officials, especially in regard to Palestine.

In other writings and statements, across the decades, we discover that Freemasonry is believed to "undermine" Islamic culture by spreading liberal democracy, movies, alcohol, pornography, women's rights, and sexual freedoms, and even through contaminating vaccines. In essence, it is believed that Freemasonry aims at spreading modern, Western culture and undermining traditional Islamic culture, especially at the bidding of international Zionists.

Ideology

Zionism and Freemasonry, Israel and the West, are believed to be intimately linked. The 1985 Tehran reprint of the *Protocols of the Elders of Zion* featured a frontispiece titled "Dream of Zionism," showing a map of the Middle East with "Greater Israel" incorporating Egypt, Syria, Iraq and Kuwait, as well as parts of Saudi Arabia, Iran and Turkey. The sinister nature of this "Dream" is underscored by the depiction of Greater Israel's boundary as a snake with eyes for scales (according to the map's legend, these represent Freemasonry)."[217] Such a map might be more reminiscent of a Dungeons and Dragons-type game than serious geopolitics, but the conspiracy theory it illustrates is highly motivating.

Although typically inveighing against "Crusaders," al-Qaeda has also attacked "Freemasonry." As the 2009 CSIS report noted, between 2008 and 2009 al-Qaeda in Yemen called for attacks against the embassies of Western nations, claiming that they "facilitated the spread of factions that run counter to Islam, including Freemasonry." The Fall 2010 edition of the online al-Qaeda magazine *Inspire* carried an article by Abu Mus Ab al Suri titled "The Jihad Experience: Open Fronts & The Individual Initiative." Al Suri tells the reader that "individual initiatives" of performing "the religious duty of jihad" have been repeated throughout Islamic history. He goes on to list numerous attacks against Jews, Americans, Russians, and Freemasons that he considers praiseworthy. Regarding the latter, he says:

In Jordan, an outstanding group consisting of four men created a cell to assassinate Freemasons in Amman, and succeeded in executing a number of them. They were subsequently arrested after clashing with the police, and some of them died as martyrs.[218]

For extreme Islamists and Jihadists, the Judeo-Masonic conspiracy theory provides a prism through which all contemporary and even past and future events can be viewed, no matter how mundane they may appear. In his *Ma'rakatuna ma'a al-Yahud* (Our Battle Against the Jews), Sayyid Qutb – one of the most influential Islamist theorists of the 20th century – says for example that the Jews' "aim is clearly shown by the *Protocols*. The Jews are behind materialism, animal sexuality, the destruction of the family and the dissolution of society."[219] Similarly, the Charter of the Hamas militant group and political party asserts that Freemasons are working for the Jews by degrading the mind of Muslims. Article 28 of the charter states explicitly that, "They [Freemasons] aim at undermining societies, destroying values, corrupting consciences, deteriorating character and annihilating Islam. It is behind the drug trade and alcoholism in all its kinds so as to facilitate its control and expansion."[220]

In Saudi Arabia, too, the school curriculum has included a lesson on the subject of the "Zionist Movement" for tenth-grade boys. This has taught that the *Protocols* is an authentic document that accurately describes the beliefs of the Jews. The lesson, like the Hamas Charter, also teaches that the Freemasons, Rotary and Lions clubs are secret organizations aiding Zionists in their bid for world domination.[221]

Although these three organizations have no connection to each other, it is not unusual to find them lumped together by Islamists. In February 2009, for example, *Forum Ulama Umat Indonesia* (Indonesia's People's Ulama Forum) demanded that President Susilo Bambang Yudhoyono ban the Rotary and Lions as a threat to Muslims. FUUI chairman Athian Ali Muhammad Da'i claimed that "The Rotary and Lions clubs are not social organizations but are part of the Freemasonry and Zionist movements, which could endanger us."[222]

However, if Middle Eastern and Asian Islamist attacks on "Freemasonry" are concerned primarily with the corruption of Muslim culture, and secondarily with politics and geopolitics, the opposite may be true in the West. When "Freemasonry" or "Freemasons" have been mentioned, it is often to explain the cause of terrorist attacks on the West, or the use of force by the USA and Britain, etc., in the Middle East. Still, here too, the term is used to refer to shadowy, powerful groups akin to a secret government.

In 2005, for example, with US and British troops in Iraq, *The Telegraph* reported that an advisor to 10 Downing Street on Muslim affairs named Ahmad Thomson had recently claimed that a "sinister" group of Jews and Freemasons had pressured then Prime Minister Tony Blair to go to war against Saddam Hussein. "Pressure was put on Tony Blair before the invasion," Thomson is reported to have said, "The way it works is that pressure is put on people to arrive at certain decisions. It is part of the Zionist plan and it is shaping events."[223] Again, Abu Hamza, a preacher at one time associated with the Finsbury Park mosque in London, is reported to have told Britain's *Independent* newspaper that the 9/11 attacks were planned by "Freemasons" – which he conflated with members of the US government – that "have loyalty to the Zionists."[224]

Terror in Turkey

As we have noted, during the early 1920s Turkey embarked on a program of reforms that would lead to the abolition of the caliphate, and the establishment of a secular (though Muslim-majority) state modeled on those of Europe. The Islamic transnational jurisdiction and the Muslim world were to be left behind. The reformists – the "Young Turks" – aspired to progress and modernity. In 1922, the office of sultan was dissolved. The following year the Republic of Turkey was proclaimed and Mustafa Kemal Ataturk was elected as its first president. In 1924, he dismissed the Caliph, Abdulmecid Efendi, and dissolved the Caliphate.

Turkey is one of the few Muslim-majority nation states that does not prohibit Freemasonry, and that tolerates the existence of a number of the fraternity's Lodges. Nevertheless, anti-Masonic rhetoric has long been part and parcel of Islamist rhetoric within Turkish politics. By the end of the 1960s, for example, the National Order Party (later the National Salvation Party) had formed and was attacking Zionism, Freemasonry, and communism.[225]

In 1992, a 40-page, full-color pamphlet titled *The Last Message* was published. On the cover was Ataturk's image, though the pamphlet, which was timed to mark the fifth centenary of the Ottoman Empire's welcoming of Jews expelled from Spain, extols the same conspiracy theory of Jews and Freemasons working to gain control of the world. Depicted in the pamphlet is the eye in the triangle found on the US dollar bill. Beneath it are five layers of a pyramid, with each representing various organizations in this conspiracy theory. At the top, dominating all of the others, are "3 Jewish Kabbalists." Next down is the Sanhedrin (or 70 elders). On the third level down are the B'nai Brith and the Bilderberg group. Beneath these are the Freemasons. On the lowest level are the Rotary and Lions clubs – those three organizations being cited in the Hamas Charter, drafted four years earlier. However, the paranoia seems to have reached even further, as the Rotary and Lions have been joined by the Diners Club.[226]

It was inevitable that Freemasonry would come into the sights of militants. In November of 2003, a wave of car and truck bombings killed 63 people, shaking Turkey. At that time, the Anadolu Ajansi news agency received a phone call from a man claiming that the attacks were the "the joint work of al-Qaida and IBDA-C [the Islamic Great Eastern Raiders' Front]." Although the targets were a synagogue (which was celebrating a bar mitzvah at the time of the attack), the British consulate, and the Turkish headquarters of HSBC Bank, the caller stated that "Our attacks on the centres of international freemasonry will continue."

Despite extreme Islamists across the globe conflating Freemasonry with whatever they dislike – especially culturally – to date, Turkey is the only country where terrorists have successfully attacked an actual Masonic building. On March 9, 2004, two Jihadist terrorists struck a Masonic Lodge in Istanbul. The attackers entered the dining hall of the building and sprayed it with bullets, after which they exploded several devices that they had strapped to their bodies. One of the terrorist's bombs failed to detonate properly and the attack did not cause the hoped-for devastation, though the impact was nonetheless considerable. Six people were injured, and a waiter was killed, along with one of the terrorists. CNN-Turk showed the surviving attacker being taken into hospital, shouting out "damn Israel."

On March 13, 2004, Al Jazeera published an English translation of a statement by the Abu Hafs al-Masri Brigades, previously published by the London-based newspaper *al-Quds al-Arabi*, in Arabic. Al Jazeera ran the statement under the heading "Purported al-Qaida statement," noting that it had been signed "Abu Hafs al-Masri/al-Qaida," and dated two days previous. This group claimed responsibility for the March 11 Madrid bombings, and praised the attack on the Turkish Masonic building, saying:

In a separate attack, Jund al-Quds [Soldiers of Jerusalem] targeted a Jewish Masonic lodge in Istanbul. Three top Masons were killed in the operation, and if it was not for technical failure all the masons would have been killed. Thanks to God anyway.[227]

According to Istanbul's governor Muammer Guler, eighteen suspects were questioned after the attack, ten of which had been formally charged at the time of his announcement. The bombers had been trained in Pakistan and Afghanistan.[228] "We don't know if they are al Qaeda camps," Guler said, "but the influence of al-Qaeda in those camps is obvious."[229]

The following year, the IBDA-C also began publishing the weekly bulletin *Kaide* (Turkish for "al-Qaeda"). In one early issue, the IBDA-C declared its "hatred [...] for the Christian-Jewish-Western imperialism," while the main article, titled "al-Qaeda is liberating the World", carried photos of terrorist attacks, under one of which it lauded the attack on the Istanbul Lodge as well as another on a hotel in Kenya "run by Jews." Spicing up the attack on the Lodge building, and, placing Jews at its center, *Kaide* now claimed that "an important Mossad official" was present during the attack.[230]

After The Arab Spring

In early January 2011, Mohamed Bouazizi, a twenty-six-year-old Tunisian street trader, sparked what was soon to become known as the "Arab Spring." Bouazizi had been unable to find regular employment although he had previously worked a number of jobs. Some reports said that he had a university degree, though his sister told the press that Bouazizi had not graduated from high school. Nevertheless, though without a license, by selling fruit and vegetables he had been able to provide his family with an income of $140 a month. When police confiscated his produce, Bouazizi doused himself in gasoline and self-immolated in a desperate protest.

After years of bottled-up anger at the country's ruling regime, Tunisia erupted with protests and violence. Soon the unrest spread to neighboring Muslim-majority states: Libya, Jordan, and Egypt. But it was the latter that really caught the Western imagination. Massive protests in the country's Tahrir Square, Cairo, flooded the news. They seemed to be ushering in a new era in which dictators would be defied and toppled. Liberty, it seemed, was dawning. Unable to quell the protests, and with increasing pressure from outside Egypt, by mid-February 2011, Hosni Mubarak had handed power over to the country's council of military leaders.

Yet, signs that Arab Spring was in trouble could be detected almost from the beginning. If the revolution meant anything, it meant pluralism – men and women, Muslims, Jews, Christians, and atheists could all come together. Yet, as Mubarak was resigning, American journalist Lara Logan was being sexually assaulted, in Tahrir Square, by a mob yelling "Jew, Jew."[231] A few days later, on February 18, Shaykh Yusuf al-Qaradawi, associated with the Islamist Muslim Brotherhood movement, held his first sermon in Egypt after years in exile. Wael Ghonim, the young pro-democracy leader who had become the face of the revolution in Egypt, was barred from the stage by the shaykh's security detail.[232]

By November, the Middle East's old paranoia about Freemasons and Zionists was bubbling up to the surface. Although not altogether novel, the New Age movement was also implicated. As Britain's *Guardian* newspaper observed, 4,500 years old, having withstood wars and revolutions, "on Friday [November 11] Egypt's Great Pyramid of Giza was confronted with what some feared would be its biggest threat yet: two crystals, a 'ceremony of love' and several hundred 'human angels' seeking to form a protective shield around the earth."

A Polish New Age organization had planned to conduct a meditation ceremony at the pyramid on the eleventh minute of the eleventh hour of 11/11/2011. They believed the ceremony would help save the world from cosmic catastrophes. Local Egyptians saw things differently, and rumors were soon circulating about a Zionist-Masonic plot. Local newspapers reported them. The activities, it was believed, "would include Masonic rituals and the attempted placing of a Jewish Star of David atop the pyramid itself." This was the final straw for the authorities, which closed the pyramid, claiming that essential maintenance work was suddenly needed.[233]

Anti-Masonic conspiracy theories were already circulating wildly among the political class and ordinary people, who wondered whether the country wasn't being manipulated by shadowy international forces. In one of the stranger theories to emerge in the wake of the Arab Spring, the Muslim Brotherhood was attacked by a group claiming to represent the international hacker network Anonymous. In a statement, the group claimed that the "Muslim Brotherhood started as a benevolent group of people with fair and just intentions" but that it had become corrupt over time. "They claim to be anti-freemasonry," the message continued, "however they follow distinct principles taken from it. If you were to leave the Brotherhood or present any threat to it, they would take […] offense and begin to intimidate you and put your life as well as your loved ones in danger."[234]

Writing in *Al Arabiya* in February 2012, Ahmed I. Abdallah told of his personal experiences on a recent visit to Egypt. "Conspiracy theories," he said, "are haunting Egyptians in a way that makes them steer away from all logic and refrain from examining the information presented to them." Abdallah had been especially struck on a shopping trip to Tahrir Square. In one store he found a television blaring out a chat show, in which the participants were claiming to be experts on all sorts of matters. "Yet, what really struck me," he said, "was a long phone call [in the show] in which the caller stressed that what is happening in Egypt is a Masonic-American-Zionist conspiracy" that involved Egyptians with Western passports. It was, of course, only the latest, localized, version of the conspiracy theory presented in the *Protocols*. Abdallah wondered if the caller even knew what Freemasonry was.[235] It is unlikely that he did since the conception of Freemasonry in Islamism and conspiracy theories is rarely related to the historical movement.

Notably, figures such as Sayyid Jamal ad-Din al-Afghani – Freemason and radical thinker – do not factor in Islamist anti-Freemasonry. When they are mentioned, it is merely as a side note, and, no matter how short, discussion about such radicals usually takes place nowhere more significant than in a post on obscure Islamist chat forums. Al-Afghani may be condemned for his membership of the fraternity, but the condemnation of Freemasonry is in no way dependent on al-Afghani or other Muslim activists that joined Masonic Lodges. As we have seen, conflated with Western power and liberal culture, Islamist anti-Freemasonry derives, ultimately, from the *Protocols* and the long tradition of European anti-Semitic and anti-Masonic conspiracy theory.

NINE

Black Nationalism in the USA

efore the end of the 19th century, British and many European
Masonic jurisdictions had accepted Jews, Egyptians, Iranians,
Indians – including those professing Hinduism and Islam – as
well as men of other nationalities and ethnicities as members of the now
global fraternal movement. However, despite the pretensions to a universal
brotherhood of man, within the world of American Freemasonry, at least,
the segregation that existed outside the Lodge affected the membership of
the fraternity. Consequently, from the late 18th century, there existed parallel,
racially segregated Masonic jurisdictions for Blacks and Whites in the USA.

With Lodges later established across the country, Black Freemasonry
would become a respected movement within the broader African-American
society, and, crucially, would not only aim to provide a sense of self-
respect and legitimacy for African history, but would eventually provide a
model, and even some of the visual trappings, for early 20th century Black
nationalist movements. Indeed, despite the domination of the White Masonic
jurisdictions, "Freemasonry," Michael A. Gomez says in *Black Crescent: The
Experience and Legacy of African Muslims in the Americas*, "was probably
critical to the promotion of a pan-African consciousness for the period [of
the late 18th century] and beyond."[236]

Unsurprisingly, discrimination against Blacks by White Freemasons, and
the claim that Black Freemasonry was illegitimate provoked resentment and
comment within the Lodges of the latter from the very beginning. Though
historically the first organization or movement for Blacks in the USA, it is this

voicing against racial discrimination, and, consequently, the sense of being specifically an African fraternity (even if Black Lodges would later accept other races), and a society for improvement of the African man, that made it in effect a proto-Black nationalist movement, albeit one that professed the ideal of a united brotherhood of man regardless of race or color of skin.

Black Masonic Lodges encouraged a sense of African community not least of all because members viewed themselves as historically as legitimate as White jurisdictions yet morally more authentic. The nature of the verbal attacks on, and arguments against, Black Freemasonry meant that defenses tended to emphasize both the historical and moral legitimacy, and to deride White racism as anti-Masonic and, not unconnected to this, irreligious. "[H]e that despises a black man for the sake of his colour, reproacheth his Maker," declared Prince Hall – the founder of Black Freemasonry in America – in a speech to an African Lodge in Charlestown on June 25, 1792.[237]

In his speech, Prince Hall traces the history, prehistory, and mythology of Freemasonry, from Old Testament stories to the Crusades, periodically noting the importance of African figures. The implication is clearly that Black history is equal to White history, and that Africans were at least as, if not more, important in the creation of the Masonic fraternity. While White Freemasons would certainly have argued the opposite, Prince Hall's speech also gives the impression that White Freemasonry is essentially schismatic, its members having forgotten their history of Blacks and Whites, and men of other races, fraternally united. Speaking of the Crusaders, who established a base on the island of Malta, Prince Hall rhetorically asked his audience of Black Freemasons to,

Query, whether at that day, when there was an African church, and perhaps the largest Christian church on earth, whether there was no African of that order; or whether, if they were all whites, they would refuse to accept them as their fellow Christians and brother Masons; or whether there were any so weak or rather so foolish, as to say, because they were Blacks, that would make their lodge or army too common or too cheap?

Prince Hall

Although details of his early life are sketchy, Prince Hall – after whom the majority Black Masonic jurisdiction would later be named – was probably born in Bridgetown, Barbados, in the British West Indies, in 1735, and grew up as a slave of William Hall of Boston. In 1770, he was freed by William Hall, who presented him with a certificate of manumission that he was, "no longer Reckoned a slave, but [had] always accounted as a free man."

Although events remain somewhat unclear, Prince Hall became a Freemason during the 1770s. According to tradition, on March 6, 1775, he and fourteen other free Black men were initiated into the Masonic fraternity by a traveling Masonic Lodge attached to a regiment under General Thomas Gage, and temporarily stationed in Boston. With the departure of the regiment not long after, Prince Hall and his fellow Black Brothers in Freemasonry were themselves granted a permit to meet as a Lodge. A formal, permanent charter was granted after the war.[238]

However, we should note that it has also been claimed that Prince Hall and his comrades were initiated by a renegade member of the regiment and traveling Lodge named John Batt, who had deserted the army, remaining in Boston after his regiment had moved on. Whatever the truth may be about the initiation, it is certain that Prince Hall was initiated into Freemasonry in 1775, and that he founded African Lodge – the first Lodge for Black men later that year. African Lodge was granted a charter by the Grand Lodge of England in 1787.[239]

Even as it grew in importance within the African-American community, Prince Hall Freemasonry – as it would later be named – would continue to see itself in much the same way as had its founder. At the very least, African history and Masonic history were regarded as intertwining. Martin Robison Delany – the first Black American granted a diploma by the medical school of Harvard University – proclaimed in 1853, in a treatise[240] delivered before

St. Cyprian Lodge, that Africa was the home of "the mysteries of Ancient Freemasonry."[241]

Yet, even as Black nationalism became more of a focus in some sectors of Prince Hall Masonry, the message of the ideal of a universal brotherhood, of opposing racism – and of the moral authenticity of Black Freemasonry, in contrast to that of Whites-only Lodges – remained, and would even eventually be aired outside of the fraternity. Most notably, in the September 1958 edition of the glossy, mainstream African-American magazine *Ebony* a number of feature articles were published that extolled Prince Hall Freemasonry and its Shriner organization, and criticized the racist attitude of White Lodges.

Accompanying these were photographs of African-American Freemasons in Masonic regalia, including Grand Lodge officers, as well as the members of Prince Hall Lodge Cosmopolitan No. 82 of Honolulu, Hawaii, which, the caption informs the reader, "lists no less than six nationalities as members." One of the articles – "White Masons Fail to Recognize Negro" – highlights the discrimination that African-Americans still faced from the dominant American Masonic jurisdictions, made up, essentially, of Caucasian brethren, and contrasts this with the relative openness of Prince Hall Lodges.

Regardless of its historical legitimacy – which the article asserts from the beginning – Prince Hall Freemasonry is presented both as a social and moral elite within African-American society. Power and legitimacy, though, are two different things. If discrimination from White Freemasonry is indicative of its closeness to power in American society, its actions are un-Masonic. "Like many other chinks in American democracy, Masonry in the U.S. today has not lived entirely up to its creed," the article asserts. If out of power, then, Prince Hall is presented as more legitimate than White Freemasonry from both an ethical and possibly even a racial perspective. White Freemasons, *Ebony* tells the reader, "have been reluctant to extend a hand of fellowship [...] in spite of their fraternal teachings of brotherly love and the fact that they all pay homage to a biblical black man, king Solomon."[242]

An article on the Black Shriners, in the same issue, claims an equally impressive lineage for this society. "The Order," *Ebony* states, "dates back to C.E. 647, and was founded by the Prophet Mohammed," and by 698,[243] "the Order was firmly established in Mecca, and ever since has been the most highly favored secret order of the Orient." The purpose of the Shriners, the magazine claims, was to "protect the weak and oppressed," and to act as judges in criminal cases. While this, had it have been correct, would more than have established its historical legitimacy, the article points out the contemporary social prominence and ethical behavior of African-American Shriners, noting that the Order had at that time "over $3 million in assets held by the group's 150 Temples" and that the African-American organization routinely distributed funding of $5,000 to doctors and medical centers for research.[244]

Black Nationalism

The USA's involvement, from 1916 to 1918, in World War I, and a decline of immigration into the US, opened the job market in the north to non-Whites. Unsurprisingly, many took the opportunity to escape the south, where Jim Crow laws mandated the separation of Whites and Blacks in public schools and other public places, on public transportation, and in regard to public drinking fountains and restrooms, etc. If the laws were justified by claims that the races were to be "separate but equal" the reality was very different, with Blacks relegated to a second-class status, suffering discrimination, and, consequently, a far greater degree of poverty than Whites. Violence at the hands of White vigilante mobs – often associated with the Ku Klux Klan – was also a common tactic to ethnically cleanse areas.

Yet, despite the hope of a better life and the expense of moving across the country, Blacks soon found that in the north discrimination, though not backed by the authorities, was still the norm. Regardless of qualification, they could only secure work in low paying, unskilled or low-skilled jobs that White workers shunned. Consequently, these migrants to the north found themselves and their families living in poverty. The overcrowded and unsanitary conditions of poor areas facilitated outbreaks of smallpox and the spread of disease. Tuberculosis, pneumonia, and venereal disease were common, and infant mortality was considerably higher for the Black population than for the White.[245]

As we have noted, because of its legitimacy within the Black community, during the early 20th century, Freemasonry in America would have a profound influence on Black nationalism. As it had in Europe during the 18th century, and in Egypt and Persia during the 19th, Freemasonry provided a practical organizational model. It also demonstrated that men could be drawn together around higher ideals, creating a society within a society. And, finally, its symbols and regalia could also be absorbed into new organizations and reinterpreted for their purposes.

One of the most important Black leaders to use some Masonic elements for the cause of Black nationalism was Marcus Garvey (1887-1940), founder of the Universal Negro Improvement Association and African Communities' League (UNIA-ACL). This organization attracted tens of thousands of members, who turned out to attend parades in the USA, Great Britain, and the Caribbean. And it also provided an intellectual foundation for Black nationalist societies and movements later on.

Garvey was born in the Jamaican coastal town of St. Ann's Bay. His mother wanted to call him "Moses" but, instead, he was named after his father, a stonemason and occasional grave digger. Garvey Sr. was an austere and authoritarian figure who had been born into slavery, and who was determined to instill in his son both a sense of the harshness of the world and the self-reliance he would need to survive in it. The younger Garvey would one day go on to preach self-reliance, not just for individuals, but for those of African descent everywhere. But, rather than stirring up fear, he would seek to inspire, encouraging Black Americans to recover their rightful sense of self-worth.

While his father had once taken the younger Garvey to a graveyard at night, leaving him stranded in freshly dug grave – taking away the ladder that Garvey Jr. had used to climb down into it – Garvey, the Black nationalist leader, sought to elevate those who followed him, socially, spiritually, and materially. He wanted the best for a people he saw as having been subjugated by Whites, whether as slaves in the southern states, discriminated against as citizens, or in employment, such as the Black laborers he had seen working on the Panama Canal. The injustice of Blacks receiving low wages for working on geopolitically important projects for the colonial powers impressed itself upon Garvey's consciousness.[246] He wanted Africans, and those of African descent, to have a nation to call their own.

According to the founding Charter of the UNIA-ACL, the organization is a "social, friendly, humanitarian, charitable, educational, institutional, constructive and expansive society, [...] founded by persons, desiring to the utmost, to work for the general uplift of the Negro peoples of the world."[247] It was shaped, in part, by the charters of fraternities including Prince Hall Freemasonry, with which Garvey was familiar, although he was not a member. And there were other aspects of the UNIA-ACL influenced by Prince Hall Freemasonry.[248] These included the names of officers. "Potentate," for example, was borrowed from the Ancient Egyptian Order of the Nobles of the Mystic Shrine's office of "Imperial Potentate."[249] And the uniforms of the UNIA-ACL strongly resemble those of American Knights Templar Freemasonry.

Garvey was close with some Black Freemasons, particularly John Edward Bruce – or "Bruce Grit" as he was affectionately known – a journalist, political activist, and historian of the African diaspora who founded the Negro Society for Historical Research and the political Afro-American league, as well as several short-lived newspapers. Bruce joined the UNIA-ACL in 1919. He was 64 at the time and became something of a father figure to Garvey, as well as a regular contributor to the organization's *Negro World* and *Daily Negro Times* newspapers.[250] Another associate and follower of Garvey's was

Arthur Alfonso Schomburg, to whom Bruce had acted as a mentor. Like the latter, Schomburg was both an advocate of Black nationalism and a staunch defender of the legitimacy of Prince Hall Freemasonry.[251]

Nevertheless, the Masonic Templar uniforms, as well as some other aspects of the fraternity, would have been familiar even to many non-Masons. During the 20th century, Masonic Knights Templar "commanderies" regularly held high street parades, with hundreds, and sometimes thousands, of its members marching in full uniform. Nor were these the only such spectacles. Though members promised to keep its initiations secret, like many others of the day, the Masonic fraternity made itself visible through other types of public events. One of these was the laying of the cornerstone of public buildings, in which Freemasons and Masonic Lodges often participated. Even President George Washington – who had been initiated into a Lodge in Fredericksburg on November 4, 1752[252] – had participated in the public laying of the Capitol cornerstone on September 18, 1793.

Such events helped to foster a sense of community, both among Freemasons and the wives and families of its members, who were otherwise excluded from the fraternity's activities – but they also helped to promote the fraternity itself, and to attract new members. Garvey and other early Black nationalists would have been aware of the community-building potential of fraternalism, pageantry, aesthetics, and symbolism. But they also probably understood the transcendental nature of Freemasonry, and of the various forms of spirituality that sometimes buffered up against it.

Both Garvey and the newspapers of the UNIA-ACL used phrases associated with the New Thought movement – which advocated positive thinking as the key to self-transformation and material success. "Let us Give Off Success and It Will Come," read a headline of Garvey's *Blackman* newspaper, "As Man Thinks So Is He."[253] Like the Prince Hall Freemasons before it, the UNIA-ACL saw manhood as dependent on the individual's ability to produce for himself, and not just to consume. This was the crux of the matter. Through discrimination, Blacks had become, in Garvey's eyes, "a race of consumers." They had to become "a race of producers." And in order to make that change they would need to "organize" – something Prince Hall Freemasons knew a lot about.

From Moorish Science to The Nation of Islam

New Thought-type positive thinking for spiritual and material transformation had emerged in Black nationalism, even before Garvey, in the shape of Moorish Science, a religious movement that also drew from Freemasonry, Rosicrucianism, and Islam. Although, in regard to the last of these, it is clear that the Ancient Egyptian Arabic Order Nobles Mystic Shrine – the version of the Shriners created by and for Black Freemasons in 1893 – was an influence on Moorish Science, we should note that, from the late 17th century, African Muslims made up a significant number of slaves brought to America, and that this culture survived, to some degree, in its new environment.[254]

The Ahmadiyya Muslims were another early community, having established a missionary training center in Chicago in 1919.[255] However, founded in India by Mirza Ghulam Ahmad – who is generally regarded by Ahmadiyyas as the Mahdi, or final prophet of Islam – the sect is markedly different from mainstream Sunni Islam, which often views it as a schism.

Moorish Science was founded by Noble Drew Ali. Little is known of his early life. Like some others that have served as modern day authorities on arcane knowledge, Ali created something of a mythology around himself, or at least appears not to have dissuaded its creation. One legend suggests that his mother was a member of the Cherokee tribe, or that he was adopted by Cherokees in early life. Another suggests that he was adopted by gypsies.[256] However, Ali was probably born Timothy Drew, on January 8, 1886, in North Carolina. His parents may have been former slaves, and his father, so one account suggests, was of Moorish extraction.

As a young man, Noble Drew Ali traveled to the north of the USA, and in either 1912 or 1913 founded the Canaanite Temple of Moorish Science in Newark, New Jersey. Around a decade later, the new faith had temples in West Virginia, Arkansas, Baltimore, Philadelphia, Chicago, Michigan, and elsewhere, with its membership numbering possibly 30,000.[257] But with growth came new challenges. Factions began to form within the movement, and, in 1925, Noble Drew Ali relocated to Chicago. There he continued to spread his doctrines, and, the following year he incorporated his organization under the name "Moorish Temple of Science."[258]

Highly unorthodox from the perspective of mainstream Sunni Islam, and perhaps more in line with the New Age and alternative spiritual movements of the 20th century, Ali even proclaimed that the faith he had founded, "honor[s] all the Divine Prophets," including not just Jesus and Muhammad but, more controversially, also Buddha and Confucius.[259]

Despite claiming that his organization practiced the Islamic faith of the ancient Moors, historians have claimed that Ali derived inspiration from a range of modern sources for the holy book of Moorish Science, the *Circle Seven Koran* – or, to give the book its full title, *The Holy Koran of the Moorish Holy Temple of Science 7, Know Yourself and Your Father God-Allah, That You Learn to Love Instead of Hate. Everyman Need to Worship Under His Own Vine and Fig Tree. The Uniting of Asia.* Accordingly, making only minor changes to superficially Islamize the texts used, the prophet of Moorish Science adopted several passages from *The Aquarian Gospel of Jesus the Christ* by Levi Dowling (1908), an essentially proto-New Age work that claimed that the young Jesus had traveled through India, learning the mysteries. (Dowling lived in Ohio, but claimed to have received revelations about Jesus from the "Akashic Record," a metaphysical record of all events past, present, and future.)

Another influence on the *Circle Seven Koran* was a work called *Unto Thee I Grant*. This book was ultimately derived from *The Economy of Human Life*, a guide to manners published in Britain in 1750. The latter was republished, in several expanded versions, during the same century, though *Unto Thee I Grant* was published in 1925 by the Ancient and Mystical Order Rosae Crucis (AMORC), an American, self-styled Rosicrucian Order based in San Jose, California. AMORC, says Mitch Horowitz, "billed it as the 'Secret Teachings of Tibet'," though the ultimate source of the text was claimed to be Pharaoh Amenhotep IV, who was believed to have authored it somewhere between 1360 and 1350 BC.[260]

We should note, however, that followers of the message of Noble Drew Ali strongly dispute these claims. Instead, they suggest that the prophet of Moorish Science was the recipient of oral traditions stemming from Muslims in India, Egypt, and Palestine, and that were kept secret until the time was right to reveal them. It was these traditions that the prophet "transmitted" through the *Circle Seven Koran* – which, according to tradition, he recited from memory to the printer of the book, much to the amazement of the latter.[261] At that time, Black Americans did, in fact, rely much more on oral transmission than on writing for the preservation of their culture and history.

Unusually for such a prominent organization in the West, Freemasonry, likewise, emphasized the importance of oral transmission, with lengthy rituals being conferred from memory. This aspect of the fraternity might well have proved appealing to African American men, who were not only accustomed to oral tradition but who were able to read their own history and metaphysics into the oral traditions of Freemasonry. It is possible, too, that modern literary references may well have provided new clothing for old ideas.

The same might also be said for dress and symbolism. And we should note that from the Black Shriners, the prophet of Moorish Science adopted the title "Noble" – used for all members of the Shrine. It is possible, too, that the use of the term "temple" was also taken from the Shriners, though this was certainly in use elsewhere. Lastly, the fez, worn by some members of the Temple of Moorish Science is similar to those worn by Shriners, and the use of Islamic and Egyptian symbolism abounds in both societies.[262]

Nevertheless, Ali cultivated a unique and visionary movement that aimed to elevate Blacks in America. For the prophet of Moorish Science, Africans and those of African descent originated in the Biblical land of Canaan. Despite being dispersed across America and elsewhere in the world, they constituted the nation of Canaanites, or, more specifically, Moabites. On entering Moorish Science, members took one of two "free national names," *El* or *Bey*.[263]

Noble Drew Ali's vision, and the organization formed around it, would influence emerging Black nationalist leaders, the most important of which was almost certainly W. D. Fard Muhammad, the founder of The Lost-Found Nation of Islam. Shrouded in mystery, beyond a few details, the life of W. D. Fard Muhammad is still a matter of debate. Although the founder of the Nation presented himself as a native of the city of Mecca, in Saudi Arabia – one of the two holy cities of Islam – the nationality and ethnicity of Fard Muhammad is still disputed.

It is certain that he was born outside of the USA, and there is some suggestion that the Nation's founder was of East Indian extraction – with family ties to the region that is now Pakistan – and that his family had been of the Ahmadiyya sect.[264] It has also been suggested that the Nation's founder was a member of the Druze,[265] the Gnostic religion, centered in Syria, influenced especially by Islam, but also by Judaism, Christianity, and ancient Greek philosophy.

Certainly, the Nation's teachings differ from orthodox Sunni Islam in significant ways. Notably, according to the Nation, Creation emerged through several emanations and, following the emergence of "Cosmic Intellect" or "Black Intellect," there appeared a divine council of Imams or scientists.[266] This is faintly reminiscent of Shi'ite esotericism. But it is closer still to the emanationist theory of Muslim philosopher Abu Nasr al-Farabi (870-950 C.E.) and some later Muslim philosophers who believed that certain cosmic "Intellects" appeared as part of the process of Creation.

The mythology of the Nation also drew from outside of Islam, not only from Moorish Science, but also possibly from Theosophy, the highly elaborate esoteric doctrine created by Mme. Blavatsky. As we have noted, its doctrines appealed to a broad audience, from the underground, though often Masonic-linked, occult scene of Great Britain, to campaigners for an independent India and pan-German nationalists and anti-Semites. Fard Muhammad had been a member of the Theosophical Society in San Francisco, as well as the Moorish Science Temple in Chicago, and Garvey's UNIA-ACL.[267]

Theosophy, based partly on Hindu philosophy, posited that time was cyclical. Arising in each epoch, according to Blavatsky, was a particular spiritual type, the highest of which, for the current age, was the Aryan – though this was intended to be understood in a symbolic or esoteric, rather than a literal or racialist, sense. For the Nation, however, Blacks were the superior. Whites, according to Nation doctrine, had been created by the evil scientist Mr. Yakub at a time of discontent among the Black nation.

In events foretold by the wise Imams, Yakub, was born in the city of Mecca. He had a large head, and an extraordinary ability for learning, starting school at the age of four and graduating from all of the city's universities at the age of 18. At that time he began preaching in the streets, attracting a large following. He also started to study the "germ of the black man, under the microscope," and discovered that it contained two genes, one black, and one brown. Separating the two, Yakub was able to breed the Red, then Yellow, and finally the White race into existence.[268]

It was in Detroit, during the 1930s, that the Lost-Found Nation of Islam got its start. Fard Muhammad was selling various wares, such as silks, door to door in the city. Women of African descent were keen to see what was for sale, and Fard Muhammad would talk to them about the lives of people in their homelands, describing, for example, what they would eat, and how this helped them to live long, healthy lives. Soon, Fard Muhammad began talking about Islam, which, he claimed, was the true religion of Africans, and about Arabic, which he claimed was their original language. Africans had been robbed of their heritage, he explained, when they had been taken on board the slave ships to America.[269]

Fard Muhammad attracted a modest following, though his teachings would gain a wider audience through the proselytizing efforts of his disciple Elijah Muhammad, who took over the leadership of the organization in 1934, after Fard Muhammad's disappearance. With Freemasonry long an influence on Black nationalism, it highly likely that some of the earliest converts to the Nation were members of the fraternity. By the late 1940s, 145 of its 172 male converts were members of the Masonic fraternity.[270] Both societies had esoteric teachings and symbols and sought to elevate their members, with Black Freemasonry since Prince Hall and the Nation presenting Black history, to African-Americans, as one of achievement, high culture, and spirituality.

Some of the Nation's leaders even "actively recruited" Freemasons, referencing Masonic symbolism and adopting its language, but this was, to some degree, inevitable. Through its rituals and regalia, Black Shriners were enmeshed in unorthodox Islamic symbolism and rhetoric, and some may have believed that the society had derived from the Prophet Muhammad himself – a claim, of course, made in the September 1958 issue of *Ebony* magazine. If so, some Black Freemasons may already have considered themselves to be, to some extent, Muslims. Certainly so, if they were devotees of Moorish Science as well.

Black Freemasons who joined the Nation probably frequently viewed it as the completion of the esoteric doctrines of Freemasonry or the Black Shriners. Notably, in a catechism written by Fard Muhammad, the founder of the Nation references the Mystic Shrine's emblem of a crescent with a curved sword above it, and, more significantly, refers to Shriners as "Moslem sons":

Q: Why does Muhammad make the devil study from 35 to 50 years before he can call himself a Moslem son and wear the greatest and only flag of the universe? And why must he add a sword to the upper part of the holy and greatest universal flag of Islam?[271]

The term "Moslem sons" would become a synonym for Shriners, and for Freemasons more broadly, in the Nation of Islam as well as in the Black nationalist movement, founded by Clarence 13X, The Nation of Gods and Earths (also called the Five-Percent Nation or the Five Percenters).[272]

The honorable Elijah Muhammad had himself been a Freemason before accepting the teachings of W. D. Fard Muhammad,[273] and, though he would inveigh against the Masonic fraternity, in 1972, he appealed to Freemasons, saying "you that have studied degrees in Masonry should not hesitate to come over [to the Nation of Islam], because we give you more than what the devil has given you"[274] – the devil being Whites. "The brothers, Fruit of Islam (FOI) are men who have learned more about Masonry than you."[275]

TEN

Anders Breivik, The Knights Templar, and Terrorism

On July 22, 2011, a large explosion rocked the government area of Oslo, Norway. This was soon followed by the shooting of 69 people – nearly half of whom were under 18 years of age[276] – on the close-by island of Utoya. Al-Qaeda-linked terrorists were suspected of being behind the attack. However, it soon turned out to be the act of a lone Norwegian national called Anders Breivik. Only hours before the attacks he had posted a 1,515-page manifesto titled *2083: A European Declaration of Independence* online, and had sent it to another 1,000 contacts. Anglicizing his name, Breivik had signed himself "Andrew Berwick" in the manifesto. He also claimed to be the "Justiciar Knight Commander for Knights Templar Europe and one of several leaders of the National and pan-European Patriotic Resistance Movement."[277]

There were "9 original founding members,"[278] Breivik claimed, adding that he had met only four of these, but that the movement had grown, and that there "might be tens, even hundreds of Justiciar Knights now spread all across Western Europe."[279] After an intensive investigation, however, Norwegian police concluded that no such network existed.

In *2083*, Breivik claims to be fighting against Islam and "Cultural Marxist" leaders in Europe that had facilitated mass immigration and the demographic and cultural transformation of the continent. Despite quoting at length a number of prominent anti-Islamic and anti-Islamist commentators, as well as mainstream news reports from the BBC and elsewhere, the inspiration for his attack came from more obvious sources. More than a dozen passages in *2083* had been copied, with only slight changes, from the manifesto of Theodore Kaczynski, the Unabomber, who terrorized the USA with a mail bomb campaign from 1978 to 1985. On trial, in April 2012, Breivik revealed that he had also studied and had drawn inspiration from al-Qaeda. For Breivik, the Jihadist network behind the 9/11 terror attacks, was "the most successful revolutionary movement in the world" and he wanted "to create a European version of al Qaeda."[280]

The modern Knights Templar will, according to *2083*, fight against the "cultural Marxist/multiculturalist regimes of Western Europe before [...] we are completely demographically overwhelmed by Muslims." In its romantic view of political violence and adoption of militant religious imagery, the organization – whether real or imagined – is in many respects a mirror image of al-Qaeda, as Breivik undoubtedly realized. The founders of the organization, the manifesto claims, decided to carry out a "large successful attack every 5-12 years [...] depending on available forces."[281]

As we will soon see, Breivik was not the first person to have claimed to be the head of the Knights Templar, either revived for some reason or alleged to have survived underground since the Middle Ages. The Crusader Order has had a peculiar hold on the romantic imagination in the West. For the occultist, the Order's significance comes from the legend that it adopted secret gnostic or occult teachings from the Middle East, and was subsequently persecuted and disbanded because of it. Some relatively recent "histories" have also claimed that the Templars acquired the Holy Grail, believed to have held the blood of Christ. A variation on this theme claims that Jesus married and had children and that his bloodline lived on through various European royal families, with the secret being protected only by the mysterious Templars.

While the mythical aura of the Crusader Order cannot be dismissed out of hand in relation to Breivik, of more immediate importance, politically, the Crusader Knight had become a popular motif of the militant end of the anti-Islamic milieu that emerged after the 9/11 attacks on New York and

Washington D.C. Breivik would certainly have known this. However, he also clearly wanted to present himself as an ideological and, to some extent, spiritual leader or warrior. To this effect, he drew in the Templars, referenced paganism, adopted Christianity as a sociopolitical identity, claimed to practice Japanese "Bushido" meditation,[282] and wore Masonic regalia for photographs included in his manifesto.

In regard to followers of the neo-pagan religion of Odinism, he says, "Even Odinists can fight with us or by our side as brothers" in the Knights Templar organization that Breivik claimed to be a founding member of. Somewhat enigmatically, he also says his primary weapon is *Mjöllnir* (the name of the hammer of the ancient Norse god Thor). But he criticizes neo-pagans, saying, that Thor's Hammer – a symbol that served a similar function to pre-Christian, Germanic tribes as the cross has for Christians – cannot unify the people of Europe, but that the cross will. For Breivik, Christianity is a political and cultural reality – born out of Europe's unique history and identity – not a religious requirement for the individual or perhaps for society as a whole. "Christian atheists,"[283] i.e., those that have grown up in Christian and post-Christian countries, were eligible to join the organization.

Freemasonry and Anti-Freemasonry

Likewise, in the manifesto, Breivik criticized Freemasonry because it is "not in any way political." Freemasons, says Breivik, "claim to be Knights of Christ yet they are not willing to sacrifice their life for the preservation of European Christendom. They do not even acknowledge that European Christendom is in the process of being deconstructed."[284] In most countries, the Masonic fraternity will admit men of any faith, including Islam. However, in Norway – which practices the "Swedish Rite" (not to be confused with the Swedenborgian Rite) – officially, only Christian men can join. Breivik had been a member of a Masonic Lodge in Oslo, and in one photo in his manifesto he appears wearing full Masonic regalia.

After the attack, and the arrest of Breivik, the Norwegian Grand Lodge put out a statement, saying that it was "appalled by the terrible crime" and expressing "sorrow and compassion" for the victims and their loved-ones. Breivik, the Grand Lodge also said, had had "minimal contact" with the fraternity,[285] and was now expelled.[286]

For Breivik, although Freemasonry contradicts his own political worldview, its rituals – rooted in antiquity – provided a kind of legitimacy of lineage. He commends Freemasonry as "keepers of cultural heritage."[287] This appears to be significant for Breivik who insists that those joining his organization must perform an initiation ceremony that is "somewhat similar to the ancient and original ritual of the Knights Templar." "This ritual," he says, "has been partly adopted and kept alive by the Freemasons and similar 'chivalric orders'."[288]

In another photograph in the manifesto, Breivik is shown wearing a ceremonial military uniform. On the arm is an emblem of a skull pierced by a dagger. Breivik calls this "the badge of the Justiciar Knight" and says, that it is "marked with the symbols of communism, Islam and Nazism on the forehead, impaled on the cross of the martyrs." On the uniform are what look like three medals. They are, in fact, three Masonic "jewels," presented to those who have obtained the Knight of Malta, Knights Templar, and Red Cross of Constantine Degrees of Freemasonry in Britain. Photographs of each appear separately in *2083*, and the web address of a British retailer of Masonic regalia is listed as a place to purchase them.

Breivik could not have received these Masonic Degrees, since they do not exist in the Swedish Rite, and he does not appear to have been involved in Freemasonry in Britain. However, he would have had no problem obtaining them as a member of the public. Such outlets do not require identification since the assumption has always been that only Freemasons would be interested in purchasing Masonic regalia.

New "Templar" Orders

The Knights Templar has an awkward though interesting association with Freemasonry. The claim that the Masonic fraternity derived from the Crusader Order was first made circa 1737 by Andrew Michael Ramsay, a tutor to Prince de Turenne, in France, and a chevalier in the Roman Catholic chivalric Order of Lazarus. Scottish by birth, Ramsay conjectured that the fraternity was rooted in Scotland and in knighthood, rather than England – where the premier Grand Lodge was founded – and stonemasonry. Ramsay may also have wished to ingratiate the Roman Catholic Church to the Masonic fraternity by proposing this history. However, if so, his attempt probably had the opposite effect, since the Church issued its first Bull, declaring membership prohibited, in 1738.[289]

In Europe, though, the idea of a knightly origin was adopted by various, often self-starting, Masonic Rites and jurisdictions. Notably, one of the earliest "high Degrees" was the so-called "Scots Master," which mixed Freemasonry with chivalry. Soon Hermeticism, Rosicrucianism, and, and other types of mysticism became an important part of Masonic ritual. Yet, since the early symbolism of Freemasonry had drawn partly, though not unsubstantially, from the Temple of Solomon, and since the Knights Templar had, historically, been encamped at its site, it was perhaps inevitable that this chivalric Order specifically would come to prominence within the Masonic milieu, at least temporarily.

A Masonic Knights Templar Degree – Christian and ascetic in nature – was being conferred by Freemasons in England and Ireland during the 1770s,[290] and still exists – albeit in modified forms – though it is generally acknowledged to be a modern invention, with no historical links to the medieval Crusader Order. At the same time, in Germany, the Rite of Strict Observance, which claimed to derive from the Templars, was already established. However, a convention of Masonic Rites, held in 1782, ruled that there was no basis for the claims made by the Strict Observance, and, mortally wounded by this declaration, it died shortly afterward.[291]

Other, non-Masonic, self-proclaimed Templar organizations have emerged, including the *Ordo Novi Templi*, founded in 1907 by a defrocked Austrian monk named Jörg Lanz von Liebenfels, to help disseminate his racialist and anti-Semitic worldview. However, it is often within the world of ceremonial occultism – which absorbed, and often misused, aspects of Freemasonry – that we find the adoption of elements of the medieval knightly Order. Since Breivik knew of Odinism, it is highly likely that he also knew of some – perhaps many – other aspects of occult tradition, most especially, the tradition of self-initiating Knights Templar organizations.

In his manifesto, Breivik states that he was present at the founding of the revived Knights Templar in London in April 2009. This, he says, is a "revolutionary conservative movement because we had lost hope that the democratic framework can solve Europe's current problems."[292] "Revolutionary conservative" was, we should note, a term used by Italian esotericist and Traditionalist Julius Evola,[293] among others that have influenced the radical-Right, though this could be a mere coincidence.

Yet, although he lambastes the Left of the political spectrum in the West, Breivik also strongly criticizes elements of the Right, especially Rightist movements inspired by René Guénon, whom Evola knew and attempted, to some degree, to emulate. Describing his Knights Templar as "revolutionary conservative," Breivik possibly place places himself very broadly within the Rightist-Traditionalist spectrum of opinion,[294] or at least sees them as overlapping in regard to its anti-liberalism, though he rejects its favorable view of Islam. Hence Breivik says,

There is also a rightist sympathy for Islam. An obvious point of agreement is of course anti-Judaism. A subtler basis for sympathy is the so-called traditionalist current, which was represented by the converts Rene Guenon and Frithjof Schuon, and still has a following: it has been idealising Islam and esp. Sufism as the preserver of the age-old philosophia pernnis [*sic*] against modernity. In Russia, some Slavophile anti-Western groups now seek an alliance with Islam against the impending Americanisation of their society. In the U.S., Christian fundamentalists and Islamic organisations are increasingly creating common platforms to speak out against trends of moral decay (abortion, pornography, etc.). Some of these phenomena of traditionalist alliance-building are quite respectable, but they are nevertheless conducive to Islam negationism.[295]

ELEVEN

Islam, Esotericism, And The Heir to The British Throne

Although still a relatively unknown intellectual figure in both the West and in the world of contemporary Islamic thought, René Guénon "has exercised profound influence in certain significant circles in a number of Islamic countries," says Seyyed Hossein Nasr, an Iranian-born scholar of Islam, "and [Guénon's] impact is very much on the rise."[296] Members of these circles either read Guénon in the original French or in translation or learned about his ideas through the writings of other major Traditionalist authors as well as a number of "Muslim-born" thinkers.

Although less influential in the Arabic-speaking world than in Iran, Turkey, Pakistan, Bosnia, or Southeast Asia, Guénon's *Crisis of the Modern World* – critical of Western modernity – as well as a number of his essays on esotericism and Sufism, have been translated into Arabic since the turn of the century.[297] Nasr himself introduced Guénon's work to Iran when he returned from studying in the USA in 1958. During the 1960s, Nasr commissioned the translation, into Farsi, of Guénon's *La Crise du monde moderne* (The Crisis of the Modern World) and *La Règne de la quantité* (The Reign of Quantity), and from the middle of the decade, he says, the ideas of Traditionalist authors "became part of the general intellectual discourse" in Iran.

If the Islamic Revolution of 1979 disrupted the growing interest in Traditionalism, it was only a temporary blip. In 1998 and 1999 Mufid University in Qom devoted two issues of its journal to the subject. These included translations of some of Guénon's articles as well as others about

Guénon himself. Also significant, a "major conference" on "Traditionalism and modernism" was held in Tehran in 2002. Guénon's books *Le Symbolisme de la croix* (The Symbolism of the Cross), *Aperçus sur l'ésotérisme islamique et le taoisme* (Insights into Islamic Esoterism and Taoism), and *Orient et Occident* (East and West) have been translated into Farsi, and a Persian-language book on Guénon's life and work has also been published.[298]

Defender of Faith

But Guénon has also had a significant if largely unacknowledged impact on some Western thinkers *vis-à-vis* Islam. Perhaps one of the most unlikely contemporary defenders of Islam, from a perspective that is at least informed by Traditionalism, is Charles, Prince of Wales. Though heir to the British throne, he is perhaps best known to Americans and many others outside of Great Britain as the former husband of Diana, Princess of Wales.

The country's monarch has traditionally been the head of the Church of England. Consequently, the prince's admiration and sympathy for Islam has sparked controversy, partly because he may one day be made king of what many still regard as a "Christian country," and, though somewhat incongruous, partly because Islam – and more especially Islamism – is not infrequently regarded as a threat to Britain's secular, liberal institutions and beliefs, such as women's equality with men.

Unlike Guénon, who had to move to Egypt to live under *shari'a*, the prince lives in a time in which *shari'a* family tribunals are operating in Britain, with their rulings on civil matters, such as inheritance, legally-binding. In 2008, when the existence of these tribunals – some of which are run from the back rooms of shops or other commercial premises – was reported[299] it provoked alarm and debate in the country, which has since been witness to campaigns by Saudi-style "morality police" patrols proclaiming areas of London and other cities "Shariah-controlled zones."[300]

With this background, the prince's views on Islam are more controversial than they might be otherwise, though he seems to be fully aware that, on a range of issues, his opinions are outside of the mainstream. In 2010, the prince published *Harmony: A New Way of Looking at Our World*, with the opening words, "this is a call to revolution"[301] – not exactly what one would anticipate from a member of the British royal family. *Harmony*'s premise is that the environmental crisis, financial crisis, and other crises of the modern world, are the result of "a crisis of perception." Man no longer knows how to live in harmony with the planet because he no longer has any knowledge of the sacred principles that it embodies, and that, for at least thousands of years, traditional cultures have revered and represented in their material culture, such as the architecture of temples, cathedrals, mosques, and so on.

The Daily Mail's Max Hastings was alarmed by *Harmony*'s message, and proclaimed, "anyone who reads the Prince of Wales' new book will have little doubt that the chief peril to our royal institution in the decades ahead lies within his well-meaning, muddled, woolly head." For Hastings, modern monarchs had to be "distant symbols of glamour, beauty and decency." The public should not know their opinions, especially if they happened to think that "revolution" – even of an internal sort – would be a good idea.[302]

In general, the prince's outlook is usually believed to be a combination of nostalgic longing for the past and slavishness to the political multicultural ideology, which holds all cultures and religions to be inherently equal and, in some sense, the same. A more thorough reading of Charles's statements and interests show that, even if he does not formally call himself a Traditionalist, his thinking approximates Guénon's Traditionalism, the doctrines and thinkers of which the prince is well aware.

But it is his sympathy for Islam that has worried especially center-Right journalists in Great Britain and, in a few cases, abroad. Daniel Pipes, an author and journalist broadly in the American neoconservative camp, has aired the suspicion that Charles might even be a secret convert to Islam.[303] Not unrelated to this, one of the biggest firestorms to erupt around the prince occurred in 2008, when Charles announced that he planned to be known as the "Defender of Faith," rather than by the official title of the "Defender of the Faith" (i.e., of the Church of England) when he ascends to the throne.

It is probably true that this change was intended, in part, to reflect the fact that Britain was no longer primarily a church-going nation,[304] but one in which Islam, Judaism, Hinduism, Sikhism, Buddhism, Zoroastrianism, etc., are active, alongside the various, dwindling denominations of Christianity, propped up only by large-scale immigration.[305] If this were the whole story, the declaration would be – and was seen to be – impeccably multicultural. Misconstrued, for many, Charles's statement has come to signify that he is out of touch with the problems of contemporary Britain. The prince would probably contend that he is looking deeper.

In a nation fracturing along lines of various competing "identities" – the religious in particular – and increasingly ill at ease with political multiculturalism, it was easy to lambaste the prince's comment as just the latest pandering to the politically correct – and some, of course, seized the moment. *The Telegraph*'s Damian Thompson complained that the heir to the throne's statement had "a whiff of vanity about it."

It was, he suggested, as if the prince were saying: "Britain is a multicultural society, so aren't you lucky that I contain multitudes?" Thompson wanted to know whether Spiritualism or the Church of Jesus Christ of Aryan Nations would be considered faiths to be defended. "How," he addressed the prince directly, "are you going to tiptoe through the theological and constitutional minefield created when unscrupulous, bizarre or extreme religions demand Royal protection – as they will?"

Thompson's main concern with the prince becoming the "defender of faith" was, perhaps not surprisingly, the erosion of the country's Christian identity, which had informed its "unwritten" Constitution and even its secular traditions. In the popular, center-Right media Christianity seemed to be under sustained assault. The concern was a valid one, although Thompson's assertion that the proposed change was "the Royal equivalent of replacing the word 'Christmas' with 'Winterval' " was grossly in error.[306] Such secularizing of Britain, and the West more broadly, profoundly disturbs the heir to the throne. Thompson had misinterpreted a small but crucial detail. The prince had expressed his desire to defend "faith," not "faiths," to be a champion, in other words, not for various competing religious and cultural groups, but for a sense of the sacred in contemporary life.

Still, not everyone believes that monarchs should be seen but not heard. Writing in *The American Spectator*, Rod Dreher defended the prince against his critics, despite being fully aware of the intellectual influences on the heir to the British throne. "It's impossible to read his words on Islam," commented Dreher, "without recalling the thought of René Guénon [...], the French traditionalist who converted to Sufi Islam and died as a sheikh in Cairo." Picking up on Charles's statement in *Harmony* that "We are not the masters of creation," Dreher concluded his article and assessment of the prince with apparent approval: "In modern Western civilization, it is hard to imagine a more profoundly conservative statement," he said, "Or a more revolutionary one."[307]

A Guénonian Prince

Defending faith, from the Traditionalist perspective (and, it would seem, from Prince Charles's perspective), could have nothing to do with the exterior, that is, with pandering to particular politicized groups. Rather, it is to defend the spirit against a modernity that has squeezed out the Divine, and turned man away from eternal and immutable truths and into a mere consumer. It is, in simpler terms, to defend the sacred against the superficial. The prince himself articulated this in his video address to the Traditionalist-oriented Sacred Web Conference held in the Canadian province of Alberta in 2006:

In these uprooted times, there is a great need for constancy; a need for those who can rise above the clamor, the din and the sheer pace of our lives to help us to rediscover those truths that are immutable and eternal; a need for those who can speak of that eternal wisdom which is called the perennial philosophy.[308]

"The perennial philosophy," we should note, is another name for Traditionalism, but in case we are in any doubt, Prince Charles continues, observing that the conference, that he is introducing, is dedicated "to a critique of the false premises of Modernity – a critique set out in one of the seminal texts of the traditionalists, René Guénon's *The Reign of Quantity*."[309] Referring to the Traditionalists, the prince contended that:

Their's [*sic*] is not a nostalgia for the past, but a yearning for the sacred and, if they defend the past, it is because in the pre-modern world all civilizations were marked by the presence of the sacred.[310]

We should recall the prince's phrase "Defender of Faith."

For Prince Charles, Traditionalism represents the prospect of "integration" in an era of "*dis*-integration, *dis*-connection and *de*-construction," and one that is, consequently, hurtling toward a "Dark Age" of environmental disaster.

In his introduction to the Sacred Web Conference, Charles reminded his audience that, "The traditionalist perspective is that we are living at the end of an historical cycle," i.e., the Kali Yuga or Dark Age. According to this doctrine, as Charles observed, at the beginning of the cycle of time all potential manifestations were latent. Emanating throughout the Ages, these manifestations descended from higher, spiritual forms to lower, and more materialistic ones. However, because of the ever-increasing distance of existence, society, etc., from eternal, spiritual laws, at a certain point collapse becomes inevitable. Yet, Charles went on, it is "through our understanding of and attachment to traditional norms of metaphysical doctrine and spiritual practice that we can, in a measure, transcend the baleful influence of the descent that is the eventual exhaustion and end of our cycle of history and prepare ourselves and the world for the beginning of the next."[311]

According to the prince, "tradition" is not something constructed by man, but "a God-given intuition" of the rhythms and harmony of opposites that can be found throughout nature.[312] Imbalance has occurred because over the last four centuries, the prince asserts, the West has become increasingly characterized "by a mechanistic approach to science." Although science is valuable, he says, it cannot "articulate matters of the soul."[313] Guénon is nowhere mentioned in *Harmony*, but the spirit of Traditionalism and esotericism more broadly is apparent: ancient traditions, Christianity, Islam, sacred geometry, ancient Egypt, and Hermeticism are all used to illustrate the prince's worldview.

Like Guénon before him, the prince believes that Islam can act as a bulwark against a type of modernity that strips man of his relationship to the Divine. We in the West must rediscover our relationship to the sacred, both have asserted. It is a task that will require us to understand not with the head but with the "heart" – a word that Charles sometimes uses when speaking of the Islamic faith. Quoting an Arab proverb, "what comes from the lips reaches the ears. What comes from the heart reaches the heart," the prince has reminded audiences (at the Open University in Cambridge in 2007, and in Oxford in 1993) both of his own sincerity and, if one reads between the lines, the necessity for what the Sufis refer to as *Tawajjuh*, or spiritual concentration.

The history of Islam and the West have long been intertwined and overlapping, and Muslims and Christians share essential beliefs – "one divine God," an afterlife, accountability for one's actions after the death of the body, etc. – Charles asserted in an article published in Britain's conservative *Telegraph* newspaper a month after the 9/11 attacks in 2001. Both sides had to be aware of the dangers of misunderstanding each other, and seeing history only from their own perspective. More daringly, considering the timing, the prince renewed his call for Westerners to "understand the Islamic world better," including "the extent to which many Muslims genuinely fear our own Western materialism and mass culture"[314] as a threat to their traditional culture and societies.

Although, in 1993, the prince spoke at the Oxford Centre for Islamic Studies, attempting to dispel Western stereotypes about Muslim countries – telling the audience, for example, that women in Turkey, Egypt, and Syria are given equal pay, and received the vote as early as women in much of Europe – his interest in Islam is not that he views it, as some multiculturalists do, as more liberal or progressive than the West. For the heir to the British throne, it is not politics that will enable the West to understand the East, or vice versa. "TADABBUR is the word […] to open our minds and unlock our hearts to each other," he declared in 1993. The Arabic term *tadabbur* refers to the contemplation of the Divine, especially through meditating upon chapters of the Qur'an (*tadabbur al-Qur'an*), on what they tell the Muslim, and how their lessons are to be implemented in daily life. *Tadabbur* is often defined as the "remembrance of God" and "remembrance of the thoughts of God."

The prince's is a gnostic, esoteric understanding of Islam. It is not primarily the faith of the *shari'a* or *fiqh* – nor of what is permitted (*halal*) and forbidden (*haram*) – or of international politics and group identity, but of the inner reality connecting man and God. It is the faith of the Islamic mystics, Rumi and Ibn Ashir, whom the prince has cited in his speeches, albeit in passing. Like the Traditionalists, Britain's heir to the throne believes that the West has focused on the external, at the expense of the inner, creating a confused and "exploitative" materialist culture. The "oneness and trusteeship of the vital sacramental and spiritual character of the world about us," the prince has said, "is surely something important we can re-learn from Islam."[315]

CONCLUSION

Secularism, Spirituality, And Struggle In The Modern Era

Though in very different ways, Freemasonry of the 18th century and the fringe Masons and Muslim revolutionaries of the 19th were seeking to answer questions that had arisen with, and in response to, the French Revolution, and its sometimes murderous attacks on the lives of the faithful. In France, Christianity especially was under attack. In the Near East, with the imposition of European powers, so was Islam.

More specifically, then, the main question thrust on both groups, was the role of religion in modernity. Many Muslim radicals wanted to see a new interpretation of Islam that would adhere to its values while absorbing the best of European intellectual tradition, not least of all to create a civilization capable of pushing out the European colonial powers from the Near East.

In some cases, although not very successfully, radical thinkers in the region used the cover of Masonic Lodges or similar societies to promote their own political programs. Freemasonry was viewed as a universal brotherhood that transcended national, religious, and cultural differences. Yet, unlike Marxism or communism, it placed God, the Divine, religious and spiritual experience, and his ability to decide for himself on such matters, at the center of man's elevation. Freemasonry held out, then, the double promise of undermining colonialism and pushing back against atheism, secularism, and materialism.

Masonic Lodges also provided a network, both internally, and to the greater esotericist and spiritualist world just beyond its somewhat porous borders. During the late 19th century and early 20th century, Islam was seen by the fledgling spiritual movements of European and America as being akin to them, or, since these movements drew from numerous religions and esoteric traditions, part of the alternative spiritual scene.

Leaving aside its political, nationalist aspects, Moorish Science fits snuggly into this milieu. In Britain, likewise, Shaykh Quilliam – a man who campaigned vigorously for the rights of Muslims under the British Empire – was immersed in Masonic and fringe Masonic esotericism, such as the Swedenborgian Rite. He also founded and promoted his own pseudo-Masonic Order of Zuzimites through various, highly specialist Masonic and esoteric journals.

The rituals and symbolism of Freemasonry do, to varying degrees, resemble those of the religions and esoteric cults, both contemporary to us and of antiquity. Islam is no exception. Hence, though no more credible than the many other theories about its roots – of which there is an inexhaustible supply – Sufi mystic and author Idries Shah has, as we saw, claimed that the Masonic fraternity originated in Sufism, and one theory – briefly aired during at the end of the 19th century – proposed that Freemasonry was rooted in the Druze religion of Syria.

Exploration and experimentation with religious symbolism and texts in the West meant that Islam would inevitably eventually have some impact on Freemasonry and, more especially, on fringe Masonry – i.e., secretive esoteric and gnostic societies modeled on the fraternity, and often founded by one or more of its members. As we saw, Crowley was influenced Sufism and drew this, to some extent, into the O.T.O. The Ancient Arabic Order of the Nobles of the Mystic Shrine (popularly known as "the Shriners") was founded by Freemasons during the late 19th century – as was the rival Mystic Order of Veiled Prophets of the Enchanted Realm.

As noted above, Shaykh Quilliam in England – like Guénon in France – was involved in an extremely obscure and secretive Masonic Rite that drew on the teachings of Christian mystic Emanuel Swedenborg. This was not the sort of society that would have benefited someone in terms of business or political contacts, as is sometimes suggested in relation to membership of the fraternity. It was of interest only to those who were dedicated to esotericism and unconventional spirituality – which, in Victorian England, would not have excluded Islam.

It will be worth mentioning here that Henry Corbin – who, from 1954 to 1974, held the chair in Islam at the Sorbonne, Paris – made a comprehensive study of Ismailism (an offshoot of Shi'a Islam) and the writing of Emanuel Swedenborg, concluding that there existed, "certain hermeneutic convergences in a writer like Swedenborg, based on the Bible, and among the Isma'ili spiritual writers in Islam, based on the Qur'an."[316] Although Quilliam was a Sunni Muslim, and, as such, may not have found in the obscure Swedenborgian Rite of Freemasonry quite the hermeneutical connection to Islam as Corbin was able to discern, it is nevertheless important that Freemasonry was able to absorb the work of esoteric thinkers, at the same time that it was able to embrace non-Christians, who saw in the Masonic Ritual a reflection of their own religious morals and practices.

In the West, at least, the notion of spirituality independent of religious authority is rooted, historically, in Freemasonry – especially its manifestation in various esoteric Rites, Orders, and rituals – and the various occult and spiritual movements to emerge from it, forming the basis of the New Age movement later on. During the 18th century, when the movement exploded in popularity across continental Europe (where Christianity was being increasingly undermined by Enlightenment thought and revolution). Unable to have total faith in the Christian doctrine, the more intellectually inquisitive and spiritually hungry Freemasons turned to non-Western and ancient religions and esoteric traditions to find the key to the Mysteries and the purpose for their own existence.

By the late 19th century, circles of Freemasons expressed an interest in religions and cultures, from the Druze to Islam, and from Hinduism to Buddhism, in articles and research papers, Masonic encyclopedias, and the rituals of the obscure but important Societas Rosicruciana. By this time,

Freemasonry had already become the first global society to embrace men of all nationalities, races, and religions.

It is one of those great ironies of history that the modern Islamist movement adopted anti-Freemasonry as part of its worldview, considering that in the shape of anti-colonial, pan-Islamic politics, Islamism begins with Muslim revolutionary and one-time Freemason Sayyid Jamal ad-Din al-Afghani, and that figures such as Shaykh Quilliam and René Guénon helped to introduce a more positive image of Islam to the West. Yet, whether joining Masonic Lodges or opposing a usually highly imaginary "Freemasonry," Muslim revolutionaries and, later, Islamists, have often been motivated by anti-colonialism, anti-Westernism, and, more specifically over the last few decades, anti-Americanism.

In the case of those joining Lodges, nearly a century or more ago, they perceived the fraternity, as we have seen, as revolutionary. Islamists and Jihadists opposing "Freemasonry" today imagine it to be the vanguard of Western powers, in league with "Zionism," meaning Israel. For the Islamist or Jihadist, "Freemasonry" is, more specifically, conflated with the culture of America and the West, especially liberal democracy, women's rights, Hollywood, and alcohol. Nevertheless, the influence of "Freemasonry" is allegedly in almost every aspect of Western culture, from comic strips[317] to Pokemon Go.[318]

Islamism has not adopted this rhetoric through an understanding of Freemasonry in the lives of al-Afghani and others. In fact, Islamist texts seem to lack even a basic knowledge of the fraternal movement, its beliefs, or history. Instead, as we saw, anti-Freemasonry was absorbed from Tsarist Russian and European anti-Semitic conspiracy theories, brought to the Middle East, and translated into Arabic, by Arab Christians.

AFTERWORD

A Time For Islamic Spirituality?

Politics and religion, and politics and spirituality, have merged also in the West. Christian spirituality has been eclipsed by the "Christian Right" or "Christian Zionism," with its faithful often seemingly more interested in geopolitics in the Middle East than in the actual teachings of Jesus. Similarly, on the opposite side of the political divide, expressions of "spirituality" frequently regurgitate, and take their orientation from whatever "progressive" talking points are currently in vogue. As Slavoj Zizek has noted, though, such popular spirituality does not equate to anti-materialism – or anti-capitalism, as he would say – but, rather, often provides a kind of psychological shield, enabling the individual to "participate in capitalist dynamics"[319] or the assumptions of Western modernity, while claiming to stand outside of it.

Hence, the popular Western conviction that "all religions" teach the same truths. While this seems, superficially, to reflect the tenets of Traditionalism and some other forms of Western-rooted spirituality – and, indeed, Allamah Tabataba'i's comprehension of gnosis as "the heart of all religions" – it is of an entirely different, and even a contrary, spirit. Since, although Western cultures now more readily defer to, and even demand public "respect" for, the world's major faiths, multiculturalism redirects neither the individual nor society as a whole toward the Divine. Instead, like looking at a faux-antique vase, pieced back together from broken fragments, the religions are perceived as ancient pieces that, together, make up – or somehow contribute to – the modern, secular, Western, political zeitgeist. As with criticisms of Islam, then, rather than preserving the sacred, defending the religious frequently means defending Western liberalism.

This perhaps explains why commentary on Islam – whether in support or critical of the faith – remains at an exceedingly low level. Rarely do we even hear about Sufism or Ismailism. Esoteric Shi'ism remains almost entirely unknown. Most do not know the difference even between Sunni and Shi'a. Fewer still realize that political Islam began during the 19th century, during colonialism, and has given birth to a range of movements, from Islamism to the pro-democracy. Shaykh Quilliam and his Ancient Order of Zuzimites, the influence of Islam on Aleister Crowley or René Guénon or the influence of Guénon on our understanding of Islam or on politics today, are either unknown or rarely acknowledged by those who work in these fields, either in academia or in foreign policy.

Nor does the West understand that groups such as al-Qaeda and ISIS are not "extremists" or "violent extremists" per se (as non-Muslim defenders of Islam, including governments, often contend) or "real Muslims" (as some of the harsher critics claim) but that they are Salafi, Takfiri, Islamist, and Jihadist. Salafi, meaning that they regard nearly all Muslims to be either deficient or in grave error in how they practice their faith. Takfiri, meaning that they believe that they have the right to apostatize, punish, and, in many cases, even to kill Muslims for their alleged deficiency or "apostasy." Islamist, because they have, as Bassam Tibi has said, "religionized politics."[320] And, Jihadist, in this context, because they believe that they or others must engage in violence, including against fellow Muslims, to establish their sociopolitical program. In other words, we are concerned with an ideology – or ideologies – rather than degrees of belief or conviction. A Salafi, Takfiri, Jihadist is not, for example, an extreme Sufi or extreme Twelver Shi'ite.

In the Middle East, Wahhabis – the Salafi movement generally referred to after its founder Muhammad ibn Abd al-Wahhab, (1703-1792) – attacked and destroyed both Sunni and Shi'ite shrines, including those of the family of the Prophet and Sufi saints, as they sought to take power.[321] Sufi shrines have been attacked by the Taliban in Afghanistan in recent years, and Shi'ites – as well as Hindus and other minorities – have found themselves persecuted by Jihadists in Pakistan.

All of this goes virtually unmentioned in the West, partly out of ignorance, and undoubtedly partly because it might provoke questions about the foreign policy of various Western governments and political parties. But, our insistence on seeing Islam through the prism of Western culture and history also means that the political Left and Right can continue to use Islam as a field on which to battle each other, which is perhaps the main benefit in an age in which the two sides have largely abandoned their principles, or, at best, are thoroughly inconsistent.

Yet, through the white noise of Western commentary, a number of Muslim thinkers have either called for the rediscovery of Islamic spirituality or – as is the case with Shaykh Abdal Hakim Murad, named Britain's most influential Muslim[322] – speak of Islam as a spiritual tradition that contrasts and is able to offset some of the worst aspects of modernity.

The well known Swiss-born Muslim intellectual Tariq Ramadan has likewise spoken of Islam and spirituality.[323] Ramadan is a complex, controversial, and interesting figure who defies easy categorization. The Islamic "reformer" – as he refers to himself – studied French literature and Western philosophy, writing his master's dissertation in philosophy on *The Notion of Suffering in Nietzsche's Philosophy*. His Ph.D. thesis, titled *Nietzsche as a Historian of Philosophy*, led him to study other major Western philosophers as well, from Socrates and Plato, through Descartes, Spinoza, Kant, Hegel, and even Marx. Around this time, Ramadan decided to move to Egypt to undertake a five-year university curriculum on Islam, and, moreover, to complete this within twelve months. Studying privately with a scholar (*'alim*) of the religion, Ramadan's days began at 5 A.M., and drew to a close between 11 P.M. and midnight.[324]

Although, as an intellectual, Ramadan is often concerned with the social implications of the Islamic textual tradition, and not its esoteric implications per se, he has nevertheless spoken of spirituality as being essential to Islam. "One should not fail to observe the revival of spirituality and of the quest for meaning among Muslim Westerners," he has asserted. The essence of Islam, he says, lies in the "millions of Muslim women and men [who] experience religion as spiritual initiation, reconciliation with meaning, and quest for the liberation of their inner selves in a global world dominated by appearances and excessive possession and consumption."[325]

Another such voice is Ali A. Allawi, a former Minister of Defense and Minister of Finance in the post-Saddam Hussein Iraq. Allawi has observed that, despite generally being seen as polar opposites, both liberal and fundamentalist Muslims have expressed the "same skepticism, if not downright hostility, towards Islam's legacy of mystical thought." So, of course, have many opponents of the faith. Yet, "Islam," Allawi says, "needs a new understanding of religion based on intuitive reasoning." This will require rediscovering, and to a greater or lesser extent, reinventing a "spiritualized language for Islam."[326]

Akbar S. Ahmed says in *Islam Under Siege* that group loyalty (*asabiyya*) has become radicalized, and now, in the shape of terrorism and inter-communal violence, threatens the security of the world. We will "need to rediscover and reemphasize the higher levels of spirituality, expressed through mysticism, which join all the great faiths," including "non-monotheistic ones like Hinduism," says Ahmed. We will "need to make a conscious attempt to rediscover the essential spiritual unity in faith that transcends ideas of group honor and identity." Moreover, he says, if we want to overcome this threat we will "need to discover the deep wells of mystic thought that lie in each civilization."[327]

I have argued that both Muslim revolutionaries and Western spiritual radicals had embarked on a journey to answer questions that arose with the French Revolution, e.g., the role of religion and spirituality in the modern, industrialized, and increasingly secular world. In some cases, such as that of René Guénon, we find Western-born individuals converting to Islam, yet involved with spirituality more broadly. We have also discovered numerous connections, during the 19th and 20th centuries, between Islam and Islamic spirituality and European and American societies, activists, and so on.

The challenge that Ahmed sees for Islam today, then, also appears to face the West, where forms of spirituality are readily available, but do not run deep. To put it bluntly, the task facing us is to rediscover how religion and spirituality – the exoteric and the esoteric – connect to each other, rather than to politics. Only then will we be able to discover for ourselves the gnosis that lies, as Allamah Tabataba'i has said, at "the heart of all religions."[328]

APPENDIX I

Islam, Europe, and The Influence of Julius Evola[329]

For those Westerners seeking an "alternative" to liberal modernity, which is "now being used as an inherently persecutory discourse," Muslim theologian Shaykh Abdal Hakim Murad has remarked, [330] it is Julius Evola that provides "a reference point."

Evola, a relatively obscure figure confined largely to the more intellectual margins of both Western esotericism and Rightist politics, saw a brief moment of nationwide fame, in the USA, in 2017, when the *New York Times*[331] picked up on a *Buzzfeed News*[332] article from the previous year. In the latter piece, Steve Bannon – "chief strategist and senior counselor" to then President-elect Donald Trump – had mentioned the Italian thinker in a comment about Russian President Vladimir Putin. Putin, Bannon suggested, has "got an adviser [i.e., neo-Eurasianist theorist Aleksandr Dugin] who harkens back to Julius Evola and different writers of the early 20th century who are really the supporters of what's called the traditionalist movement."

People sometimes say things less accurately in conversation or speeches than they might in writing, since, of course, the mind can sometimes go blank, and, in the moment, the speaker might forget an important detail. However, from the brief – and much-hyped – comment, Bannon's knowledge seems to be somewhat cursory, and at least partly wrong. Bannon suggested, quite unbelievably, that Traditionalism "really eventually metastasized into Italian fascism." Although, given space to write in one of the fascist newspapers, Evola criticized the movement for not being Traditionalist enough, but Traditionalism was not, in fact, a significant influence on the Italian political movement in question. Notably, Benito Mussolini himself had begun his political career as an active socialist.

However, since his public mention of Evola, it has been suggested[333] that Bannon is not only familiar with the Italian Traditionalist, and with the work of René Guénon, but that his worldview has been shaped, to a greater or lesser extent, by their ideas. But, if so, Bannon is unlike them in important ways.[334] Most especially, Bannon is often considered to be strongly opposed to Islam, while Traditionalism has always been sympathetic to it.

Since the main theme of this book is the historical connection between Freemasonry and Islam in the modern era, it will be worth mentioning that Evola, like many on the "Right," during the preceding century, was hostile to Freemasonry. In his *Men Among The Ruins*, for example, he references *The Protocols* and its anti-Semitic and anti-Masonic conspiracy theory, which he sees as illustrating, metaphysically, the heart of the "occult war." This war, Evola claimed, was being waged between more, if imperfectly, Traditional nations and cultures and those representing "democracy," modernity, and anti-Traditional values. Besides its role in the "occult war," the Italian esotericist and political theorist condemned the Masonic fraternity for creating what, in his view, was an ersatz aristocracy of knighthoods, chivalric titles, and so on. Yet, for Evola, neither Judaism nor Freemasonry could be considered permanent foes since it was possible, he believed, that anti-Traditional forces might eventually turn against them.

However, the Italian Traditionalist did express approval of Islam, including in regard to the concept of Jihad as both an internal and an external "struggle" – though this was during World War II, when Evola was writing for pro-fascist newspapers, in the hope of winning the movement away from its most vulgar elements and turning it toward a more authentically Traditionalist perspective.[335] Nor can we ignore the fact that Evola also referenced, positively, Jewish mysticism – most particularly the Cabala – as well, in his writing on alchemy and Hermeticism.

Yet, despite the complexity of Evola's thought, as Shaykh Murad has noted, he has influenced some counter-cultural groups and thinkers. Politically, Evola's main influence has been on the "New Right" (*Nouvelle Droite*) movement that emerged with G.R.E.C.E. (*Groupement de recherche et d'études pour la civilization*), a think tank founded by French intellectual Alain de Benoist in response to demonstrations and riots by Left-wing activists in 1968. Evola's thought can also be seen in the writings of Italian organization Raido, and in the *Political Soldier* pamphlet (1984) of Derek Holland, an intellectual of the (British) National Front.

Holland went on to become one of the founders of the International Third Position, whose principal enemies were viewed as capitalism and communism (with Zionism perhaps regarded as the foundation of these modern socio-economic systems). Notably, the ITP, and the National Front only slightly earlier, embraced Islamic and Third World states in what they regarded as their common cause, with one 1988 issue of *National Front News* announcing a new alliance between the nationalist party and Colonel Muammar Gaddafi of Libya, Ayatollah Khomeini, and the Nation of Islam. The new alliance was not necessarily embraced by those endorsed by the nationalist newspaper. During the same year, National Front fundraisers visited Gaddafi in Tripoli. However, the Libyan leader decided not to support the party.

Mass immigration from the Middle East and perhaps, ultimately, what appears to be the emergence of unaccountable governments disinterested in, if not hostile to, the electorate, has spurred the growth of new movements hostile to Islam, some of them emerging from the New Right milieu, and others arguably classical liberal – wanting to secure women's rights and gay rights, etc.

Considering Traditionalism's relationship to Islam (especially in the figure of Guénon), yet also considering Evola's influence on the counterculture, can there be a bridge between the faith and the Traditionalist-influenced counterculture? Shaykh Murad comments that,

Evola... somebody who is in many ways inimical to an Islamic perspective... [is] nonetheless someone who has had a very significant role in triggering the counterculture — it's not a Left-wing counterculture, it's not a Right-wing counterculture, but it is a counterculture, which has continued to this day, and which, unfortunately... has moved in the direction of forms of xenophobia. But, nonetheless, his discourse and the discourse of that cloud of thinkers around him... represents a vision that can offer Muslims at least pause for thought.

The British shaykh also remarks that the Traditionalist-inspired counterculture represents a "missed opportunity," presumably to win its members over to a more sympathetic view of Islam, and toward a more spiritual and less racialist and IQ-focused worldview. Later, Shaykh Murad comments that, besides unaccountable governments in Europe, what is really at the heart, or the root, of the counterculture is the destruction of the sacred, and the erasing of meaning, in the modern world.

"So the [...] present-day advocates of the Evola attempt to 'ride the tiger,' [they want] to try [to] find forms whereby the world can be resacralized," says Shaykh Murad. Protests against mass immigration or the acceptance of hundreds of thousands of asylum seekers represent only the outward form of a deeper anxiety. "[T]hey are deeply uneasy about what they are, where they are going, the political elite that's leading them to more and more blandness, away from Tradition."

While Left-wing journalists and spokespeople often loudly denounce popular "Right-wing" movements as "racist," the latter frequently criticizes "the Left" for, in essence, failing to consistently promote its values, or, to put it another way, for failing to be consistently or sufficiently Left-wing in relation to Islam or Muslim immigration in the West. As such, the majority of "Right-wing," anti-Islamic or anti-Islamist groups – which may well have no connection to Right-wing movements of the type inspired by Evola – appear to position themselves as a kind of traditional Left. To pull off this sleight of hand, such groups insist that women's rights, gay rights, free speech, and so on, represent traditional Western or national values, which must be defended in order to ensure the continuation of individual rights, etc.

All of this is quite different to movements inspired by Evola, which sought not only to establish a new political reality but to create a new type of man. This figure would be a "political soldier" – an intellectual warrior, an ascetic that shuns modern excesses, sacrificing comforts and pleasures for a more austere, authentic, and in some sense "Traditional" life.

The influence of Evola can be seen on such contemporary, Traditionalist-influenced – though, in the West, highly controversial – thinkers as Dugin. In contrast to anti-Islamic movements, Dugin focuses his criticism toward Saudi Wahhabism and terrorist movements such as ISIS (or "Daesh") while supporting Traditional and conservative Islamic culture, especially Sufism and Shi'ism. Indeed, it would seem that these thinkers regard the support for Traditional Islamic cultures as an important bulwark against "American liberalism" and "Americanization" – of which Dugin is especially critical – and, as such, as ultimately supportive of an eventual resacralization in the West.

APPENDIX II

The Freemasonry On Bin Laden's Bookshelf[336]

There was at least one big surprise among Osama bin Laden's personal library, declassified in May 2015 by the Director of the Office of National Intelligence. Bin Laden, al-Qacda's one-time leader, had a copy of *The Secret Teachings of All Ages* by Manly Hall (1928), a classic of New Age or alternative spiritual thought. Was bin Laden a closet New Ager? No. Did he agree with the thesis of *The Secret Teachings*? Again, no.

Indeed, while Hall's book presents the notion of a universal knowledge to be found in Freemasonry, Judaism ("Qabbalah"), the Knights Templar (Crusader) Order, and among the ancient Greek philosophers, etc., in 1998, Bin Laden had, with other Jihadist leaders, published a "fatwa" under the name of "World Islamic Front for Jihad Against Jews and Crusaders." An al-Qaeda training manual discovered in 2005 states that the movement's battle "does not know Socratic debates..., Platonic ideals..., nor Aristotelian diplomacy. But it knows the dialogue of bullets, the ideals of assassination, bombing, and destruction, and the diplomacy of the cannon and machine-gun." All of this makes it clear that al-Qaeda's ideology is more or less the exact opposite of Hall's worldview.

Although I was surprised that bin Laden owned a copy of *The Secret Teachings* – a particular, lengthy, and somewhat romantic book – I was not surprised that bin Laden had an interest in at least some of the subjects it covers. I believe he had read at least some of the book's more than forty chapters, and that it was of importance to him, especially its commentary on the subjects of Islam and Freemasonry. Chapters on the pyramids, astrology, and so on, probably interested bin Laden less, if at all.

Relying heavily on Western sources, and quoting extensively, the chapter on Islam is rather weak (Hall was more of a mystic than a scholar). Bin Laden may well have welcomed the author's criticism of the negative "attitude of Christendom toward Islam." But any believing Muslim would be offended by Hall's contention that, "The arcana of Islam may […] be demonstrated to have been directly founded upon the ancient pagan Mysteries performed at the Caaba centuries before the birth of the Prophet" and that "many of the ceremonials now embodied in the Islamic Mysteries are survivals of pagan Arabia." (According to Islam, Muhammad received the Qur'an from the Angel Gabriel, not from pre-existing pagan traditions, which, from a mainstream Islamic perspective, were committing *shirk* — the sin of practicing idolatry or polytheism.)

In my view, the chapters about Freemasonry are laborious, focusing on various alleged ancient influences more than on the history of the centuries-old fraternity itself. But why would bin Laden own such a book? It is probable that, although not interested in the Islamic scholarship in itself, bin Laden believed *The Secret Teachings* accurately represented the "Masonic" or Western view of Islam. In other words, that — as with many of the other books bin Laden owned – he believed it gave some insight into the mindset of the enemy. Notably, another book allegedly owned by bin Laden was *Bloodlines of the Illuminati* by Fritz Springmeier.[337]

What bin Laden's bookshelf seems to confirm is that the Islamist worldview is more complex than is generally believed, being influenced by, among other things, Western conspiracy theories about Freemasonry. But the lack of comment by journalists and scholars about the al-Qaeda leader's ownership of *The Secret Teachings* tells us that our understanding of Islamism and Jihadism, or the relationship of Islam and "the West," will not change anytime soon.

Endnotes

1   Nasr, Vali, *The Shia Revival: How Conflicts Within Islam Will Shape the Future*, W. W. Norton & Company, New York, 2006, p. 37.

2   Tabataba'i, Sayyid Muhammad Husayn, *Shi'ah* (Sayyid Husayn Nasr, Trans.), Ansariyan

Publications, Qum, Islamic Republic of Iran, 2002, p. 219.

3   Ibid., p. 208.

4   Nasr, Vali, *The Shia Revival: How Conflicts Within Islam Will Shape the Future*, 2006, p. 74. See also Lalljee, Yousuf N., ed., *Ali the Magnificent*, Ansariyan Publications, Qum, Islamic Republic of Iran, original publication date unknown, third reprint 2006.

5   Tabataba'i, *Shi 'ah*, 2002, p. 133.

6   Ibid., p. 133

7   Amir-Moezzi, Mohammad Ali, *The Divine Guide in Early Shi'ism: The Sources of Esotericism in Islam*, (trans. David Streight, State University of New York Press, New York, 1994, p. 43.

8   Ibid., p. 12.

9   Daftary, Farhad, ed., *Intellectual Traditions in Islam*, I.B. Tauris & Co. Ltd. in association with The Institute of Ismaili Studies, London, 2000, pp. 89- 90.

10   Köprülü, Mehmet Fuat, *The Origins of the Ottoman Empire*, State University of New York Press, Albany, 1991, p. 100.

11   Shaw, Stanford J., *History of the Ottoman Empire and Modern Turkey: Volume 1, Empire of the Gazis: The Rise and Decline of the Ottoman Empire 1280-1808*, Cambridge University Press, Cambridge, 1976, pp. 4-5.

12   Momen, Moojan, *An Introduction to Shi'i Islam*, Yale University Press, New Haven, 1987, p.90 and p. 208.

13   Trimingham, J. Spencer, *The Sufi Orders in Islam*, Oxford University Press, 1998, p. 136.

14   Ernst, Carl W., Sufism: *An Introduction to the Mystical Tradition of Islam*, Shambhala, Boston, 2011, p. 26.

15   McGregor, R. S., ed., *Devotional Literature in South Asia: Current Research, 1985-1988- Papers of the Fourth Conference on Devotional Literature in New Indo-Aryan Languages Held at Wolfson College, Cambridge, 1-4 September*, Cambridge University Press, Cambridge, 1992, p. 184.

16   Ernst, Carl W., *Sufism: An Introduction to the Mystical Tradition of Islam*,

Shambhala, Boston, 2011, pp. 20-21.

17   Ibid., p. 19. See also Farhadi, A. G. Ravan, *Abdullah Ansari of Herat (1006-1089 Ce): An Early Sufi Master*, Routledge, 1996, p. 47.

18   Pourjavady, Reza, *Philosophy in Early Safavid Iran (Islamic Philosophy, Theology and Science)*, Brill, Leiden, 2011, p. 7.

19   Bashir, Shahzad, *Sufi Bodies: Religion and Society in Medieval Islam*, Columbia University Press, New York, 2011, p. 91.

20   Green, Nile, *Sufism: A Global History*, Wiley-Blackwell, Chichester, 2012, p. 101.

21   Brown, John P., *The Darvishes: Or Oriental Spiritualism*, Routledge, 2008, p. VII.

22   Schimmel, Annemarie, *The Triumphal Sun: a Study of the Works of Jalâloddinn Rumi*, State University of New York, 1993, pp. 73-74.

23   Islam Awareness, http://www.islamawareness.net/Isra/hadith.html.

24   Glassé, Cyril, *Concise Encyclopedia of Islam*, Rowman & Littlefield Publishers, 2008, "Night Journey," p. 395 and p. 473.

25   Katz, Steven T., ed., *Comparative Mysticism: An Anthology of Original Sources*, Oxford University Press, Oxford, 2013, p. 19.

26   Schwartz, Stephen, *The Other Islam: Sufism and the Road to Global Harmony*, Doubleday, New York, 2008, p. 117.

27   Chittick, William C. (foreword by Nasr, Seyyed Hossein), *The Sufi Doctrine Of Rumi*, World Wisdom, Inc., 2005, p. 20.

28   Schimmel, Annemarie, *The Triumphal Sun: a Study of the Works of Jalâloddinn Rumi*, 1993, p. 237. See also Baljon, Johannes Marinus Simon, *Religion and Thought of Shāh Walī Allāh Dihlawī: 1703 – 1762*, Brill, Leiden, 1986, p. 106, footnote 11.

29   Ibid., p. 237.

30   Northrup, Linda S., "The Bahri Mamluk sultanate, 1250-1390," published in *The Cambridge History of Egypt, Volume One: Islamic Egypt, 640-1517*, Petry, Carl F., ed., Cambridge University Press, 2008, p. 267.

31   Donner, Fred McGraw, *Muhammad and the Believers: At the Origins of Islam*, Belknap Press of Harvard University Press, Cambridge, Mass., 2010, p. 112.

32   Smith, Huston, *Islam: A Concise Introduction*, HarperSanFrancisco, San Francisco, 2001, p. 84.

33   Chittick, William C., *The Sufi Path of Knowledge: Ibn Al-'Arabi's Metaphysics of Imagination*, State University of New York Press, Albany, 1989, p. 102

34   Yadav, Rama Sankar, and Mandal, B.N., *Global Encyclopaedia of Education*, Vol 1, Global Vision Publishing House, p. 67

35   Hanif, N., *Biographical Encyclopaedia of Sufis: Africa and Europe*, Sarup & Sons, New Delhi, 2002, p. 20

36   Muhaiyaddeen, M. R. Bawa, *To Die Before Death: The Sufi Way of Life*, The

Fellowship Press, Philadelphia, 1997, p. 23.

37   Shah, Idries, *The Sufis*, Anchor Books, New York, 1971, pp. 412-414.

38   Trimingham, J. Spencer, *The Sufi Orders in Islam*, 1998, p. 14.

39   Ibid., pp. 24-25.

40   Eliade, Mircea, *The Forge and the Crucible: The Origins and Structure of Alchemy*, University Of Chicago Press, Chicago, 1979.

41   McIntosh, Christopher, *The Rosicrucians: The History, Mythology, and Rituals of an Esoteric Order*, Red Wheel Weiser, York Beach, 1998, pp. 21-22.

42   See "Confessio Fraternitatis", published in Yates, Frances, *The Rosicrucian Enlightenment*, Routledge, London, 1972, p. 255.

43   Yates, Frances, *The Rosicrucian Enlightenment*, 1972, pp. 235-238.

44   See "Fama Fraternitatis", published in Yates, Frances, *The Rosicrucian Enlightenment*, 1972, pp. 238-240.

45   Lewis, Bernard, *The Muslim Discovery of Europe*, p. 32, Weidenfeld and Nicolson, London, 192.

46   Akerman, Susanna, *Rose Cross Over the Baltic*, Brill, Leiden, 1998, p. 41.

47   Ibid., p. 51.

48   Anderson, James, *The Constitutions of the Free-Masons*, London, 1723, p. 24,.

49   Ibid., p. 45.

50   Ibid., p. 28,.

51   Bogdan, Henrik, Western *Esotericism and Rituals of Initiation*, State University of New York Press, Albany, 2007, pp. 84-85.

52   Yatim, Mohamad A., "Freemasonry and The Mystic Schools of the East," published in the July 2013 issue of *Living Stone*.

53   Richard Netton, Ian, *Allah Transcendent: Studies in The Structure and Semiotics of Islamic Philosophy, Theology, and Cosmology*, Curzon Press, Richmond, United Kingdom, 1994, pp. 256-266.

54   Shah, Idries, *The Sufis*, 1971, p. vii.

55   Ibid., p. 206.

56   Nasr, Seyyed Hossein, *The Heart of Islam: Enduring Values for Humanity*, Harper One, San Francisco, 2004, p. 180.

57   Burton, Sir Richard Francis, *First Footsteps in East Africa: Or, An Exploration of Harar*, Longman, Brown, Green, and Longmans, 1856, p. 361, footnote.

58   Smith, Rev. Haskett, "The Druses of Syria and Their Relation to Freemasonry" published in the *Ars Quatuor Coronatorum*, Vol. IV, 1891.

59   Ambelain, Robert, *Franc-maçonnerie d'autrefois*, Robert Lamont, Paris 1988, pp. 39-40.

60   Shute, John Raymond, ed., *LVX, Being the Transactions of the North Carolina College, Societas Rosicruciana in U.S.*, Vol I, part I, 1933, p. 18.

61   Millar, Angel, *Freemasonry: Foundation of the Western Esoteric Tradition*,

Salamander and Sons, Brisbane, 2014.

62   Hilderbrandt, Otto F., *A Peep Into the Mystic Realm*, Supreme Council M.O.V.P.E.R., Chicago, Illinois, 1960, p. 13.

63   Stillyard, B. H., *The Secret Ritual of the Secret Work of the Ancient Arabic Order of the Nobles of the Mystic Shrine*, published by John G. Jones, 1914, p. 22.

64   *Detroit Masonic News*, May 1921, Volume II, Number 5.

65   Albert Gallatin Mackey, Robert Ingham Clegg, William James Hughan, *Mackey's History of Freemasonry*, Masonic History Company, 1921, pp. 1973-1983.

66   Nance, Susan, *How The Arabian Nights Inspired The American Dream, 1790-1935*, University of North Carolina Press, Chapel Hill, 2009, pp. 95-99.

67   Ibid., p. 95.

68   Ibid., pp. 95-102.

69   Rose, H. A., *A Glossary of the Tribes and Castes of the Punjab and North-West Frontier Provinces*, Asian Educational Services, New Delhi, 1911, p. 554.

70   Goodrick-Clarke, Nicholas, *The Occult Roots of Nazism*, New York University Press, New York, 2004, pp. 135 – 143.

71   Flowers, Stephen E., *The Practice of the Ancient Turkish Freemasons*, Runa Raven, 2011.

72   Crowley, Aleister (edited by Hymenaeus Beta), *Magick: Liber Aba*, Weiser Books, Boston, 1997, p. lvii.

73   Martin P. Starr, *The Unknown God: W.T. Smith and the Thelemites*, The Teitan Press, Inc., Bolingbrook, Illinois, 2003, p. 100.

74   Crowley, Aleister, *The Confessions of Aleister Crowley: An Autohagiography*, (edited by John Symonds and Kenneth Grant), Penguin, 1989, p. 451.

75   Ibid., p. 446.

76   Crowley, Aleister, *The Scented Garden of Abdullah The Satirist of Shiraz* (from the introduction by Martin P. Starr), The Teitan Press, Chicago, 1991, p. 8.

77   Ibid., pp. 5-13.

78   Ibid., 1991, p. 7.

79   Yusuf Ali (translation), The Holy Quran,1934.

80   Crowley, Aleister, *The Book of The Law*, Ch. III, 28.

81   Crowley, Aleister, *The Book of The Law*, Ch. III, 7-8.

82   Ali, Yusuf (Trans.), The Holy Quran,1934, Surah VIII, 60.

83   Crowley, Aleister, *Magick Without Tears*, Ch. 23.

84   Crowley, Aleister, *Magick: Liber Aba*, Weiser Books, Boston, Masachusetts, USA, 1994, p. 433.

85   Crowley, Aleister, *The Confessions of Aleister Crowley: An Autohagiography*, Penguin, 1989, p. 388.

86   Aleister Crowley (Hymenaeus Beta, ed.), *Magick: Liber ABA, Book 4*, Weiser Books, 2nd revised edition, York Beach, Maine, 1998, p. lxv.

87   Yarker, John, "Arab Masonry", published in Ars Quatuor Coronatorum, Vol.

XIX, 1908, p. 243.

88   Gould, S. C., *Notes and Queries: A Monthly of History, Folk-Lore, Mathematics, Literature, Art, Arcane Societies, Etc.*, Vol. 25, 1900, pp. 215-216.

89   Harland-Jacobs, Jessica L., *Builders of Empire: Freemasons and British Imperialism, 1717-1927*, The University of North Carolina Press, Chapel Hill, 2007, p. 76.

90   Gould, Robert Freke, *The History of Freemasonry*, Vol. IV, pp. 142-143, John C. Yorston & Co., Publishers, 1896.

91   Rich, Paul, *The Invasions of the Gulf: Radicalism, Ritualism, and the Shaikhs*, p. 139, Allborough Press, Cambridge, UK, 1991.

92   Kedourie, Elie, *Afghani and 'Abduh: An Essay on Religious Unbelief and Political Activism in Modern Islam*, Frank Cass & Co. Ltd., New York, 1966, p. 20.

93   Ágoston, Gábor, ed., and Masters, Bruce Alan, ed., *Encyclopedia of the Ottoman Empire*, Facts on File, 2008, "Abd al-Qadir al-Jazairi," p. 4.

94   Commins, David Dean, *Islamic Reform: Politics and Social Change in Late Ottoman Syria: Politics*, Oxford University Press, New York, 1990, pp. 26-28.

95   Bouyerdene, Ahmed, *Emir Abd El-Kader: Hero and Saint of Islam*, World Wisdom, 2012, pp. 196-198. See also David Dean Commins, *Islamic Reform : Politics and Social Change in Late Ottoman Syria: Politics*, Oxford University Press, 1990, pp. 29.

96   Cole, Juan R. I., *Colonialism and revolution in the Middle East: social and cultural origins of Egypt's Urabi movement*, p. 138, The American University in Cairo Press, Egypt, 1999.

97   Pryce-Jones, David, *The Closed Circle: An Interpretation of the Arabs*, p. 87, Harper Perennial, a division of Harper-Collins Publishers; an Edward Burlingame book, 1991.

98   Kedourie, Elie, *Afghani and 'Abduh: An Essay on Religious Unbelief and Political Activism in Modern Islam*, 1996, pp. 18-19.

99   Algar, Hamid, "An Introduction to the History of Freemasonry in Iran," published in *Middle East Studies*, Vol. Six, No. three, published by Frank Cass & Co. Ltd., London, October 1970, p. 281.

100   Keddie, Nikki R, *An Islamic Response to Imperialism: Political and Religious Writings of Sayyad Jamāl ad-Din "al-Afghāni". Incl. a Translation of the "Refutation of the materialists"*, Berkeley U. A., University of California, 1983, p. 43.

101   Blunt, Wilfrid Scawen, *Secret History Of The English Occupation Of Egypt - Being A Personal Narrative Events*, p. 63, Peffer Press, 2007.

102   Charfi, Mohammed, *Islam and Liberty: The Historical Misunderstanding*, p. 81 and pp. 84-85, Zed Books, London, 2005.

103   Gould, Robert Freke, *The History of Freemasonry*, Vol. IV, pp. 142-143, John C. Yorston & Co., Publishers, 1896.

104   Kedourie, Elie, *Afghani and 'Abduh: An Essay on Religious Unbelief and*

Political Activism in Modern Islam, 1996, p. 18.

105   See my *Freemasonry: Foundation of the Western Esoteric Tradition*, Salamander and Sons, 2014.

106   Kudsi-Zadeh, A. Albert, 'Afghani and Freemasonry in Egypt,' published in the Journal of the American Oriental Society, vol. 92, Number 1, January-March 1972.

107   Keddie, Nikki R, *An Islamic Response to Imperialism: Political and Religious Writings of Sayyad Jamāl ad-Din "al-Afghāni"*, 1983.

108   Hourani, Albert, *Arab Thought in the Liberal Age 1798-1939* Cambridge University Press, Cambridge, New York, 1983, p. 134.

109   Ibid., p. 135.

110   Ibid., pp. 130-139.

111   Germain, Eric, "Southern Hemisphere Diasporic Communities in the Building of an International Muslim Public Opinion at the Turn of the Twentieth Century," published in *Comparative Studies of South Asia, Africa and the Middle East*, Vol. 27, No. 1, 2007, Duke University Press.

112   Geaves, Ron, *Islam in Victorian Britain: The Life and Times of Abdullah Quilliam*, Kube Publishing, Leicestershire, 2010, p. 108.

113   Ibid., p. 109.

114   *The Freemason (Illustrated): A Weekly Journal of Freemasonry, Literature, Science, and Art*, Vol. XL., November 16, 1901, p. 600.

115   Howe, Ellic, "Fringe Masonry in England 1870-85," published in *Ars Quatuor Coronatorum*, 1972.

116   Voorhis, Harold V. B., ed., *Collectanea*, Volume 1, The Grand College of Rites of the United States of America, 1947, p. 21.

117   Germain, Eric, "Southern Hemisphere Diasporic Communities in the Building of an International Muslim Public Opinion at the Turn of the Twentieth Century," 2007.

118   *Luzac's Oriental List*, Vol. XVII, January to December, 1906. Luzac & Co., 1906., p. 296.

119   Gould, S. C., ed., *Rosicrucian Brotherhood*, Vol. II, No. I, January 1908.

120   Quilliam, W. H. Abdullah, "Ancient Order of Zuzimites: Aims, Objects, and Usages"; *The Kneph*, Vol. I, p. 47, June 1881. Republished in S. C. & L. M. Gould, *Notes and Queries: A Monthly of History, Folk-Lore, Mathematics, Literature, Art, Arcane Societies, Etc.*, Vol. XVIII, 1900.

121   Voorhis, Harold V. B., ed., *Collectanea*, Volume 1, The Grand College of Rites of the United States of America, 1947, pp. 137-141.

122   Ibid., p. 129. The Zuzimite Ritual is quoting John Robinson, D. D., "Friendship," *A Theological, Biblical, and Ecclesiastical Dictionary*, printed for Longman, Hurst, Rees, Orme, and Brown, London, 1815.

123   Guénon, René, *The Crisis of the Modern World*, Sophia Perennis, Ghent, New York, 2001, p. 36.

124   Herlihy, John, ed., with an introduction by Lings, Martin, *The Essential René Guénon: Metaphysics, Tradition, and the Crisis of Modernity*, World Wisdom, Inc. and Sophia Perenis, USA, Bloomington, Indiana, 2009, pp. 206- 211.

125   Ibid., pp. 237- 242.

126   Guénon, René, *Theosophy: History of a Pseudo-Religion*, Sophia Perennis, Hillsdale, New York, 2004, p. 104.

127   Herlihy, John, ed., with an introduction by Lings, Martin, *The Essential René Guénon: Metaphysics, Tradition, and the Crisis of Modernity*, World Wisdom, Inc. and Sophia Perenis, USA, Bloomington, Indiana, 2009, pp. 275-281.

128   Sedgwick, Mark, *Against The Modern World: Traditionalism and the Secret Intellectual History of the Twentieth Century*, Oxford University Press, Oxford, 2004, p. 77, and pp. 74-80.

129   Waterfield, Robin, René Guénon and the Future of the West: The Life and Writings of a 20th-Century Metaphysician, Sophia Perennis, Hillsdale, NY, USA, 2005, p. 25.

130   Gilbert, R. A., "Chaos Out of Order: The Rise and Fall of the Swedenborgian Rite," published in *Ars Quatuor Coronatorum*, Vol. 108, 1995.

131   Paul Chacornac (translated by Cecil Bethell), *The Simple Life of René Guénon*, Sophia Perennis, Hillsdale, New York, 2004, p. 22.

132   The Knight Kadosh, a Masonic degree.

133   Waterfield, Robin E., *René Guénon and the Future of the West: the Life and Writings of a 20th-Century Metaphysician*, Sophia Perennis, 1987, second edition 2002, pp. 23-35.

134   Jawad, Haifaa A., *Towards Building A British Islam: New Muslims' Perspectives*, Bloomsbury, London, 2012, pp. 31-34.

135   Fitzgerald, Michael Oren, with a foreword by Stoddart, William, *Frithjof Schuon: Messenger of the Perennial Philosophy*, World Wisdom, Inc., 2010, p 27.

136   Ibid., p 32.

137   Jawad, Haifaa A., *Towards Building A British Islam: New Muslims' Perspectives*, 2012, pp. 85-94.

138   Sedgwick, Mark, *Against The Modern World: Traditionalism and the Secret Intellectual History of the Twentieth Century*, 2004, p. 126.

139   Ibid., p. 128.

140   Ibid., p. 171. See also pp. 83-93.

141   Moin, Baqer, *Khomeini: Life of the Ayatollah*, Thomas Dunne Books, an imprint of St. Martin's Press, New York, 2000, p. 18.

142   Martin, Vanessa, *Creating an Islamic State: Khomeini and the Making of a New Iran*, I. B. Tauris, New York, 2000, p. 29.

143   Hossein Nasr, Seyyed, *The Garden of Truth: The Vision and Promise of Sufism, Islam's Mystical Tradition*, HarperOne, New York, 2007, pp. 224-225.

144   Martin, Vanessa, *Creating an Islamic State: Khomeini and the Making of a New Iran*, 2000, p. 32.

145   Lorentz, John H., *The A to Z of Iran*, Scarecrow Press, Inc., a subsidiary of the Rowman and Littlefield Publishing Group, Inc., 2007, pp. 104-105
146   Moin, Baqer, *Khomeini: Life of the Ayatollah*, 2000, p. 43.
147   'Azimi, Mohammad Reza, ed. and L. Limba, Mansoor, ed., *The Wine of Love, Mystical Poetry of Imam Khomeini*, trans. A'wani, Ghulam-Rida and Legenhausen, Muhammad, with an introduction by Legenhausen, Muhammad, The Institute for Compilation and Publication of Imam Khomeini's Works, reproduced with permission by the Ahlul Bayt Digital Islamic Library Project team, http://www.al-islam.org/wine-of-love/2.htm
148   Algar, Hamid, trans., *Islam and Revolution: Writings and Declarations of Imam Khomeini (1941-1980)*, Mizan Press, 1981, p. 425. See also *The Wine of Love, Mystical Poetry of Imam Khomeini*.
149   'Azimi, Mohammad Reza, ed. and L. Limba, Mansoor, ed., *The Wine of Love, Mystical Poetry of Imam Khomeini*.
150   Algar, Hamid, trans., *Islam and Revolution: Writings and Declarations of Imam Khomeini (1941-1980)*, Mizan Press, 1981, p. 422.
151   Ibid., p. 416.
152   Afary, Janet, *The Iranian Constitutional Revolution, 1906-1911: Grassroots Democracy, Social Democracy, and the Origins of Feminism*, Columbia University Press, New York, 1996, p. 30.
153   Mowat, C. L., ed., *The New Cambridge Modern History Volume 12: The Shifting Balance of World Forces, 1898–1945*, Cambridge University Press, 1968, p. 275.
154   Munson, Henry, *Islam and Revolution in the Middle East*, Yale University Press, 1989, p. 41.
155   Afary, Janet, *The Iranian Constitutional Revolution, 1906-1911: Grassroots Democracy, Social Democracy, and the Origins of Feminism*, 1996, p. 33.
156   Bayat, Mangol, *Iran's First Revolution: Shi'ism and the Constitutional Revolution of 1905-1909*, Oxford University Press, New York, 1991, p. 57.
157   Axworthy Michael, *A History of Iran: Empire of the Mind*, Basic Books, a member of Perseus Books Group, New York, 2008, p. 198.
158   Afary, Janet, *The Iranian Constitutional Revolution, 1906-1911: Grassroots Democracy, Social Democracy, and the Origins of Feminism*, 1996, p. 39.
159   Lorentz, John H., *The A to Z of Iran*, Scarecrow Press, a subsidiary of The Rowman & Littlefield Publishing Group, Inc., p. 224, "National Front."
160   Wiesehofer, Josef, *Ancient Persia*, I. B. Tauris & Co Ltd, New York, 1996, reprinted 2006, p. xi.
161   Pollack, Kenneth, *The Persian Puzzle: The Conflict Between Iran and America*, Random House, New York, 2004, p. 6 and pp. 37-38.
162   Moin, Baqer, *Khomeini: Life of the Ayatollah*, Thomas Dunne Books, 2000, pp. 54-55.
163   Cronin, Stephanie, ed., *The Making of Modern Iran: State and Society*

Under Riza Shah, 1921-1941, Routledge. 2003, p. 198.

164   Moin, Baqer, *Khomeini: Life of the Ayatollah*, Thomas Dunne Books, 2000, p. 55.

165   Yann, Richard, "Ayatollah Kashani: Precursor of the Islamic Republic?", trans. Keddie, Nikki R., published in *Religion and Politics in Iran: Shi'ism from Quietism to Revolution*, Yale University Press, 1983, p. 104.

166   Lorentz, John H., *The A to Z of Iran*, Scarecrow Press, Plymouth, 2007, p. 224, "National Front."

167   Bill, James A., *The Eagle and the Lion: The Tragedy of American-Iranian Relations*, Yale University Press, New Haven 1989, p. 69.

168   Martin, Vanessa, *Creating an Islamic State: Khomeini and the Making of a New Iran*, I. B. Tauris, New York, 2000, p. 56.

169   Moin, Baqer, *Khomeini: Life of the Ayatollah*, Thomas Dunne Books, 2000, pp. 75-79.

170   Martin, Vanessa, *Creating an Islamic State: Khomeini and the Making of a New Iran*, I. B. Tauris, New York, 2000, p. 32.

171   Bill, James A., *The Eagle and the Lion: The Tragedy of American-Iranian Relations*, Yale University Press, New Haven 1989, pp. 147-148.

172   Moin, Baqer, *Khomeini: Life of the Ayatollah*, Thomas Dunne Books, 2000, p. 100.

173   Algar, Hamid, trans., *Islam and Revolution: Writings and Declarations of Imam Khomeini (1941-1980)*, Mizan Press, 1981, pp. 16-17.

174   Aghaie, Kamran Scot, *The Martyrs of Karbala: Shi'i Symbols and Rituals in Modern Iran*, University of Washing on Press, Seattle, 2004, p. 87.

175   Glasse, Cyril, and Smith, Huston, *New Encyclopedia of Islam: A Revised Edition of the Concise Encyclopedia of Islam*, AltaMira Press, Walnut Creek, CA, 2003, p. 259.

176   Martin, Vanessa, *Creating an Islamic State: Khomeini and the Making of a New Iran*, I. B. Tauris, New York, 2000, p. 64.

177   Moin, Baqer, *Khomeini: Life of the Ayatollah*, Thomas Dunne Books, 2000, pp. 138-139.

178   The American Presidency Project, "Tehran, Iran Toasts of the President and the Shah at a State Dinner," http://www.presidency.ucsb.edu/ws/?pid=7080#axzz2gcFnMVTf

179   Taheri, Amir, *The Spirit of Allah: Khomeini and the Islamic Revolution*, Adler & Adler, Bethesda, Maryland, 1986, p. 225-226.

180   Ganji, Babak, *Politics of Confrontation: The Foreign Policy of the USA and Revolutionary Iran*, I. B. Tauris, London, 2012, p. 48.

181   Koya, Abdar Rahman, ed., *Imam Khomeini: Life, Thought and Legacy*, Islamic Book Trust, Malaysia (in cooperation with Crescent International, Canada), 2009, p. 44.

182   Taheri, Amir, *The Spirit of Allah: Khomeini and the Islamic Revolution*,

1986, p. 227-228.
183   Encyclopaedia Iranica, December 15, 2000, 'FREEMASONRY, iv. THE 1979 REVOLUTION'; http://www.iranica.com/articles/freemasonry-iv-the-1979-revolution
184   Algar, Hamid, 'An Introduction to the History of Freemasonry in Iran, published in *Middle East Studies*, Vol. Six, No. three, 1970, p. 285-287.
185   Buchan, James, *Days of God: The Revolution in Iran and Its Consequences*, Simon & Schuster, New York, 2013, p. 165.
186   Ridgeon, Lloyd, and trans. Van der Bos, Matthijis, *Religion and Politics in Modern Iran: A Reader*, I. B. Tauris, pp. 149-150.
187   O'Kane, Rosemary H. T, *Terrorism*, Pearson, Harlow, UK, 2001, p. 33.
188   Bayat, Asef, *Making Islam Democratic*, Stanford University Press, California, 2007, p. 71.
189   Moin, Baqer, *Khomeini: Life of the Ayatollah*, Thomas Dunne Books, 2000, p. 52.
190   Nasr, Vali, *The Shia Revival: How Conflicts Within Islam Will Shape the Future*, 2006, p. 120.
191   Berry, Mike and Greg Philo, *Israel and Palestine: Competing Histories*, Pluto Press, London, 2006, p. 1.
192   Ibid., p. 17.
193   Ibid., 10-11.
194   Stillman, Norman A., "Anti-Judaism and Antisemitism in the Arab and Islamic World Prior to 1948," published in *Antisemitism: A History*, Lindemann, Albert S., ed., and Levy, Richard S., ed., Oxford University Press, New York, 2010, pp. 218-219.
195   Hause, Steven C. and Maltby, William, *Western Civilization: A History of European Society*, Wadsworth, 2005.
196   Jewish Virtual Library, "French Revolution"; http://www.jewishvirtuallibrary.org/jsource/judaica/ejud_0002_0007_0_06791.html
197   Konrad Heiden, *The Fuhrer*, Beacon Press, Boston, p.15.
198   Ben-Itto, Hadassa, *The Lie That Wouldn't Die: The Protocols of the Elders of Zion*, Vallentine Mitchell, London, 2005. See also the History of the *Protocols of the Learned Elders of Zion*; http://www.freemasonry.bcy.ca/texts/protocols.html, and B'nai B'rith Anti-Defamation Commission Inc., http://www.antidef.org.au/www/309/1001127/displayarticle/1001415.html
199   Nilus, Sergiei, and Marsden, Victor E. (translator), *Protocols of the Learned Elders of Zion*,Liberty Bell Publications, 1922, p. 19.
200   Ibid., p. 21.
201   Wistrich, Robert S., *From Ambivalence to Betrayal: The Left, the Jews, and Israel*, University of Nebraska Press, 2012, pp. 9-11.
202   Levy, Richard S., *Antisemitism: A Historical Encyclopedia of Prejudice and Persecution*, ABC-CLIO, Santa Barbara, California, 2005, p. 250.

203   Goodrick-Clarke, Nicholas, *The Occult Roots of Nazism*, 2004, pp. 123-130.
204   Ibid., p. 133.
205   Ibid., p. 150.
206   From Protocol III: "I can tell you to-day that our goal is close at hand. Only a small distance remains, and the road less traveled by us will complete the cycle of the symbolic snake that represents our people. When this circle is completed, all European governments will be enclosed in its coils as in a vise."
207   *National Geographic News*, September 11, 2006, Brian Handwerk, 'Anti-Semitic "Protocols of Zion" Endure, Despite Debunking'; http://news.nationalgeographic.com/news/2006/09/060911-zion.html
208   *Reuters*, March 30, 2010, "Timeline: Female suicide bombers"; http://uk.reuters.com/article/2010/03/30/us-russia-metro-women-idUKTRE62T3WX20100330.
209   Johnson, Michael, *All Honourable Men: The Social Origins of War in Lebanon*, I. B. Tauris, 2002, pp. 149-150.
210   Berry, Mike and Philo, Greg, *Israel and Palestine: Competing Histories*, 2006, pp. 6-19.
211   Mattar, Philip, *The Mufti of Jerusalem: Al-Hajj Amin Al-Husayni and the Palestinian National Movement*, Columbia University Press, New York, 1992, p. 74.
212   Berry, Mike and Philo, Greg, *Israel and Palestine: Competing Histories*, 2006, pp. 23-30.
213   *National Post*, Bell, Stewart, "Islamist Extremists view Freemasons as the enemy: report", March 31, 2011, http://news.nationalpost.com/2011/03/31/islamist-extremists-view-freemasons-as-the-enemy-report.
214   See Arthur Versluis, *The New Inquisitions: Heretic-Hunting and the Intellectual Origins of Modern Totalitarianism*, Oxford University Press, 2006.
215   *New Straits Times*, Omar, Amin, "Ordinary Treatise on the Islamic State", February 15, 1991, http://news.google.ca/newspapers?id=r7oTAAAAIBAJ&sjid=UJADAAAAIBAJ&pg=6895,3625664&dq
216   Heimbichner, Craig and Parfrey, Adam, *Ritual America: Secret Brotherhoods and Their Influence on American Society: A Visual Guide*, Feral House, Port Townsend, WA, 2012, p. 175. Also Themwl.org, "Muslim World League Islamic Fiqh Council, Resolutions of Islamic Fiqh Council, Makkah Mukarramah, From 1st to 18th Sessions During 1398-1427H (1977-2006)"; http://themwl.org/downloads/Resolutions-of-Islamic-Fiqh-Council-1.pdf.
217   *Washington Jewish Week*, Pipes, Daniel, "The fantasy of 'Greater Israel' ", July 6, 1989, http://www.danielpipes.org/5337/the-fantasy-of-greater-israel
218   Inspire, Suri, Abu Mus Ab al, "The Jihad Experience: Open Fronts & The Individual Initiative", fall 2010,
219   Memri, Special dispatch No. 25, "Contemporary Islamist Ideology Authorizing Genocidal Murder", January 27, 2004, http://www.memri.org/bin/

articles.cgi?Page=archives&Area=sr&ID=SR2504. Also cited in Haim, S.G., "Sayyid Qutb," Asian and African Studies, 16, 1982, pp. 155-156.
220   Yale Law School, The Avalon project, *Hamas Covenant 1988*, http://avalon. law.yale.edu/20th_century/hamas.asp.
221   *2008 Update: Saudi Arabia's Curriculum of Intolerance*, Center for Religious Freedom of Hudson Institute with the Institute for Gulf Affairs; http://www.hudson.org/content/researchattachments/attachment/656/saudi_textbooks_final.pdf
222   *The Jakarta Post*, "Hard-line clerics demand ban on Rotary, Lions clubs", February 2, 2009, http://www.thejakartapost.com/news/2009/02/02/hardline-clerics-demand-ban-rotary-lions-clubs.html
223   *The Telegraph*, Helm, Toby, "Jews and Freemasons controlled war on Iraq, says No 10 adviser", 12 September 2005, http://www.telegraph.co.uk/news/uknews/1498217/Jews-and-Freemasons-controlled-war-on-Iraq-says-No-10-adviser.html
224   *The NewStatesman*, Cohen, Nick, "Is fascism behind the terror?", April 12, 2004, http://www.newstatesman.com/node/147692
225   Margulies, Ronnie and Yildizoglu, Ergin, "The Resurgence of Islam and the Welfare Party in Turkey", published in *Political Islam: Essays from the Middle East Report*, p.144-154.
226   Zeldis, Leon, "The Protocols of the Elders of Zion: Anti-Masonry and Anti-Semitism", published in *Heredom: The Transactions of the Scottish Rite Research Society*, vol. 7, Morris, Brent, ed., Washington, D.C., 1998.
227   Al Jazeera, "Purported al-Qaida statement", March 13, 2004; http://english.aljazeera.net/archive/2004/03/20084914326902740.html
228   Al Jazeera, "Bombers attack Istanbul Masonic lodge", http://www.aljazeera.com/archive/2004/03/20084914247975106.html, March 10, 2004
229   CBS News, March 16, 2004, Jarrett Murphy, 'Turks Say Terror Plot Foiled'; http://www.cbsnews.com/stories/2004/03/16/world/main606596.shtml
230   Memri, "Kaide' ('Al-Qaeda') Magazine Published Openly in Turkey," August 7, 2005, http://www.memri.org/report/en/0/0/0/0/0/0/1432.htm
231   *New York Post*, "Michael Shain, Don Kaplan, and Kate Sheeny, 'CBS reporter's Cairo nightmare: Lara Logan set upon by mob in brutal sex attack", February 16, 2011, http://www.nypost.com/p/news/international/cbs_reporter_cairo_nightmare_pXiUVvhwIDdCrbD95ybD5N
232   Filiu, Jean-Pierre, *The Arab Revolution: Ten Lessons from the Democratic Uprising*, Oxford University Press, Oxford, p. 100.
233   *The Guardian*, Shenker, Jack, "Egyptian Pyramid Closes Briefly Over 11/11/11 Rumour Mill", November 11, 2011, http://www.guardian.co.uk/world/2011/nov/11/egypt-great-pyramid-closes-111111
234   IkhwanWeb, "International Anonymous Hacker Group Threatens to 'Destroy The Muslim Brotherhood' ", November 22, 2011, http://www.ikhwanweb.

com/article.php?id=29161&ref=search.php

235   Al Arabiya News, Ahmed I. Abdallah, "Translators are Traitors", February 14, 2012, http://english.alarabiya.net/views/2012/02/14/194659.html

236   Gomez, Michael A., *Black Crescent: The Experience and Legacy of African Muslims in the Americas*, Cambridge University Press, New York, 2005, p. 244..

237   *Charge Delivered to the Brethren of the AFRICAN LODGE On the 25th of June, 1792 At the Hall of Brother WILLIAM SMITH IN Charlestown By the Right Worshipful Master PRINCE HALL, Printed at the Request of the Lodge. Printed and Sold at the Bible and Heart, Corphill, Boston*, date unknown.

238   Kaplan, Sidney and Kaplan, Emma Nogrady, *The Black Presence in the Era of the American Revolution*, University of Massachusetts Press, 1989, pp. 202-103.

239   Révauger, Cécile, *Black Freemasonry: From Prince Hall to the Giants of Jazz*, Inner Traditions, Rochester, Vermont, 2016, pp. 13-14.

240   Levine, Robert S. (Editor), *Martin R. Delany: A Documentary Reader*, The University of North Carolina Press, Chapel Hill, NC, 2003, pp. 49-67.

241   Révauger, Cécile, *Black Freemasonry: From Prince Hall to the Giants of Jazz*, Inner Traditions, Rochester, Vermont, 2016, p. 49.

242   *Ebony*, "White Masons Fail to Recognize Negro", a Johnson Publication, September 1958, pp. 28-29.

243   The date appears in the article as 1698, but this is too late, and must be an error.

244   *Ebony*, "Fun Loving Shriners are Social, Charitable Group," a Johnson Publication, September 1958, pp. 30-31.

245   Gomez, Michael A., *Black Crescent: The Experience and Legacy of African Muslims in the Americas*, 2005, pp. 208.

246   Horowitz Mitch, *Occult America: The Secret History of How Mysticism Shaped Our Nation*, Bantam Books, New York, New York, 2009, pp. 132-133.

247   Garvey, Marcus, *The Marcus Garvey and Universal Negro Improvement Association Papers, Volume XI: The Caribbean Diaspora, 1910-1920*, Hill, Robert A., ed., Duke University Press, Durham, 2011, p. ixxxv.

248   Gomez, Michael A., *Black Crescent: The Experience and Legacy of African Muslims in the Americas*, 2005, p. 244.

249   Grant, Colin, *Negro with a Hat: The Rise and Fall of Marcus Garvey*, Oxford University Press, Oxford, 2010, p. 119.

250   BlackPast.org, Irons, Stasia Mehschel, "Bruce, John Edward (1856-1924).", http://www.blackpast.org/aah/bruce-john-edward-1856-1924

251   Sinnette, Elinor Des Verney *Arthur Alfonso Schomburg, Black Bibliophile & Collector: A Biography*, Wayne State University, Detroit, 1989, p. 27.

252   Mackey, Albert G., *An Encyclopedia of Freemasonry And Its Kindred Sciences Comprising The Whole Range of Arts, Sciences And Literature As Connected With The Institution*, Vol. 2, The Masonic History Company, New York, 1919, p. 838.

253 Horowitz Mitch, *Occult America: The Secret History of How Mysticism Shaped Our Nation*, 2009, p. 134.
254 Dannin, Robert, *Black Pilgrimage to Islam*, Oxford University Press, Oxford, 2002, p. 17.
255 Dannin, Robert, *Black Pilgrimage to Islam*, Oxford University Press, Oxford, 2002, p. 35.
256 Gomez, Michael A., *Black Crescent: The Experience and Legacy of African Muslims in the Americas*, 2005, pp. 203-205.
257 Ibid., pp. 206-207.
258 Ibid., p. 215.
259 Gomez, Michael A., *Black Crescent: The Experience and Legacy of African Muslims in the Americas*, 2005, p. 234.
260 Horowitz Mitch, *Occult America: The Secret History of How Mysticism Shaped Our Nation*, 2009, p. 141.
261 Hopkins-Bey D.M., A., *Prophet Noble Drew Ali: Saviour of Humanity*, Ali's Men publishing and Azeem Hopkins-Bey, USA, 2014.
262 Gomez, Michael A., *Black Crescent: The Experience and Legacy of African Muslims in the Americas*, 2005, p. 247.
263 Ibid., pp. 218-219.
264 Knight, Michael Muhammad, *Blue-Eyed Devil: A Road Odyssey Through Islamic America*, Soft Skull Press, Brooklyn, 2009, p. 92.
265 Gardell, Mattias, *In the Name of Elijah Muhammad: Louis Farrakhan and The Nation of Islam*, Duke University Press, Durham, 1996, p. 182.
266 Ibid., p. 181.
267 Majid, Anouar, *We Are All Moors: Ending Centuries of Crusades against Muslims and Other Minorities*, University of Minnesota Press, Minneapolis, 2009, p. 80.
268 Muhammad, Elijah, *Message to the Blackman in America*, Secretarius MEMPS Publications, 2009.
269 Curtis IV, Edward E., *Black Muslim Religion in the Nation of Islam, 1960-1975*, The University of North Carolina Press, Chapel Hill, 2006, p. 2.
270 Allen, Jr., Ernest, "Identity and Destiny: The Formative Views of the Moorish Science Temple and the Nation of Islam", published in *Muslims on the Americanization Path?* (Yvonne Yazbeck Haddad and John L. Esposito (editors), Oxford University Press, Oxford, 2000, p. 181.
271 Allen, Jr., Ernest, "Identity and Destiny: The Formative Views of the Moorish Science Temple and the Nation of Islam", published in *Muslims on the Americanization Path?* (Yvonne Yazbeck Haddad and John L. Esposito (editors), Oxford University Press, Oxford, 2000, p. 181.
272 *The Positive Seed*, 9th Issue, May 1999.
273 Clegg, Claude Andrew, *An Original Man: The Life and Times of Elijah Muhammad*, St. Martin's Press, New York, 1998, p. 71.

274   Ibid., p. 72.
275   Muhammad, Elijah and Makr Hakim, Nasir, ed., *The Secrets of Freemasonry*, Secretarius MEMPS Publications, Phoenix, Arizona, 1994, p. 24.
276   *The Guardian*, Townsend, Mark, "Survivors of Norway shootings return to island of Utøya", August 20, 2011, http://www.theguardian.com/world/2011/aug/21/utoya-anders-behring-breivik-norway
277   Berwick, Andrew, *2083: A European Declaration of Independence*, London, 2011, p. 16.
278   Ibid, p. 1362.
279   Ibid, p. 1362.
280   *The Independent*, "Anders Breivik studied terror strategies on internet, court hears", Saturday July 12, 2014, http://www.independent.co.uk/news/world/europe/anders-breivik-studied-terror-strategies-on-internet-court-hears-7665054.html
281   Berwick, Andrew, *2083: A European Declaration of Independence*, 2011, p. 1379.
282   *Mail Online*, Lowe, Kristine and Henley, Charlotte, "Last year Anders Breivik killed 77 people –now it's room service, his own suite and Japanese meditation", April 14, 2012, http://www.dailymail.co.uk/news/article-2129914/Last-year-Anders-Breivik-killed-77-people-s-room-service-suite-Japanese-meditation.html
283   Berwick, Andrew, *2083: A European Declaration of Independence*, 2011, p. 829.
284   Ibid, p. 1369.
285   Freemasons For Dummies Blogspot, Hodapp, Christopher, "Norwegian Terror Suspect's Masonic Membership", July 23, 2011, http://freemasonsfordummies.blogspot.com/2011/07/norwegian-terror-suspects-masonic.html
286   Freemason Information, "Norwegian Order of Freemasons expel Breivik", July 25, 2011, http://freemasoninformation.com/2011/07/norwegian-order-of-freemasons-expel-breivik/
287   Berwick, Andrew, *2083: A European Declaration of Independence*, 2011, p. 1363.
288   Ibid, p. 1116.
289   Millar, Angel, *Freemasonry: A History*, Thunder Bay Press, San Diego, California, 2005, pp. 158-161.
290   Waite, Arthur Edward, *A New Encyclopedia of Freemasonry*, Volume 2, p. 226.
291   Millar, Angel, *Freemasonry: Foundation of the Western Esoteric Tradition*, 2014.
292   Berwick, Andrew, *2083: A European Declaration of Independence*, 2011, p. 1436.
293   Evola, Julius, and Moynihan, Michael, ed., *Men Among The Ruins: Postwar*

Reflections of a Radical Traditionalist, Stucco, Guido, trans., Inner Traditions, Rochester, Vermont, 2002, p. 31.

294   For a different opinion, see Sedgwick, Mark, "Breivik's 'European Declaration of Independence' "; http://traditionalistblog.blogspot.com/2011/07/breiviks-european-declaration-of.html

295   Berwick, Andrew, *2083: A European Declaration of Independence*, 2011.

296   Nasr, Seyyed Hossein, *Islam in the Modern World: Challenged by the West, Threatened by Fundamentalism, Keeping Faith with Tradition*, Harper One, New York, 2010, p. 363.

297   Nasr, Seyyed Hossein, *Islam in the Modern World: Challenged by the West, Threatened by Fundamentalism, Keeping Faith with Tradition*, 2010, pp. 364-365.

298   Ibid, pp. 366-367.

299   *Mail Online*, Hickley, Matthew, "Islamic sharia courts in Britain are now 'legally binding' ", September 15, 2008, http://www.dailymail.co.uk/news/article-1055764/Islamic-sharia-courts-Britain-legally-binding.html

300   *Mail Online*, Camber, Rebecca, "'No porn or prostitution': Islamic extremists set up Sharia law controlled zones in British cities", July 28, 2011, http://www.dailymail.co.uk/news/article-2019547/Anjem-Choudary-Islamic-extremists-set-Sharia-law-zones-UK-cities.html

301   Charles, Prince of Wales, *Harmony: A New Way of Looking at the World*, HarperCollins, New York, New York, USA, 2010, p. 3.

302   *Mail Online*, Hastings, Max, "Why Prince Charles is too dangerous to be king: In a landmark essay MAX HASTINGS tells why this increasingly eccentric royal could imperil the monarchy", December 18, 2010, http://www.dailymail.co.uk/debate/article-1339707/Prince-Charles-dangerous-king-This-eccentric-royal-imperil-monarchy.html

303   Danielpipes.org, Pipes, Daniel, "Is Prince Charles a Convert to Islam?", November 3, 2009, http://www.danielpipes.org/blog/2003/11/is-prince-charles-a-convert-to-islam

304   *Mail Online*, Doughty, Steve, "Just 800,000 worshippers attend a Church of England service on the average Sunday", March 21, 2014, http://www.dailymail.co.uk/news/article-2586596/Just-800-000-worshipers-attend-Church-England-service-average-Sunday.html

305   *The Guardian*, Gledhill, Ruth, "Church attendance has been propped up by immigrants, says study", June 3, 2014, http://www.theguardian.com/world/2014/jun/03/church-attendance-propped-immigrants-study

306   *The Telegraph*, Thompson, Damian, "Prince Charles's plan to become 'Defender of Faith' will help destroy our Christian identity", November 14, 2008, http://blogs.telegraph.co.uk/news/damianthompson/5718748/Prince_Charless_plan_to_become_Defender_of_Faith_will_help_destroy_our_Christian_identity/

307   *The American Conservative*, Dreher, Rod, "Philosopher Prince: The revolutionary anti-modernism of Britain's heir apparent", March 12, 2012, http://

www.theamericanconservative.com/articles/philosopher-prince/
308   SacredWeb.com, "Sacred Web Conference : An Introduction from His Royal Highness The Prince of Wales, September 23rd and 24th, 2006, Myer Horowitz Theatre, University of Alberta. Edmonton, Alberta", http://www.sacredweb.com/ conference06/conference_introduction.html
309   Ibid.
310   Ibid.
311   Ibid.
312   Princeofwales.gov.uk, Charles, Prince of Wales, "A speech by HRH The Prince of Wales titled 'Islam and the West' at the Oxford Centre for Islamic Studies, The Sheldonian Theatre, Oxford", October 27, 1993, http://www. princeofwales.gov.uk/media/speeches/speech-hrh-the-prince-of-wales-titled-islam-and-the-west-the-oxford-centre-islamic
313   Charles, Prince of Wales, *Harmony: A New Way of Looking at the World*, 2010, p. 10.
314   Princeofwales.gov.uk, Charles, Prince of Wales, "An article by HRH The Prince of Wales for the Daily Telegraph supplement on Islam", November 15, 2001, http://www.princeofwales.gov.uk/media/speeches/article-hrh-the-prince-of-wales-the-daily-telegraph-supplement-islam
315   Princeofwales.gov.uk, Charles, Prince of Wales, "A speech by HRH The Prince of Wales titled 'Islam and the West' at the Oxford Centre for Islamic Studies , The Sheldonian Theatre, Oxford", October 27, 1993, http://www.princeofwales. gov.uk/media/speeches/speech-hrh-the-prince-of-wales-titled-islam-and-the-west-the-oxford-centre-islamic
316   Corbin, Henry, *Swedenborg and Esoteric Islam*, (Swedenborg Studies / No. 4), Fox, Leonard, trans., Swedenborg Foundation, West Chester, Pennsylvania, 1999.
317   Yahya, Harun (Adnan Oktar), *Global Freemasonry: The Masonic Philosophy Unveiled And Refuted*, Global Publishing, (available at http://www. harunyahya.com/en/Books/677/global-freemasonry), p. 85.
318   *Freemasons For Dummies*, July 20, 2016, "Saudi Clerics Issue Fatwa Against 'Masonic' Pokemon GO"; http://freemasonsfordummies.blogspot. com/2016/07/saudi-clerics-issue-fatwa-against.html.
319   Zizek, Slavoj, *The Universal Exception*, Continuum, London, 2006, p. 253.
320   Tibi, Bassam, *Islam and Islamism*, Yale University Press, New Haven, 2012, p. 239.
321   Allen, Charles, *God's Terrorists: The Wahhabi Cult and the Hidden Roots of Modern Jihad*, Da Capo Press, Cambridge, Massachusetts, 2006, pp. 45-52.
322   *The Independent*, August 19, 2010, "Timothy Winter: Britain's most influential Muslim - and it was all down to a peach"; http://www.independent. co.uk/news/people/profiles/timothy-winter-britains-most-influential-muslim-and-it-was-all-down-to-a-peach-2057400.html

323   Gulfnews.com, Ramadan, Tariq, "Contemporary Muslims are in need of spirituality", February 21, 2012, http://gulfnews.com/opinions/columnists/contemporary-muslims-are-in-need-of-spirituality-1.983759

324   Ramadan, Tariq, *What I Believe*, Oxford University Press, Oxford, 2010, pp. 3-12.

325   Ibid., p. 33.

326   Allawi, Ali A., *The Crisis of Islamic Civilization*, Yale University Press, New Haven, 2009, pp. 259-260.

327   Ahmed, Akbar S., *Islam Under Seige: Living Dangerously in a Post-Honor World*, Polity Press, Cambridge, UK, 2003, pp. 164-165.

328   Tabataba'i, *Shi 'ah*, 2002, p. 133.

329   Adapted from an article published by *People of Shambhala*, http://peopleofshambhala.com/islam-europe-and-evola-riding-the-tiger-of-modernity/

330   Cambridge Muslim College, "Shaykh Abdal Hakim Murad - Riding the Tiger of Modernity"; https://www.youtube.com/watch?v=07Ien1qo_qI.

331   *New York Times*, Jason Horowitz, February 10, 2017, "Steve Bannon Cited Italian Thinker Who Inspired Fascists"; https://www.nytimes.com/2017/02/10/world/europe/bannon-vatican-julius-evola-fascism.html?_r=0

332   BuzzFeed News, J. Lester Feder, November 15, 2016, "This Is How Steve Bannon Sees The Entire World"; https://www.buzzfeed.com/lesterfeder/this-is-how-steve-bannon-sees-the-entire-world?utm_term=.lx75VognA#.dlZ64lZDP

333   *Vanity Fair*, July 17, 2017, Joshua Green, "Inside The Strange Origins Of Steve Bannon's Nationalist Fantasia"; https://www.vanityfair.com/news/2017/07/the-strange-origins-of-steve-bannons-nationalist-fantasia.

334   Peopleofshambhala.com, July 24, 2017, Alexander Shepard, "Does Bannon Accurately Reflect the Views of Guenon and Evola?"; http://peopleofshambhala.com/does-bannon-accurately-reflect-the-views-of-guenon-and-evola/

335   Evola, Julius (introduction by John B. Morgan IV), *Metaphysics of War: Battle, Victory and Death in The World of Tradition*. Arktos, United Kingdom, 2011.

336   Adapted from an article published by *Eurasia Review*, http://www.eurasiareview.com/23052015-the-freemasonry-on-bin-ladens-bookshelf/

337   Office of the Director of National Security, "Bin Laden's Bookshelf"; https://www.dni.gov/index.php/resources/bin-laden-bookshelf?start=4

INDEX

A

'Abduh, Muhammad, 54-56
Adam (prophet), 12, 13
al-Afghani, Jamal ad-Din, 1, 50-55, 58, 84-85, 96, 124, 160
Afghanistan, 46, 58, 121, 163
Ahmad, Mirza Ghulam,
Ahmadiyya, 133, 136
Alawites, 31
Alchemy, 11, 12, 15, 17, 36-37, 168
Ali, Noble Drew, 2, 133-136
Allah, Ibn 'Ata', 13-14
Allied Masonic Degrees, 59
Ancient and Accepted Scottish Rite, 32
Ancient and Mystical Order Rosae Crucis (AMORC), 135
Ancient Arabic Order of the Nobles of the Mystic Shrine, 32-35, 43, 158
Ancient Egyptian Order of the Nobles of the Mystic Shrine, 131, 133, 135, 138
Ancient Order of Zuzimites, 64-67, 158, 162
      Freemasonry and, 64-65
      Ritual of, 64-67
Anderson, James, 23-24
Anti-communism, 37, 120, 144, 169
Anti-Islamic, 84, 141-142, 170, 171
Anti-Masonic, 24, 26, 70, 73-74, 115-124, 126, 143, 160, 168
      Islamist, 115-124
      Terrorism and, 117, 119-122
Anti-modern, 37
Anti-Semitism, 101-102, 106-107, 110-112, 137, 146, 168
Archer, Captain J. H. Lawrence, 60
Ars Quatuor Coronatorum, 27, 28, 43, 64
Aryan, 37, 86-87, 112, 115, 137, 152
'Ashura, 92
Asiatic Society, 41
al-Azhar (university), 52, 54, 55

B

Bacon, Francis, 21
Balustre, The,
Bannon, Steve, 167-168
Barruel , Augustin, 103-105, 107
Batin, 7, *see also Esoteric*
Bektashi (Sufi Order), 10, 31, 34, 37
Bin Laden, Osama, 173-174
Black nationalism, 125, 128-130, 132-133, 138
Blake, William, 61
Blavatsky, Mme. Helena, 35, 70, 87, 137
Book of The Law, see Liber AL vel Legis
Borujerdi, Ayatollah Muhammad Hossein, 89-90
Breivik, Anders, 141-147
Burckhardt, Titus, 2, 75

C

Cabala, 19, 21, 22, 24-27, 36, 65, 168
Cairo, 34, 36, 40-41, 47, 50, 52-53, 71, 74, 122, 153
Caliphate, 38, 54, 86, 113, 119
Canadian Security Intelligence Service (CSIS), 115, 116, 117
Charles, Prince of Wales, 2, 150-156
Chemical Wedding of Christian Rosenkreutz, The, 17
Circle Seven Koran, 2, 134-135, *see also Moorish Science*
Compagnonnage, 17
Corbin, Henry, 159
Crowley, Aleister, 4, 26, 37-42, 158, 162
      Abdullah el Haji (pseudonym), 39
      Aiwass, 40-42
      Caliphate and, 38
      Mansur al-Hallaj and, 38
      Scented Garden of Abdullah The Satirist of Shiraz, 39-40
      Sufism and, 4, 26, 38-40, 42, 158

D

Damascus, 19, 47-48, 101
Damcar, 21
Détré, Charles, 72
Dhikr, 13-14, 78
Dhu'l-Nun, Abu'l-fayd b. Ibrahim, 15

Dreyfus, Captain Alfred, 106
Druze, 27, 28, 35, 48, 136, 158, 159
Druze Masonry, 28
Dugin, Aleksandr, 167, 171

E

Egypt, 6, 15, 16, 19, 37, 45, 49, 50-58, 74, 102, 117, 122-124, 130, 135, 150, 155, 156, 163
Egyptian deities, 40, 66-67
Egyptian symbolism, 61, 66, 135
Eliade, Mircea, 17
Encausse, Gerard, 62
Entezam, Seyyed 'Abdollah, 97
Esoteric, 1-4, 6-10, 13, 15, 25-32, 34-38, 43, 44, 47, 55, 57-64, 66, 69-70, 72-74, 78, 91, 137, 138, 156, 158-159, 163, 165
Esotericism, 7, 15, 17, 26-27, 29-31, 37, 58, 61, 69, 73, 136, 149, 155, 158-159, 162-163, 165, 167
Etudes Traditionelles (journal), 71
Evola, Julius, 146, 167-171
        Guénon and, 146, 168-169
        Influence on Right-wing politics, 169
        Occult war, 168
Exoteric, 7, 9, 12, 83, 165

F

Fama Fraternitatis, 19-20
Faramushkhaneh, 51
Feiziyeh (seminary), 81, 91
Fez (city), 19
Fez (hat), 33, 135
Fiqh, 8, 82, 156
Five Percenters, *see Nation of Gods and Earths*
Fleming, Dr. Walter M., 34-35
Florence, William J., 34-35
Freemasonry, 1-3
        Different religions and, 3, 23, 29, 31, 160
        Globalism and, 3
        Iran and, 97, 117
        Islam and, 1-2, 23-31, 34, 37, 40, 46, 50, 133, 158-160, 168,
        Islamist anti-American conspiracy theory and, 115-116

      Masonic building, terrorist attack on, 119-122
      Muslims and Hindus initiated into, 3, 23, 125
      Sufism and, 26-27, 31, 36, 40, 69, 97, 158
Freethinkers, 50, 86
Freethinking, 46
Fringe Masonry, 2, 26, 31, 35, 42-43, 58-64, 70, 72-73, 157-158
Fritsch, Theodor, 110
Futuwwa, 16

G

Gabriel (angel), 5, 12, 40, 63, 73, 174
Gaddafi, Colonel Muammar, 169
Garvey, Marcus, 130-133, 137
Germanic Order, 36, 110
Gnosis, 7, 12, 15, 69, 161, 165
Gnosticism (Islamic tradition of), 6, 11, 80, 81, 99
Goetia, 66
Golden Dawn, *see Hermetic Order of The Golden Dawn*
Grand Orient (Masonic jurisdiction), 48-51, 53, 73
Grande Loge Swedenborgienne de France, 72
Grotto, *see Mystic Order of the Veiled Prophets of the Enchanted Realm*
Guénon, René, 2, 69-78, 146, 149-155, 158, 160, 162, 164-169
      Cairo and, 71, 74, 153
      Freemasonry and, 70, 73
      Sufism and, 74-76, 149

H

Haganah, 114
Hall, Prince, 126-127
Haqiqa, 7, 8, 70
Haqiqa muhammadiyya, 13
Henry IV (Masonic Lodge), 48-49,
Hermetic Order of The Golden Dawn, 4, 37, 62, 72, 73
Hermeticism, 1, 28, 64, 145, 155, 168
Herzl, Theodor, 107
Hinduism, 23, 28, 57, 62, 69, 71, 76, 77, 78, 125, 152, 159
Hitler, Adolf, 87, 110
Howe, Ellic, 64
Hussein, Saddam, 94, 119, 164
al-Husseini, Haj Amin, 113-114

I

IBDA-C, 120-121, *see also al-Qaeda*
Imamate, 6-8
Indra (Vedic deity), 71
Iran, 9, 10, 33, 38, 54, 79-99, 117, 149,
    Allies and, 88
    CIA and, 89
    Constitutional Revolution and, 85-86
    Guénon's writing and, 149
    Iraq and, 94-95, 98
    Islamic Revolution and, 81-83, 91, 93-94, 96-98, 149
'Irfan, 79-82, 91, 98-99, *see also Gnosis*
Isis (Egyptian deity), 40, 66-67,
ISIS (Jihadist militia), 62, 71
Ismailis, 7, 27, 35, 159, 162

J

al-Jazairi, Abd al-Qadir, 2, 46-50
Jesus, 5, 13, 16, 23, 24, 77, 134, 142, 161
Judeo-Masonic conspiracy theory, 104-111, 116-120

K

Kali Yuga, 154
Karbala (battle at), 92
Kellner, Carl, 4, 37
Khomeini, Ayatollah Ruhollah Musavi, 79-99, 169
    Childhood and education, 79-80
    Islamic gnosticism and, 80-82, 99
    Islamic Revolution and, 82, 93-94, 96, 98
    Paris and, 95
    White Revolution and, 91
Kipling, Rudyard, 60
Kneph (journal of the Antient and Primitive Rite of Masonry), 64
Knights Templar,
    Anders Breivik and, 141-146
    Anti-Masonry and, 104
    Black nationalism and, 131-132
    Masonic, 32, 131-132, 144-145

L

Liber AL vel Legis, 40-41,
Lings, Martin, 2, 77-78
Lions Club, 91, 118, 120
Liverpool Muslim Institute, 57, 63
Loge Symbolique Humanidad, 72

M

MacKenzie, Kenneth, 43-44, 60
Magic, 15, 42, 66
Magick, 37
Mahdi, 6, 133
Martinism, 28
Martinist Supreme Council, 62
Marx, Karl, 106, 163
Marxism, 88, 111, 157
Marxists, 89, 93, 95, 106, 110, 141, 142
Mathers, Samuel Liddell MacGregor, 4, 37
Mecca, 5, 6, 35, 42, 47, 129, 136, 137
    Liber AL vel Legis and, 41
Mecca Temple (Shriners), 34,
Mevlevi (Sufi Order), 36
Mjöllnir, 143
Moorish Science, 2, 133-138, 158
Mosaddeq, Muhammad, 89
Muhaiyaddeen, M. R. Bawa (Sufi shaykh), 15
Muhammad (Prophet), 5, 10, 12, 14, 63, 174
    'Ali and, 6, 8,
    Biography by Martin Lings, 2, 78
    Night journey, 11-12
    Receives revelation, 5, 40, 63, 73, 174
Muhammad, Elijah, 138-139
Mystic Order of the Veiled Prophets of the Enchanted Realm, 32-33, 158

N

Naqshbandi (Sufi Order), 12, 13, 70
Nation of Gods and Earths, 139
Nation of Islam, 2, 136-139
    Teachings of, 136
Nationalsozialistische Deutsche Arbeiterpartei, see Nazi Party

Nazi ideology, 115
Nazi Party, 87, 110, 112,
      Anti-Masonry and, 110-111, 115
      Protocols of The Elders of Zion and, 110-111
Nazi Scouts, 113
Ne'matollahi (Sufi Order), 97
New Age (movement), 1, 2, 62, 123, 134, 159, 173
New Right, 169
New Thought (movement), 1, 132-133

O
Occult, 4, 22, 36-37, 40, 42, 44, 58, 66, 70, 72, 73, 137, 142, 146, 159,
Odinism, 143, 146
Ordo Novi Templi, 146
Order of Ishmael, 35, 42-43
Order of Lazarus, 145
Ordo Templi Orientis, 4, 37, 62, 72
Osiris, 40, 66-67

P
Palestine, 20, 101, 102, 106, 113-114, 116, 135
Philosopher's Stone, 12
Plato, 91, 163
Pohl, Hermann, 36-37
Proofs of a Conspiracy, 104
Protocols of the Elders of Zion, 102, 106-111, 116-118, 124, 168

Q
Qadiriyya (Sufi Order), 47
al-Qaeda, 117, 121, 122, 141, 142, 162, 173, 174
Qom, 80-83, 88, 91, 92, 149
Quilliam, Shaykh Abdullah, 2,
      Ancient Order of Zuzimites and, 64-65, 158, 162
      Conversion to Islam, 57
      Freemasonry and, 53, 57-66, 72-73, 158-160
      John Yarker and, 60, 61, 64, 72-73
      Swedenborgian Rite and, 61-62, 64, 72-73, 158-159
Qutb, Sayyid, 118

R

Ramsay, Andrew Michael, 145
Rawson, Albert. 35, 43
Reuss, Theodor, 4, 37, 62, 72
Rite National Espagnol, 72
Rite of Memphis and Misraim, 28, 64, 72
Rite of Strict Observance (Masonic), 145
Robison, John, 104
Rose Croix (Masonic Degree), 22
Rose, Edward, 45
Rosenkreutz, Christian, 19-21
Rosicrucian manifestos, 19-22
Rosicrucianism, 1, 17, 28, 36, 64, 133, 145
Rotary Club, 118, 120
Rumi, Jalal ad-Din, 11, 12, 80, 156
Runes, 22, 36, 37

S

Sat Bhai (Order), 59-60, 64
Schuon, Frithjof, 75-78, 146
        Guénon and, 76, 78
        Initiation into Sufism, 77
von Sebottendorff, Baron Rudolf, 36-37, 110
Secret Chiefs, 42
Sefer Jezira, 22
Shadhiliyya (Order), 13
Shah, Idries, 15-16, 26-27, 158
Shah, Nasir al-Din, 84-85, 96
Shahada, 14, 24-26
Sheikhs of the Desert, Guardians of the Kaaba, Guardians of the Mystic Shrine (fraternity), 35
Shi'ism, 6-8, 80, 89
        Esotericism, 6-8, 136, 162
        Revolutionary, 93-94
        Sufism and, 27
        "Twelver," 6-7, 162
Shiraz, 10, 87, 92,
Shriners, 32, 34-35, 158
        African-American, 128-129, 133, 135, 138
        "Moslem Sons," 139

Sufism and, 34, 158
Spiritualism, 70, 152
Sufism, 2, 4, 5-17, 26-27, 31, 34, 36, 38, 40, 47, 69-70, 74, 75-78, 97, 146, 149, 158, 162, 171
  Alchemy and, 11, 12, 15
Sunni Islam, 5, 6, 8, 13, 16, 50, 56,80, 133, 134, 136, 159, 162
Swedenborg, Emanuel, 61, 63
Swedenborgian Rite of Phremasonry, 61, 72
Swedenborgian Rite (Primitive and Original), 72
Syrian Social National Party, 111

T
Tabataba'i, Allamah Sayyid Muhammad Husayn, 6-7, 161, 165, 175, 192
Tasawwuf, 9, *see also Sufism*
Taxil, Leo, 73
Thelema, 4, 40
Theosophical Society, 35, 87, 137
Theosophy, 70-71, 137
Third Reich, 88, 111, 113-114
Thule Society, 110
Traditionalism, 2, 69-70, 149-151, 154-155, 161, 167-169
Trump, Donald, 167
Typhon (Egyptian deity), 66

U
UNIA-ACL, 130-132, 137

V
Vajra, 71

W
Waite, A. E., 64
Westcott, William Wynn, 4, 37, 61
Western esotericism, 26, 31, 159, 167
World Islamic Front for Jihad Against Jews and Crusaders, 173, *see also al-Qaeda*

Y
Yarker, John, 35, 43, 60-61, 64, 72-73

Z
Zahir, 7, *see also Exoteric*
Zarathustra (prophet), 86
Zizek, Slavoj, 161
Zoroastrianism, 44, 86, 152
Zuzimite (term), 65

ABOUT THE AUTHOR

Angel Millar is the author of *Freemasonry: Foundation of the Western Esoteric Tradition* (2014) and *Freemasonry: A History* (2005). His writing has also been published in *The Journal of Indo-European Studies*, *Quest* magazine, and *Philalethes: The Journal of Masonic Research*, among others.

Millar also frequently lectures on Freemasonry, esotericism, and related subjects to both public and private audiences. For more information on his work, or to contact the author, you can visit his website, angelmillar.com.

CPSIA information can be obtained
at www.ICGtesting.com
Printed in the USA
BVHW040847230519
549121BV00017B/441/P

9 780999 324707